JESUS CHRIST, THE SON OF GOD

VOLUME 3

VOLUME 3

JESUS CHRIST, THE SON OF GOD

THE WITNESS OF THE GOSPELS

STEVEN R. MCMURRAY

Acknowledgments

I am profoundly grateful for the help and suggestions of my sweet wife, Lorna. She has willingly read almost every page and made invaluable suggestions. Her insight cannot be overstated, and her support has been unwavering.

I am likewise grateful for the wonderful and insightful help of the lead editor, Suzy Bills. She is a marvelous editor and contributed much toward the writing of this book and its publication. I am so grateful for her help and encouragement. Rather than just dealing with punctuation and grammar, which she did very well, she made my rather complex sentences simple without altering the meaning and suggested changes to the order of certain paragraphs and sentences. She was willing to move sentences and paragraphs when needed and was insightful and willing to challenge statements and make suggestions. Yet she was easy to work with and very encouraging and supportive. I could not have had a better editor.

I am also grateful for the invaluable assistance of Christina Crosland for carefully checking each footnote against each quoted or reference passage of scripture and editing the same where necessary. Given the number of footnotes, this task was daunting and somewhat tedious. Christina also typeset this volume, designed the cover, and created the table of contents. She has been marvelous to work with.

Thanks also need to be given to Rebecca Timmons, who has laboriously proofread this volume, and to Emma Ebert, who skillfully created the index.

I very much appreciate their help and encouragement. Also, thanks to all others who encouraged me to complete and publish this book and to those who will assist with the completion of the additional volumes.

Table of Contents

Chapter 36

CONCLUSION OF GALILEAN MINISTRY; FEAST OF TABERNACLES

Christ had shared His witness and gospel with those in Galilee and the surrounding areas, thus fulfilling His Father's will. Many had been converted, while many others had rejected Christ and His teachings. Around this time, He sent the Seventy to Judea and Perea, where they helped bring others to Christ and were also strengthened themselves—as is the Father's plan. Next, Jesus would go to Jerusalem for the Feast of Tabernacles as a further witness to those of that city. His major objectives now were to teach the gospel to the people in those areas and to give His personal witness that He was the promised Messiah.

Jesus Sends Out the Seventy (Luke 10:1–12)

Christ's mortal ministry was rapidly coming to an end. His message needed to extend beyond those He could teach Himself. In addition, He needed to establish the administrative foundation for His Church. Therefore, He appointed men as Seventies[1] to assist in the great work of spreading His gospel message.

---

1. It is impossible to determine how many men Jesus first called to be in the Seventy since this priesthood office does not necessarily contain seventy individuals. Nevertheless, Luke 10:1 states that Jesus appointed "seventy," which may imply that He in fact called seventy individuals.

Based on the scriptural record, it is impossible to determine when and where Jesus sent forth the Seventy.[2] Farrar and Talmage indicated that Jesus sent the Seventy after He attended the Feast of Tabernacles in Jerusalem.[3] Edersheim and McConkie indicated that Jesus commissioned the Seventy while in Galilee prior to attending the feast.[4] Galilee seems more reasonable as the location because it offered a calmer environment in which to select, call, and ordain the Seventy, as well as divide them into companionships and determine where they should go. If Galilee was the location, Jesus may have sent forth the Seventy before He departed for the Feast of Tabernacles, or He may have sent them afterward, so they could attend this major Jewish feast. Of more importance than the time and place of this occurrence is the fact that Jesus selected, appointed, and sent forth the Seventy to assist in establishing the pattern for moving His great work forward. Luke's record is as follows:

> **Luke 10:1–12.** After these things the Lord appointed other seventy also, and sent them two and two before his face into every city and place, whither he himself would come. Therefore said he unto them, The harvest truly is great, but the labourers are few: pray ye therefore the Lord of the harvest, that he would send forth labourers into his harvest. Go your ways: behold, I send you forth as lambs among wolves. Carry neither purse, nor scrip, nor shoes: and salute no man by the way. And into whatsoever house ye enter, first say, Peace be to this house. And if the son of peace be there, your peace shall rest upon it: if not, it shall turn to you again. And in the same house remain, eating and drinking such things as they give: for the labourer is worthy of his hire. Go not from house to house. And into whatsoever city ye enter, and they receive you, eat such things as are set before you: and heal the sick that are therein, and say unto them, The kingdom of God is come nigh unto you. But into whatsoever city ye enter, and they receive you not, go your ways out into the streets of the same, and say, Even the very dust of your city, which cleaveth on us, we do wipe off against you: notwithstanding be ye sure of this, that the kingdom of God is come nigh unto you. But I

---

2. See Edersheim, *Life and Times of Jesus the Messiah*, p. 561.

3. See Farrar, *Life of Christ*, p. 408; Talmage, *Jesus the Christ*, p. 398.

4. See Edersheim, *Life and Times of Jesus the Messiah*, p. 567; McConkie, *Mortal Messiah*, vol. 3, p. 99.

say unto you, that it shall be more tolerable in that day for Sodom, than for that city.

Jesus sent the companionships into every place where He would go.[5] The wording suggests that the Seventy were to preach in the areas that Jesus would be in during the remaining months of His mortal ministry, including Judea, located on the western side of the Jordan River, and Perea, located on the eastern side. The Seventy were to prepare the way for Christ and to serve as additional witnesses of His divinity. They must have been men with firm faith and testimonies and with a willingness to leave their families and other duties and prepare the way for the Lord.

The Savior's charge to the Seventy was almost the same in substance as the charge He gave to the Apostles prior to their first mission.[6] He told the Seventy that the harvest would be truly great despite the relatively small number of Seventy in so large a geographical area and the shortness of their missions. Jesus also counseled the Seventy to pray to the Father and implied that they should rely on the inspiration they received. Their prayers were to focus on the success of their missions and the missions of the other members of the Seventy, for the harvest would be great. Further, Jesus warned that the Seventy would be among "wolves"—those who sought to destroy the Seventy and their message—yet they were to remain humble and submissive to the spiritual directions they would receive. That charge likely encouraged the Seventy to search their souls to determine the depth of their faith and commitment.

Jesus told the Seventy, as He had directed the Apostles, that they were to go forth simply and modestly, without money or means to carry items needed for their missions. They were to wear sandals, not shoes or other costly apparel; humility in appearance was essential. They were not to stop to visit those whom the Seventy knew, for they needed to keep their focus on their missions.

Jesus also told the Seventy that as laborers, they must be "worthy of [their] hire"; that is, they needed to be diligent in their service for the Lord.

---

5. The Seventy were to be witnesses of Jesus to prepare the minds and hearts of the people to see Jesus and hear His gospel.

6. See Matt. 10; 11:1; Mark 6:7–13; Luke 9:1–6; see also chapter 27 in volume 2 of this series.

He counseled them to not go arbitrarily from house to house but instead to go where the Spirit directed. Jesus might have been implying that they were not to focus on seeking out better accommodations or food. The Seventy were to eat whatever was offered to them so that they would not offend. Like all other missionaries, the Seventy were to leave peace with those who accepted the Seventy and their message. The peace that they were to leave was a witness of Christ.

Jesus also directed these priesthood holders to heal the sick and to declare that the kingdom of God would soon come. When the Seventy met those who rejected the gospel message, the Seventy were to wipe the dust from their feet and warn the nonbelievers that their fate would be dreadful. However, they were warned that they needed to be sure and certain of complete rejection, for they were on the Lord's errand and must remain receptive to inspiration.

Also of significance is the fact that the Seventy were to go to every place where Christ would thereafter go. Based on this instruction, it is evident that much of Jesus's ministry in Judea and Perea is unrecorded in scripture.

Jesus was making it clear that members of His Church were to be missionaries and not to merely observe the Sabbath. The Seventy, unlike the Apostles prior to their first mission, were not directed to preach only to the Jews.[7] Christ's gospel message was (and is) to go to all the world. As the Lord said to His Apostles on the Mount of Olives shortly prior to His death: "And this gospel of the kingdom shall be preached in all the world for a witness unto all nations; and then shall the end come."[8] After His Resurrection, Christ instructed His Apostles to "go ye into all the world, and preach the gospel to every creature."[9] And as He said to His Apostles prior to His final ascension into heaven: "But ye shall receive power, after that the Holy Ghost is come upon you: and ye shall be witnesses unto me both in Jerusalem, and in all Judea, and in Samaria, and unto the uttermost part of the earth."[10] Thus, much of the counsel Jesus gave to the early Seventies is applicable to

7. Subsequently, Jesus directed the Apostles to "go ye into all the world" (Mark 16:15) and to "teach all nations" (Matt. 28:1).

8. Matt. 24:14.

9. Mark 16:15; see also Matt. 28:19.

10. Acts: 1:8.

modern-day missionaries as they go throughout the world. Helping bring others to Christ is one of the great missions and responsibilities of The Church of Jesus Christ of Latter-day Saints.

The office of the Seventy was a building block in Christ's original Church and is likewise in His Church today. The Lord described the role of the Seventy in The Church of Jesus Christ of Latter-day Saints as follows: "The Seventy are also called to preach the gospel, and to be especial witnesses unto the Gentiles and in all the world."[11]

Just as the original Seventy worked hand in hand with Christ in taking the gospel to those who would believe, Christ is laboring with His missionaries today, in preparation for His glorious Second Coming. As recorded in a parable in the Book of Mormon, the Lord declared: "This is the last time that I shall nourish my vineyard; for the end is nigh at hand, and the season speedily cometh."[12] The same parable states that "the Lord of the vineyard labored also with [His servants]; and they did obey the commandments of the Lord of the vineyard in all things."[13] The Lord has also promised those who serve as missionaries: "I will go before your face. I will be on your right hand and on your left, and my Spirit shall be in your hearts, and mine angels round about you, to bear you up."[14] Presumably, that is the same in the spirit world.

Jesus Upbraids Certain Cities in Galilee (Matt. 11:20–24; Luke 10:13–16)

As Jesus came to the conclusion of His Galilean ministry, He singled out three cities—Bethsaida, Capernaum, and Chorazin—for special condemnation because they lacked faith notwithstanding His many miracles in those areas. Bethsaida was located on the eastern shore of the Sea of Galilee, Capernaum was located on the northeastern shore of the Sea of Galilee, and Chorazin[15] was located north of Capernaum. The following is Matthew's record:

---

11. D&C 107:25.
12. Jacob 5:71.
13. Jacob 5:72.
14. D&C 84:88.
15. Chorazin was an ancient town in the hills about two miles north of Capernaum, above the northwestern shore of the Sea of Galilee (see *HarperCollins Bible Dictionary*, s.v. "Chorazin"). The only biblical reference to Chorazin is in Matthew 20.

Matthew 11:20–24. *Then began he to upbraid the cities wherein most of his mighty works were done, because they repented not: Woe unto thee, Chorazin! Woe unto thee, Bethsaida! For if the mighty works, which were done in you, had been done in Tyre and Sidon, they would have repented long ago in sackcloth and ashes. But I say unto you, It shall be more tolerable for Tyre and Sidon at the day of judgment, than for you. And thou, Capernaum, which art exalted unto heaven, shalt be brought down to hell: for if the mighty works, which have been done in thee, had been done in Sodom, it would have remained until this day. But I say unto you, That it shall be more tolerable for the land of Sodom in the day of judgment, than for thee.*

As Christ reflected on all of His labor and miracles in Galilee, He must have been filled with deep sadness and sorrow that so many in this region had rejected Him and His gospel message. He likely lamented over these cities in Galilee in the same way that He lamented over Jerusalem: "O Jerusalem, Jerusalem, thou that killest the prophets, and stonest them which are sent unto thee, how often would I have gathered thy children together, even as a hen gathereth her chickens under her wings, and ye would not!"[16]

Christ foresaw the judgment that would come upon those who chose not to repent. He explained that if the mighty works He had done in the three cities had been done in Sodom, it would not have been destroyed but would have remained down through the centuries. Just as Isaiah foretold the fall and destruction of Babylon, Christ foresaw the destruction of these cities. Isaiah said of Babylon and its king, "That thou shalt take up this proverb against the king of Babylon, and say, How hath the oppressor ceased! The golden city ceased! The Lord hath broken the staff of the wicked, and the sceptre of the rulers."[17] Likewise, Christ upbraided the three Galilean cities; in particular, He criticized Capernaum, where He had performed so many miracles.

Each of these cities has long since been destroyed and now lies in rubble. Jesus's warning was applicable not only to people in His time but to those today who reject Him, His gospel, and His Church after having seen miracles in their lives or the lives of others and felt the confirmation of the Holy Ghost. Of course, there is always hope and room for repentance.

---

16. Matt. 23:37; see also Luke 13:34.
17. Isa. 14:4–5.

Notwithstanding Jesus's condemnation of some of the major cities in Galilee, many in the area did believe in Him, and His gospel began to spread throughout the land as the Seventy went forth.

Christ's Brethren (Kinsmen) Encourage Christ to Attend the Feast (John 7:2–9)

Jesus's Galilean ministry was now concluded. He would forever leave the area where He was raised as a boy and where most of His public ministry, including His teachings and miracles, had occurred. It was now autumn,[18] the last autumn of Jesus's life in mortality. Approximately six months had passed since the Apostles had returned from their missions, and many in Galilee were making preparations for the annual caravans to attend the Feast of Tabernacles in Jerusalem.[19] The following is John's account of the discussion Jesus had with certain of His "brethren" or kinsmen, who encouraged Him to attend the feast openly:

> **John 7:2–9.** Now the Jews' feast of tabernacles was at hand. His brethren therefore said unto him, Depart hence, and go into Judaea, that thy disciples also may see the works that thou doest. For there is no man that doeth any thing in secret, and he himself seeketh to be known openly. If thou do these things, shew thyself to the world. For neither did his brethren believe in him. Then Jesus said unto them, My time is not yet come: but your time is alway ready. The world cannot hate you; but me it hateth, because I testify of it, that the works thereof are evil. Go ye up unto this feast: I go not up yet unto this feast; for my time is not yet full come. When he had said these words unto them, he abode still in Galilee.

Jesus's brethren urged Him to attend this great annual feast in order to openly demonstrate His miraculous powers. John's record states that these brethren did not believe in Him. The word brethren may refer to Jesus's biological brothers: James, Joses, Juda, and Simon.[20] If some or all of these individuals were the ones referred to, then it seems that they did not believe or that neither Mary, Joseph, or Jesus had fully told the family of His divine

---

18. See Farrar, *Life of Christ*, p. 372.
19. See Farrar, *Life of Christ*, p. 372.
20. See Mark 6:3.

birth and who He was.[21] The term brethren may also refer to other close relatives, such as cousins or uncles. If James and Juda were among those who did not believe, they were obviously fully converted after Christ's Resurrection, since the books of James and Jude in the New Testament are attributed to these brothers of Jesus.

With some unbelief, Jesus's brethren said, "If thou do these things . . ."[22] These brethren, like so many others, sought for additional signs and proof for themselves and for others. These brethren wanted Jesus to publicly perform miracles to verify His claimed divinity. On many occasions, Jesus told those He healed to not tell anyone what had occurred. These brethren's motives were not pure.

Jesus then plainly told these men that His time had not yet come, implying that openly attending the Feast of Tabernacles would accelerate Jewish leaders' hatred of Him and would result in His ministry being cut short of what He had determined was necessary. He was the one to decide when and where He went.

Moreover, He warned these men that their time for being tested was now. Would they believe in Jesus as they stood in His presence? This question applies to all who seek to counsel the Lord.

Christ did not say He would not attend the Feast of Tabernacles; rather, He said that He would not "yet" attend. Later, Christ attended the feast, initially somewhat secretly. The specifics of this feast will be considered in this chapter, and what Christ did at the feast will be considered in the next two chapters.

The Feast of Tabernacles

It is beneficial to reflect on the various individual and family activities involved in the Feast of Tabernacles and to consider their rich symbolism today as people prepare for the Savior's return to the earth.[23] This feast, or festival, symbolized Jehovah's mercy in delivering the ancient Israelites from

---

21. Luke 2:19 states, "And Mary kept all these things, and pondered them in her heart."

22. These words are somewhat similar to those Satan had previously told Jesus (see Matt. 4:3, 6, 9; Luke 4:3, 7, 9).

23. See Zech. 14:16.

bondage and leading them through the desert to the promised land. The feast also pointed to Christ's mortal ministry, particularly His sacrifice for all, and symbolically taught of His future Second Coming. Thus, the feast's rich symbolism was designed to help the Jews, and all others, to remember Jehovah (Christ). The feast encouraged a renewed fellowship with Jehovah. This festival, along with the other two required festivals, were to be "unto the Lord."[24] The festival was also called the Feast of Ingathering because it involved celebrating the harvest and remembering God's bounty in providing food.[25]

Jews throughout Palestine and from other surrounding nations made a "required pilgrimage to Jerusalem three times a year: at the Festival of Unleavened Bread (Passover), the Festival of Weeks (Pentecost), the Festival of Tabernacles (Deut. 16:16; cf. Exo. 23:13–17; 34:18–23). . . . In NT times, large crowds of pilgrims are depicted as coming to Jerusalem for such festivals (Luke 2:41–45; John 12:20) . . . and the joy of the occasion would be marked by singing and rejoicing."[26]

The feast was a time for Jews to come together to make sacrifices with the assistance of priests and to participate in the events and rituals associated with the feast. Participating together gave the Jews a sense of belonging to something larger than their own local synagogue. "In a figurative sense, the NT also portrays the Christian life as a journey toward a heavenly city (Heb. 11:13–16; cf 1 Pet. 1:17; 2:11)."[27] There is some similarity in The Church of Jesus Christ of Latter-day Saints during general conference; people all over the world listen to Church leaders provide instruction and may sense they are part of something much larger than their own wards or branches.

The pilgrimage was also a time to reflect on the ancient Israelites' wandering in the desert for forty years[28] and God's mercy in delivering the

---

24. Lev. 23:39; see also Judg. 21:19; Ezek. 45:23. Of course, the Israelites also celebrated other feasts, such as the Feast of Trumpets, the Feast of Purim, and the Feast of Dedication, as well as observed weekly Sabbaths and other celebratory events (see *HarperCollins Bible Dictionary*, s.v. "Tabernacles, Festival of"; Smith, *Bible Dictionary*, s.v. "festivals").

25. Remembering God and Christ are recurrent themes in the scriptures. See "remember" in scripture concordances for numerous references.

26. See *HarperCollins Bible Dictionary*, s.v. "pilgrimage."

27. *HarperCollins Bible Dictionary*, s.v. "pilgrimage."

28. See Num. 14:33–34; 32:13; Deut. 2:7; 8:2; Josh. 5:6.

Israelites from Egyptian bondage.[29] The pilgrimage was a time to remember that God provided needed water and food in the desert.[30] It was a time to remember God's mercy in providing a way for those who were bitten by fiery serpents to be healed.[31] It was a time to remember the commandments written by the finger of God on Mount Sinai.[32] It was a time to remember that God enabled the Israelites to conquer their enemies upon arriving in the promised land.[33] It was also a time to reflect on one's own life and recommit to always remember God and to keep His commandments.[34]

The Feast of Tabernacles was celebrated for eight days, beginning on the fifteenth of Tishri (September/October).[35] Josephus wrote that the Feast of Tabernacles was a "most holy and most eminent feast" for the Hebrews.[36] Presumably because of the feast's importance, Solomon's temple was dedicated during this feast.[37]

The Lord directed that the Israelites dwell in booths during the feast, that their "generations may know that I made the children of Israel to dwell in booths, when I brought them out of the land of Egypt."[38] The booths were to be made of "pine branches, and myrtle branches, and palm branches, and branches of thick trees," according to Nehemiah 8:15, or "boughs of

29. See Ex. 3:8; 18:8–10.

30. See Ex. 16:15, 31–35; 16:31.

31. See Num. 21:6–9; 1 Ne. 17:41; Alma 33:19.

32. See Ex. 31:18.

33. See Josh. 1:1–5; see also the book of Joshua overall; *HarperCollins Bible Dictionary*, s.v. "festivals" and "Tabernacles, Festival of"; Smith, *Bible Dictionary*, s.v. "Tabernacles, Feast of."

34. Today, the sacrament prayers are also reminders of Christ's body and blood, which were sacrificed for all people (see D&C 20:77, 79).

35. See *HarperCollins Bible Dictionary*, s.v. "Tabernacles, Festival of"; Smith, *Bible Dictionary*, s.v. "festivals."

36. Josephus, *Antiquities*, 8,4,1.

37. When Solomon completed his temple, "he also wrote to the rulers and elders of the Hebrews, and ordered all the people to gather themselves together to Jerusalem, both to see the temple which he had built, and to remove the ark of God into it" (see Josephus, *Antiquities*, 8,4,1; see also 1 Kgs. 8). The "ark of the covenant of the Lord" was to be brought "out of the city of David, which is Zion" (see 1 Kgs. 8:1).

38. Lev. 23:43; see also Neh. 8:14.

goodly trees,"[39] according to Leviticus 23:40. These items were materials that God, not humans, had made. [40]

The booths were placed wherever there was space. Even those who had homes in Jerusalem constructed booths on the roofs of their houses. The booths served as a reminder of the shelters under which Israelite families lived while in the wilderness. Therefore, the booths helped the Jews to remember the importance of the family unit. In the Feast of Tabernacles, the Jews used the Hebrew word *sukkah* for both booth and for tabernacle.[41] It is interesting to note that the tabernacle that served as a portable temple in the wilderness was holy and that Jehovah gave strict rules regarding the service to be performed in the tabernacle and how it was to be transported. Therefore, the booths also reminded the Jews that the home should likewise be a place of holiness.

Every seventh year during the Feast of Tabernacles, parts of the Torah were read publicly.[42] Reading from the word of God was a vivid reminder of His commandments, of the fact that He lives, and of the importance of the scriptures.

The Lord decreed that the "first day [of the Feast of Tabernacles] shall be a sabbath, and on the eighth day shall be a sabbath."[43] Additionally, the Lord directed that this feast was to be a celebration of the "gather[ing] in the fruit of the land."[44] No work was to be done, and the Israelites were to "afflict [their] souls."[45]

---

39. Lev. 23:40.

40. The phrase "boughs of goodly trees," according to Talmage, "had come to be understood as citron fruit, which every orthodox Jew carried in one hand while, in the other he bore a leafy branch or a bunch of twigs known as the 'lulab,' when he repaired to the temple for the morning sacrifice, and in the joyous processions of the day" (Talmage, *Jesus the Christ*, p. 394).

41. The Hebrews also used the words *ohel* or *mishkan* for the tabernacle (see Young, *Analytical Concordance*, s.v. "booth" and "tabernacle").

42. See Deut. 31:10–11. When the Jews returned to Jerusalem after the Babylonian captivity, Ezra read from the "book of the law of God" each of the seven days of this feast (see Neh. 8:18).

43. Lev. 23:39.

44. Lev. 23:39.

45. Lev. 23:32; Num. 29:7.

The feast began with a holy convocation, which is a type of religious meeting.[46] During the week of festivities, all the courses of priests[47] were employed in turn.[48] On the eighth day, there was a solemn assembly that served to conclude the feast, and the priests would offer a burnt offering of "one bullock, one ram, seven lambs of the first year without blemish . . . and one goat for a sin offering."[49]

During the Feast of Tabernacles, more public burnt offerings were made to the Lord than during any other feast. On the first day of the feast, thirteen young bullocks, two rams, fourteen young lambs, and one young goat were offered as burnt offerings to the Lord.[50] Burnt offerings were a symbol of the Atonement.[51] On each subsequent day, the same sacrifice was made except that one fewer bullock was offered, so that on the seventh day only seven bullocks were offered, for a total of seventy bullocks sacrificed. In addition, on the fifth, sixth, and seventh days, one adult goat was to be

---

46. Num. 29:12.

47. "The earliest historical record of any division of the priesthood belongs to the time of David. . . . It can be established that the priesthood was divided into twenty-four 'courses' or orders[,] . . . each of which was to serve in rotation for one week, while the further assignment of special services during the week was determined by lot. . . . There were not fewer than 24,000 stationed permanently at Jerusalem, and 12, 000 at Jericho" (Smith, *Bible Dictionary*, s.v. "priests, classification"). "Sacrificial functions were discharged by the descendants of Aaron, while the other Levites held subsidiary roles. . . . Chief among the duties of the priests was the performance of sacrifices. . . . Ordinary priests performed these daily functions, but the high priest was entrusted with the sin offerings, especially that of the Day of Atonement. . . . [They] pronounced the priestly blessing . . ., blew trumpets on festive occasions such as holidays and new moons, and blew the . . . ram's horn . . . on the Day of Atonement. . . . The priests also were in charge of maintenance of the temple. . . . The collection of tithes and other obligatory temple donations was administered by the priests. . . . Purification rites were performed by a priests, [and] the priests were charged with diagnosing leprosy" (*HarperCollins Bible Dictionary*, s.v. "priests").

48. See Farrar, *Life of Christ*, p. 372; see also 1 Chr. 24:1–19.

49. Num. 29:36, 38; see also vv. 35, 37.

50. Burnt offerings were made at regularly appointed times: daily in the morning and evening (see Ex. 29:38–42; Num. 28:3–4), with a double portion on the Sabbath (see Num. 28:9–10), and monthly at the new moon (see Num. 28:11–15). Burnt offerings were also made at seasonally appointed times, such as at the Feast of the Passover, Feast of the Harvest, and Feast of Tabernacles; on the first day of the New Year; and on the Day of Atonement.

51. As an angel taught Adam, "This thing [sacrifice] is a similitude of the sacrifice of the Only Begotten of the Father, which is full of grace and truth" (Moses 5:7). See also Lev. 1:4; 14:20; Heb. 9:11–15; 1 Pet. 1:19; 2 Ne. 11:4; 25:24–27; Jacob 4:5; Jarom 1:11; Mosiah 3:15.

offered instead of a young goat.[52] Of this successive decrease in offerings, Edersheim wrote: "Indeed, the whole symbolism of the Feast, beginning with the completed harvest, for which it was a thanksgiving, pointed to the future. The Rabbis themselves admitted this. The strange number of sacrificial bullocks—seventy in all—they regarded as referring to 'the seventy nations' of heathendom."[53]

All of the sacrifices were male animals without blemish, symbolic of Christ, who was in the world but without sin[54] and was the great and last sacrifice.[55] Further, just as the animals' blood and bodies were sacrificed upon the altar, Christ sacrificed His body and blood in Gethsemane and on the cross. As He felt the awful weight of the Atonement, He shed great drops of blood from every pore.[56]

The animal sacrifices were made on a stone altar unhewn by human hands so that the altar remained unpolluted.[57] The altar's construction points to the creation of this earth by God through His Only Begotten Son, not humans or random scientific principles. God has allowed His children to reside here during their mortal lives, but the world is His creation. Further, the altar was to be a reminder to the Jews that God was the one who provided "a great and last sacrifice."[58]

One of the notable ceremonies during the feast was the daily procession to the pool of Siloam, where a priest filled his golden pitcher with the water to use for the day's sacrifice. The procession then returned to the temple. The return was timed such that the procession would arrive just as the priests were laying the pieces of the sacrifice on the great altar of burnt offering, toward the close of the morning sacrifice service.[59] The priest who had gotten water from the pool of Siloam mixed the water with wine and

---

52. See Num. 29:7–34.
53. Edersheim, *Life and Times of Jesus the Messiah*, p. 577; see also Farrar, *Life of Christ*, p. 372.
54. See Lev. 1:3.
55. Alma 34:10, 13–14; see also vv. 11–12, 15–16.
56. See Luke 22:44.
57. See Ex. 20:25.
58. See Gen. 22:8; Alma 34:10–16.
59. See Talmage, *Jesus the Christ*, p. 394.

then poured the mixture on the sacrificial offering.[60] This act, in effect, was a priesthood ordinance. The Jews believed that pouring the mixture over the sacrifice was symbolic of the outpouring of the Lord's spirit on the people. Additionally, pouring the water on the sacrifices was a reminder that Christ was baptized by recognized priesthood authority and that all people must be baptized by immersion as part of the perquisites to inherit the kingdom of God.[61] Further, the wine made the mixture red, signifying that Christ bled and died for all and that He would "[trod] the winepress alone."[62] The color also symbolized that when He returns, He will be "red in his apparel, and his garments like him that treadeth in the wine-vat."[63]

The overall ceremony was a reminder that Christ is the Living Water.[64] As both Ezekiel and Zechariah prophesied, when the Savior returns again to the earth, living waters will flow from Jerusalem to the Sea of Galilee and to the Dead Sea and will heal the waters of the Dead Sea.[65] Additionally, "in the barren deserts there shall come forth pools of living water; and the parched ground shall no longer be a thirsty land."[66] Further, Christ will lead His disciples to "living fountains of waters" and will "wipe away all tears from their eyes."[67]

As the people traveled to and from the pool of Siloam, they sang or chanted the Hallel.[68] Singing together during this festival, including while traveling to the temple and altar of sacrifice, taught the not-so-obvious lesson that all people are connected and are children of Heavenly Father. They need each other's help, support, and instruction. People need to learn to serve and to accept service. This truth is reflected in John Donne's poem "No Man Is an Island":

---

60. This ceremony was omitted on the eighth day of the festival (see Talmage, *Jesus the Christ*, p. 394).

61. See John 3:5; 2 Ne. 31.

62. Isa. 63:3.

63. D&C 133:48.

64. See John 4:1–26; John 7:38; Jer. 2:13; D&C 63:23.

65. See Ezek. 47:8–9; Zech. 14:8.

66. D&C 133:29.

67. Rev. 7:17.

68. See Ps. 113–118. These psalms consist of praise and thanksgiving to the Lord and were also sung at the Passover.

No man is an island,
Entire of itself,
Every man is a piece of the continent,
A part of the main.
If a clod be washed away by the sea,
Europe is the less.
As well as if a promontory were.
As well as if a manor of thy friend's
Or of thine own were:
Any man's death diminishes me,
Because I am involved in mankind,
And therefore never send to know for whom the bell tolls;
It tolls for thee.[69]

At night during the Feast of Tabernacles, four golden lamps on four golden candlesticks were lit and kept burning in the temple's Court of the Women.[70] The lights were a reminder that Jehovah is the Light of the World[71] and that His disciples should also be a light to the world. The lamps burned with oil, which was also symbolic. For example, oil was used to sanctify Aaron and his sons when they were ordained to the priesthood.[72] Additionally, oil is representative of the spiritual strength needed to abide the day of Christ's return to the earth.[73]

As the priest arrived at the temple, he entered through the Water Gate, which was named for this ceremony and went straight into the Court of the Priests. The priest was welcomed by the sound of trumpets played by other priests.[74] On the last day of the feast, the priests walked the perimeter of the altar not just once, as they did on the other days of the feast, but seven times, as if they were compassing the gentile city of Jericho as did the ancient Israelites before obtaining the promised land.[75] The priests officiated at the

---

69. Donne, Meditation XVII, *Devotions upon Emergent Occasions.*

70. See Dummelow, *Bible Commentary*, p. 787.

71. See John 8:12; 9:5.

72. See Lev. 8:12.

73. See Matt. 25:1–13.

74. See Talmage, *Jesus the Christ*, p. 394. Each day of the feast, the temple trumpets sounded twenty-one other times, in an inspiring and triumphant blast (see Farrar, *Life of Christ*, pp. 372–373).

75. See Talmage, *Jesus the Christ*, p. 395.

altar not only because they had authority but also as a subtle reminder that their authority came from God.

The Feast of Tabernacles will be held around the time of Christ's Second Coming and thereafter, as prophesied by Zechariah. When the Lord returns at the Second Coming, people will gather to Jerusalem to worship Him. Zechariah prophesied, "And it shall come to pass, that every one that is left of all the nations which came against Jerusalem shall even go up from year to year to worship the King, the Lord of hosts, and to keep the feast of tabernacles."[76] Many in the nations of the earth that fought against Israel will finally accept Christ as the promised Messiah, "and the Lord shall be king over all the earth: in that day shall there be one Lord, and his name one."[77]

The latter-day Feast of Tabernacles that Zechariah prophesied of may differ from the prior ones in that animals might not be sacrificed, since Christ is the "great and last sacrifice."[78] As the Lord taught the people in the Americas following His Resurrection: "And ye shall offer up unto me no more the shedding of blood; yea, your sacrifices and your burnt offerings shall be done away, for I will accept none of your sacrifices and your burnt offerings. And ye shall offer for a sacrifice unto me a broken heart and a contrite spirit. And whoso cometh unto me with a broken heart and a contrite spirit, him will I baptize with fire and with the Holy Ghost, even as the Lamanites, because of their faith in me at the time of their conversion, were baptized with fire and with the Holy Ghost, and they knew it not."[79] What may very well be required of those who participate in this Feast of Tabernacles are a broken heart and a contrite spirit. They will honor and worship Him in Jerusalem. Certainly, at least some will shout praises to the "King of kings, and Lord of lords," as John saw in vision.[80]

Like the Jews of Jesus's day who traveled to Jerusalem for the Feast of Tabernacles, members of The Church of Jesus Christ of Latter-day Saints make a pilgrimage—to temples. For some, the distance is short, whereas for others the distance is long, requiring significant time and expense.

---

76. Zech. 14:16.
77. Zech. 14:9.
78. Alma 34:10, 13–14.
79. 3 Ne. 9:19–20.
80. Rev. 19:16; see also 1 Tim. 6:15; JST 1 Tim. 6:15.

Nevertheless, faithful members of the Church prepare themselves and are drawn to the temple, where they are served by others and where they serve those who have passed on to the spirit world. When in the temple, Church members perform sacred ordinances, make covenants, ponder Christ's life, and worship Him. In doing so, they are spiritually refined.

In Jesus's day, those who traveled long distances to the Feast of Tabernacles had to be prepared for the journey with food and clothing. Saints today must also be prepared. Similarly, just as residents of Jerusalem received those traveling to the city in caravans, Church members today need to be willing to help those in need, whatever the circumstances may be.

Rather than booths prepared in the desert of Sinai or at Jerusalem, members of The Church of Jesus Christ of Latter-day Saints invite the Spirit and the Light of Christ into their homes and learn of Him to better prepare themselves and their families for His return to the earth, when the faithful will shout, "Hosanna."

The theme that permeates all the events of the Feast of Tabernacles— and almost all scripture—is Christ. Considering the events that occurred during the Feast of Tabernacles, their symbolism, and what will most certainly come, this feast is well worth reflecting on. Doing so can help individuals to strengthen their testimonies and the testimonies of family members and to be prepared for the Savior's glorious return to the earth.

Chapter 37

JESUS ATTENDS THE FEAST OF TABERNACLES

Now was the time for Jesus to leave the area where He had grown up and where He had often taught and performed miracles. The time for His Atonement, betrayal, and Crucifixion were drawing near—about six months away. He likely looked upon the area of Galilee with both fondness and sadness: fondness because of those who believed; sadness because of those who rejected Him. Yet He remained focused on what lay ahead and what He came to the earth to do. As Isaiah wrote, Jesus "set [His] face like a flint"[1] and departed Galilee.

Jesus Departs for Jerusalem (Luke 9:51; John 7:10)

From Galilee, Jesus headed toward Jerusalem for the Feast of Tabernacles. Both Luke's and John's brief accounts follow:

Luke 9:51. And it came to pass, when the time was come that he should be received up, he steadfastly set his face to go to Jerusalem.

John 7:10. But when his brethren were gone up, then went he also up unto the feast, not openly, but as it were in secret.

Jesus and His Apostles Are Rejected in a Samaritan Village (Luke 9:52–56)

Many of Jesus's disciples and His "brethren" had already left for Jerusalem. Presumably these brethren were the same men who had entreated

---

1. Isa. 50:7.

Him to go to the Feast of Tabernacles and openly display His power.[2] The Apostles knew that certain of the scribes, Pharisees, and members of the Sanhedrin sought Jesus's life and that if He appeared openly at the Feast of Tabernacles, His enemies would likely try to find occasion to take Him and put Him to death. The Apostles may have also been afraid that their lives were likewise in danger. They were likely amazed that Jesus would go where His life might be taken. Regardless of the danger, Jesus would travel to Jerusalem because He needed to testify of Himself there.

Rather than taking the more common route along the Jordan Valley, Jesus chose to take the shorter route through Samaria. The Jews often passed through Samaria but seldom availed themselves of Samaritan hospitality, even though the rabbis had taught that the Samaritan lands, roads, waters, and dwellings were clean[3] and even though Samaritans typically received travelers when requested. The following is Luke's account of what transpired during Jesus's travel through Samaria:

> **Luke 9:52–56.** And [Jesus] sent messengers before his face: and they went, and entered into a village of the Samaritans, to make ready for him. And they did not receive him, because his face was as though he would go to Jerusalem. And when his disciples James and John saw this, they said, Lord, wilt thou that we command fire to come down from heaven, and consume them, even as Elias did? But he turned, and rebuked them, and said, Ye know not what manner of spirit ye are of. For the Son of man is not come to destroy men's lives, but to save them. And they went to another village.

Jesus sent messengers ahead, presumably some of His Apostles, likely to seek lodging, food, and water for Jesus and the rest of the group. Previously when Jesus was in Samaria, residents of the city of Sychar had accepted Him as the Messiah. But on this latter occasion, when many Jews were traveling to Jerusalem through Samaria for the Feast of Tabernacles, things were different. Though the Samaritans expected a Messiah, those in the village that the messengers went to believed that Jesus could not be the One because He was going to Jerusalem instead of to their holy Mount Gerizim. The Samaritans therefore rejected the messengers Jesus sent.

---

2. See John 7:2–9.
3. Dummelow, *Bible Commentary*, p. 750.

When James and John saw that the people rejected Christ and those with Him, the two Apostles impetuously asked Jesus if they could call down fire from heaven to consume the villagers, as Elias (Elijah) had previously done in Samaria.[4]

On a previous occasion, Jesus had called James and John "sons of thunder,"[5] a name that may imply they had strong personalities and often were impatient. Because they sought to destroy those in the Samaritan village, the Lord rebuked these Apostles. Jesus taught them again that He had not "come to destroy men's lives, but to save them." The Apostles needed to learn and relearn this lesson because they were soon to embark on missions again, they held the priesthood power and authority of God, and the priesthood should not be misused.

In the Sermon on the Mount, Jesus had taught that "whosoever shall smite thee on thy right cheek, turn to him the other also."[6] Now, He showed His Apostles—particularly James and John—what this teaching meant in practice.[7]

Jesus's statement that He came not to destroy but to save all people encompasses the purpose of every person's life on earth. People are not here to be condemned by God but to complete the steps necessary to gain eternal salvation. Indeed, God's work and glory is for all people to gain eternal life,[8] not to stop their eternal progression. In teaching James and John, Jesus was demonstrating His and His Father's unbounding love for all people. His statement can provide the basis of faith in God, for no matter a person's circumstances and no matter what he or she may have done or not done, Heavenly Father and Jesus Christ are always there with open arms.

---

4. In the days of Elijah, the king of Samaria was ill and sent messengers to ask the god of Ekron whether the king would recover. The angel of the Lord told Elijah to go to the king and declare that he should have inquired of the God of Israel and that the king would surely die. Upon hearing this message, the king sent two captains and their soldiers to arrest Elijah and thus dishonor the Lord. When the armies found Elijah on a hill in Samaria, the prophet called down fire from heaven to destroy the armies. (See 2 Kgs. 1:1–17.)

5. Mark 3:17.

6. Matt. 5:39.

7. Jesus again showed what this lesson meant in practice as He hung on the cruel cross and declared, "Father, forgive them; for they know not what they do" (see Luke 23:34).

8. See Moses 1:39.

Similarly, Jesus implicitly taught that people should not condemn others, though it is often easy to do so. Disciples of Christ should lift others and help them find salvation, not tear them down, no matter what they have done.

After Jesus and His Apostles were rejected, they went to another village. Had the group not traveled through Samaria on their way to the Feast of Tabernacles, the Apostles may not have had the opportunity to learn in practice a most important lesson—a lesson that is important for all to understand.

Jesus Likely Goes to Bethany (Luke 10:38–42)

It is possible that before attending the Feast of Tabernacles in Jerusalem, Jesus and His Apostles went past Jerusalem, over the Mount of Olives, and on to Bethany, which is approximately two miles to the east of Jerusalem.[9] Edersheim wrote:

> Again, from the narrative of Christ's reception in the house of Martha, we gather that Jesus had arrived in Bethany with His disciples, but that He alone was the guest of the two sisters (Luke 10:38). We infer that Christ had dismissed His disciples to go into the neighboring City for the Feast, while Himself tarried in Bethany. Lastly, with all this agrees the notice in St. John 7:14, that it was not at the beginning, but "about the midst of the feast," that 'Jesus went up into the Temple.' Although travelling on the two first restive days was not actually unlawful, yet we can scarcely conceive that Jesus would have done so—especially on the Feast of Tabernacles; and the inference is obvious, that Jesus had tarried in the immediate neighborhood, as we know He did at Bethany in the house of Martha and Mary.[10]

Their brother, Lazarus, had likely left for Jerusalem to attend the feast.

The Jews Seek Jesus at the Feast (John 7:11–13)

Presumably, Jesus's brethren arrived in Jerusalem for the feast before He did, since He left Galilee after they did. Some of the Jews may have recognized these brethren or Jesus's Apostles and may have inquired of

---

9. See *HarperCollins Bible Dictionary*, s.v. "Bethany."

10. See Edersheim, *Life and Times of Jesus the Messiah*, p. 573. John is the only Gospel writer who recorded the account of Jesus at the Feast of Tabernacles; therefore, precise chronology is difficult to determine.

them or simply discussed among themselves whether Jesus had come or was coming to the feast. The following is John's account:

John 7:11–13. Then the Jews sought him at the feast, and said, Where is he? And there was much murmuring among the people concerning him: for some said, He is a good man: others said, Nay; but he deceiveth the people. Howbeit no man spake openly of him for fear of the Jews.

Of course, Jesus had not told His brethren whether He would come, and at this point He had either not arrived or had not made His arrival publicly known. Perhaps the Jews were curious about whether Jesus was coming because they thought He would perform great miracles for them. Despite the Jews' curiosity, they did not voice their questions before the leaders of the Jews, apparently fearing what might happen to Jesus and to those who expressed curiosity.

It is likely that those asking about Jesus's potential appearance had varying perceptions of Him. Presumably, some of these Jews believed that He was the Messiah; some thought that He was a good man or a great prophet; some did not care who He was; some were skeptical; and some said He was a deceiver, ascribed His miracles to Beelzebub, and sought to take His life. From what transpired later at the feast, many of those present presumably had neither sought nor received a spiritual witness of Jesus as the Son of God. They had apparently failed to understand that they could ask God whether Jesus was the Christ, as He had declared. They had been blinded to spiritual things by their religious literalism and the numerous rabbinical rules and regulations, which did not promote faith and the things of the Spirit. The Jews had been taught that fastidiously adhering to the rabbinical rules was the only requirement for salvation.

Likewise, many people today are blinded to the truth that Jesus is the Messiah. As Paul taught, many are "tossed to and fro, and carried about with every wind of doctrine, by the sleight of men, and cunning craftiness, whereby they lie in wait to deceive."[11] Many are distracted by the things of the world or are focused on themselves, their circumstances, and their social and political causes. It would be beneficial for all to take time to pause, ask God, recognize answers, and believe.

---

11. Eph. 4:14; see also James 1:6.

The Feast of Tabernacles was particularly important for Jews who lived outside of the Jerusalem area. They came from regions throughout the Mediterranean, and upon arriving in Jerusalem for the feast, they paid a temple tax or contribution.[12] These individuals were joined by those coming from Galilee, Decapolis, Samaria, Perea, and Judea.

The Feast of Tabernacles pointed to Christ and His Atonement. The following is an observation from Edersheim:

> It must have been a stirring scene, when from out of the mass of Levites, with their musical instruments, who crowded the fifteen steps that led from the Court of Israel to that of the Women [at the temple] stepped two priests with their silver trumpets. As the first cockcrowing intimated the dawn of morn, they blew a threefold blast; another on the tenth step, and yet another threefold blast as they entered the Court of the Women. And still sounding their trumpets, they marched through the Court of the Women to the Beautiful Gate. Here, turning round and facing westwards to the Holy Place, they repeated: "Our fathers, who were in this place, they turned their backs on the Sanctuary of Jehovah, and their faces eastward, for they worshipped eastward, the sun; but we, our eyes are towards Jehovah." "We are Jehovah's—our eyes are towards Jehovah."[13]

Those who came were looking for the promised Messiah, whom they expected would free them from the bondage of Rome. Jesus was the hoped-for Messiah and came to this feast, which was to honor Him, but most of the Jews did not recognize who He really was, notwithstanding His many miracles. In the Jews' hope for a deliverer, they failed to comprehend the symbolism of the feast. Jesus came with a very different purpose and earthly mission than that for which the Jews hoped. He did not come with the purpose of delivering them from Roman bondage. He came to teach His pure gospel and to give His personal witness of both the Father and Himself. He came as the "great high priest,"[14] the "great and last sacrifice,"[15]

---

12.   Edersheim wrote: "For this [the Feast of Tabernacles] was pre-eminently the Feast for foreign pilgrims, coming from the farthest distance who Temple-contributions were then received and counted" (Edersheim, *Life and Times of Jesus the Messiah*, p. 576).

13.   Edersheim, *Life and Times of Jesus the Messiah*, p. 577.

14.   Heb. 4:14; see also 9:11–14.

15.   Alma 34:10, 13–14.

the "bread of life,"[16] the "living water,"[17] and the "light of the world,"[18] all of which were symbolized in the events of this feast.

Jesus Teaches at the Temple and Gives a Key to Gaining Knowledge of God (John 7:14–18)

As Jesus arrived in Jerusalem, He may have seen the smoke from sacrifices rising to the heavens and may have smelled the burning flesh. He may have seen the procession of the priests and others going to or from the waters of Siloam. He may have seen those who carried a palm branch in their right hand and fruit in their left hand while they marched.[19] He may have heard the priests playing silver trumpets. He would have seen multitudes of people who had come from afar and were dressed in the clothing of their localities. When Jesus went to the temple midweek, He likely sat in one of the large halls that opened out to the temple courts. While at the temple, He taught all who would listen.[20]

How marvelous it would have been to hear Jesus teach at the temple. His instruction was valuable for those who were present and is also valuable for all people today. Indeed, John—the only Gospel writer to record these events—did so in part for people in the latter days. John's account begins as follows:

John 7:14–18. Now about the midst of the feast Jesus went up into the temple, and taught. And the Jews marvelled, saying, How knoweth this man letters, having never learned? Jesus answered them, and said, My doctrine is not mine, but his that sent me. If any man will do his will, he shall know of the doctrine, whether it be of God, or whether I speak of myself. He that speaketh of himself seeketh his own glory: but he that seeketh his glory that sent him, the same is true, and no unrighteousness is in him.

John's record does not indicate what the first part of Jesus's sermon focused on. Jesus likely taught the principles He had taught so many times before, including faith, repentance, and the way to live. He likely addressed

---

16. John 6:25.
17. John 4:10.
18. John 8:12.
19. See Edersheim, *Life and Times of Jesus the Messiah*, p. 582.
20. See Farrar, *Life of Christ*, p. 375.

the principles He had taught in His Sermon on the Mount and may also have addressed prophecies concerning the coming of the Messiah. He likely taught things that appealed to the hearts and spirits of those who were spiritually receptive, not the tedious rules and regulations of the Pharisees, priests, and rabbis. He may also have relied heavily on the scriptures, for John's record states that the people marveled because of His knowledge of the scriptures despite not being taught by the rabbis. Once again, the people failed to understand that He was the Jehovah of the Old Testament. It was He who gave the law to Moses. And it was He who enabled inspiration and revelation to flow to the prophets. Christ did not need instruction from the rabbis; they should have looked to Him for divine instruction.

Jesus then identified a key to obtaining knowledge of God: if a person would "do His will," the person would know that the principles Jesus taught were of God. Jesus then gave another truth to the Jews: Those who speak of themselves seek their own glory, not the glory of God. Those who are humble, don't boast, and seek the glory of God are among the righteous. This teaching was a direct condemnation of the Jewish leaders who constantly sought status, wealth, and costly robes and homes rather than the glory of God, whom they claimed to serve.

Jesus Addresses the Jews' Desire to Kill Him (John 7:19–24)

Jesus then confounded the reasoning and pricked the conscience of the unbelieving Jews. John recorded Jesus's words as follows:

John 7:19–24. Did not Moses give you the law, and yet none of you keepeth the law? Why go ye about to kill me? The people answered and said, Thou hast a devil: who goeth about to kill thee? Jesus answered and said unto them, I have done one work, and ye all marvel. Moses therefore gave unto you circumcision; (not because it is of Moses, but of the fathers;) and ye on the sabbath day circumcise a man. If a man on the sabbath day receive circumcision, that the law of Moses should not be broken; are ye angry at me, because I have made a man every whit whole on the sabbath day? Judge not according to the appearance, but judge righteous judgment.

First, Jesus reminded them of their law, which Jehovah had given Moses on Mount Sinai. That law's fifth commandment states, "Thou shalt not kill."[21] Christ then condemned the thoughts and intentions of those listening by bluntly stating that none of them kept the law they so revered because they sought to kill Him without just cause. In response, the people denied that anyone sought to kill Jesus, and they accused Him of being possessed by the devil.

Despite this denial, some of the Jews did indeed seek to kill Jesus, using the false justification that He had violated the rabbinical understanding of the law of Moses. For example, Jesus had healed a man on the Sabbath, and shortly after this healing, He had told the Jews that "my Father worketh hitherto, and I work."[22] The Jews considered this declaration blasphemy. Of course, Jesus was the only one who could not be guilty of blasphemy for claiming to be the Son of God.

Jesus then explained that the accusations against Him were unjust, for what He had done on the Sabbath was good: He had healed a man, which was not unlawful.[23] How could making a man whole be a defilement of the Sabbath? Further, how could healing a man with only a word be classified as work? Jesus then referred to the exemption that permitted priests to circumcise on the Sabbath. Wasn't healing someone an act of even greater good? Christ declared, "Judge not according to the appearance, but judge righteous judgment." He was teaching that the Jews needed to look to the spirit of the law, not to the multitude of extraneous rules. Unfortunately, many of the Jews were hypocrites and had lost the true meaning of the Sabbath. Their pride prevented them from believing.

Jesus Testifies of Himself (John 7:25–31)

Some of those who heard Jesus teach at the temple were confused as to why the leaders of the Jews neither said nor did anything about Jesus teaching in the temple. Presumably, there was little doubt in the people's minds that the Jewish leaders sought Jesus's life. Some wondered whether

21. Ex. 20:13.
22. John 5:17.
23. See John 5:1–9.

the Jewish leaders believed that Jesus was the promised Messiah and were thus afraid to take action. John's account states the following:

> **John 7:25–31.** Then said some of them of Jerusalem, Is not this he, whom they seek to kill? But, lo, he speaketh boldly, and they say nothing unto him. Do the rulers know indeed that this is the very Christ? Howbeit we know this man whence he is: but when Christ cometh, no man knoweth whence he is. Then cried Jesus in the temple as he taught, saying, Ye both know me, and ye know whence I am: and I am not come of myself, but he that sent me is true, whom ye know not. But I know him: for I am from him, and he hath sent me. Then they sought to take him: but no man laid hands on him, because his hour was not yet come. And many of the people believed on him, and said, When Christ cometh, will he do more miracles than these which this man hath done?

According to Geikie, those present may have also said, "'Do not the Rabbis tell us . . . that the Messiah will be born at Bethlehem, but that He will be snatched away by spirits and tempests soon after His birth, and that when He returns the second time no one will know from whence He has come?'"[24] The Jews assumed that Jesus had been born in Nazareth, where He was raised to manhood. But if the Jews had merely asked Jesus where He was born, they would have learned the truth about His miraculous birth. They would have discovered that He was born in Bethlehem, which was the prophesied birthplace of the Messiah, and that His birth was without equal in all the annals of history. The Jews needed to accurately determine the facts to judge righteously, but they did not.

It is interesting to note that some of the Jewish leaders who were alive when Jesus was born may have ignored or long forgotten hearing of the testimony of the shepherds who had received the witness of an angel and were present shortly after Jesus's birth.[25] Some may also have ignored or forgotten the testimonies of Simeon[26] and Anna[27] at the temple in Jerusalem shortly after Jesus's birth. Additionally, some may have forgotten about or disregarded hearing of the Wise Men coming from the east in search of the

---

24. Geikie, *Life and Words of Christ*, vol. 2, p. 274.
25. See Luke 2:9–18.
26. See Luke 2:25–35.
27. See Luke 2:36–38.

king of the Jews—a visit that must have caused some wonderment among those in Jerusalem at the time. It is likely that these events related to Jesus's birth had not been recorded, and it seems that more than thirty years later, the stories were forgotten. Alternatively, perhaps the stories were ignored, especially by those who wanted to take Jesus's life.

In response to those at the temple who wondered why the Jewish leaders did not prevent Jesus from speaking, He declared in essence that they thought they knew He came from Nazareth. He further declared that He did not come to the Feast of Tabernacles of His own accord; rather, His Father had sent Him. Implied is an assertion that God was Jesus's father. That day in the temple courts, Jesus bore His divine and solemn witness of the Father. Jesus taught the people that His doctrine was the Father's doctrine and that the Father had taught Jesus and sent Him to the earth. Jesus also taught that He knew the Father; that the Father is "true," meaning, among other things, that He exists and possesses all truth; and that the Jews did not really know Jesus even though they stood in the temple courts with Him. What a simple yet profound message of the unique and divine relationship between Jesus Christ and His Father. And what a sad commentary regarding those who would not believe.

However, not all who were in the temple had deaf ears. Many were spiritually touched by Jesus's witness of Himself and of the Father, and consequently they believed. They also believed because He had performed miracles that none other than the Christ could have performed. Others, however, thought that Jesus was only a prophet—they asked whether, when Christ came, He would perform more miracles than Jesus had.

Today, if Christ were to appear in modern clothing and with hair cut short and were to speak from the grounds of one of the temples, would those who heard recognize Him? Would they believe? Would their eyes be opened and would their hearts burn within them, as did the hearts of the two disciples on the road to Emmaus as they walked with the risen Lord?[28]

---

28. See Luke 24:13–32.

Jesus Declares, "Where I Am, Thither Ye Cannot Come" (John 7:32–36)

While Jesus was still in the temple, certain of the leaders of the Pharisees learned of what those who were listening to Him were saying. John's record states the following:

> **John 7:32–36.** The Pharisees heard that the people murmured such things concerning him; and the Pharisees and the chief priests sent officers to take him. Then said Jesus unto them, Yet a little while am I with you, and then I go unto him that sent me. Ye shall seek me, and shall not find me: and where I am, thither ye cannot come. Then said the Jews among themselves, Whither will he go, that we shall not find him? will he go unto the dispersed among the Gentiles, and teach the Gentiles? What manner of saying is this that he said, Ye shall seek me, and shall not find me: and where I am, thither ye cannot come?

According to Farrar, Jewish leaders frequently met in their stone hall within the temple courts. By means of emissaries, these leaders were kept advised of all that Jesus did and said. By this process, they "watched His every movement with malignant rage."[29] The Jewish leaders knew that if Jesus rose in the minds of the people, the Jewish hierarchy would fall. However, the leaders also knew there was a risk in arresting Jesus publicly, because the people who supported Him might revolt. Moreover, there had been no meeting or decree of the Sanhedrin directing that Jesus be arrested, nor could He have justly been arrested without a formal meeting, accusation, witnesses, and examination. Nevertheless, the chief temple officials and priests sent officers or members of the temple police to arrest Jesus and bring Him before the Sanhedrin.

The presence of these officers caused no interruption in Jesus's teaching, although it is reasonable to assume that Jesus knew of the officers' presence and purpose. Notwithstanding the presence of these officers, Jesus boldly told those who were listening that He would only be with them for a little while longer and that after His death and Resurrection He would return to His Father and would be out of the reach of those who sought Him.

---

29. Farrar, *Life of Christ*, p. 378.

Those who heard failed to understand; they wrongly supposed that Jesus would soon leave Judea and perhaps go northward to the Gentiles. This conclusion may have accelerated the Jewish leaders' eventual arrest and false trial of Jesus, for they would not have wanted Him to escape and then later return.

Jesus Declares That He Is the Living Water (John 7:37–44)

John's record indicates that Jesus taught again on the eighth day of the feast. On this occasion, He declared that He was the Living Water.[30]

> **John 7:37–44.** In the last day, that great day of the feast, Jesus stood and cried, saying, If any man thirst, let him come unto me, and drink. He that believeth on me, as the scripture hath said, out of his belly shall flow rivers of living water. (But this spake he of the Spirit, which they that believe on him should receive: for the Holy Ghost was not yet given; because that Jesus was not yet glorified.) Many of the people therefore, when they heard this saying, said, Of a truth this is the Prophet. Others said, This is the Christ. But some said, Shall Christ come out of Galilee? Hath not the scripture said, That Christ cometh of the seed of David, and out of the town of Bethlehem, where David was? So there was a division among the people because of him. And some of them would have taken him; but no man laid hands on him.

In declaring that He was the Living Water, Jesus was comparing Himself to an important ceremony that occurred during the first seven days of the feast. On these days, a great procession headed to and from the waters of Siloam, where a priest dipped a golden goblet into the water. The priest then returned to the temple, mixed the water with wine, and poured the mixture over a sacrificial offering. This ceremony did not occur on the eighth and final day of the feast. Jesus must have been saddened that the Jews focused on this ceremony but did not recognize Him as the one who had instituted it.[31] Nor did they comprehend on the eighth day of the feast, when the priest brought no water from Siloam, the meaning of Jesus's statement that

---

30. This feast day was not the first time Jesus had declared that He was the Living Water. He had delivered the same message when speaking to a woman at a well in the Samaritan city of Sychar (see John 4:12–14).

31. See Geikie, *Life and Words of Christ*, vol. 2, p. 276.

those who thirst spiritually should come to Him and drink of the spiritual water that He freely offered, with the result that they would be filled to overflowing with His water of life.

The pool of Siloam had special significance in relation to Christ as the Living Water. "'Siloam' is a later Greek form of 'Shiloah.'"[32] The related word *Shiloh* is "a description of Messiah, as the Prince of Peace; or as the '*Seed*' of Judah."[33] Isaiah prophetically referred to the waters of Shiloah when he warned King Ahaz of Judah not to form an alliance with King Rezin of Syria and King Pekah of Israel: "Forasmuch as this people refuseth the waters of Shiloah that go softly, and rejoice in Rezin and Remaliah's son; now therefore, behold, the Lord bringeth up upon them the waters of the river, strong and many, even the King of Assyria, and all his glory." The "waters of Shiloah" Isaiah spoke of symbolized the "house of David, much reduced in its apparent strength, yet supported by the blessing of God."[34] In essence, Isaiah told King Ahaz to trust in the Lord, no matter what fierce enemy was threatening the kingdom.

Jesus alone was the Living Water that would deliver people from the powers of evil, in whatever form, and lead the righteous to the peace of eternal life. The process of drawing water from the pool of Siloam and then using the water as part of the sacrifice had far deeper meaning than the Jews then understood.

Jesus's statement that He is the Living Water was particularly relevant to those at the feast because the feast took place in the autumn, when the Jerusalem area was dry. After declaring that He was the Living Water, Jesus stated that those who believed in Him would have rivers of water flowing from their bellies. John parenthetically noted that this water was the influence, witness, and power of the Holy Ghost. Jesus's symbolic use of the word *belly* is important; a person's belly is deep inside. Likewise, the Holy Ghost would flow to the depths of a person. Further, Jesus indicated that the influence of the Holy Ghost would not be a trickle or small stream but a river. In other words, the influence of the Holy Ghost would be abundant and powerful in the lives of those who believed. Joseph Smith's inspired translation makes

---

32. *HarperCollins Bible Dictionary*, s.v. "Siloam tunnel."
33. Young, *Analytical Concordance*, s.v. "Shiloh."
34. Clarke, *Commentary*, vol. 2, p. 61.

it clear that the Holy Ghost would come to those who believe, "after Jesus was glorified."[35]

In response to Jesus's teachings on this last day of the feast, division arose again among the people. Some said that Jesus was indeed a prophet or the promised Messiah, while others blindly said that Jesus was from Galilee and therefore could not be the seed of David or be the Messiah. They had not taken the opportunity to learn the truth or to feel in their hearts the witness that Christ had borne of Himself. Some of those who did not believe desired to take Him at that time, but John recorded that "no man laid hands on him." It was simply not His time.

The People Are Divided (John 7:45–53)

The officers who were sent to arrest Jesus returned to the chief priests and Pharisees without Him and were questioned about why they had not brought Him. John's account states:

> **John 7:45–53.** Then came the officers to the chief priests and Pharisees; and they said unto them, Why have ye not brought him? The officers answered, Never man spake like this man. Then answered them the Pharisees, Are ye also deceived? Have any of the rulers or of the Pharisees believed on him? But this people who knoweth not the law are cursed. Nicodemus saith unto them, (he that came to Jesus by night, being one of them,) Doth our law judge any man, before it hear him, and know what he doeth? They answered and said unto him, Art thou also of Galilee? Search, and look: for out of Galilee ariseth no prophet. And every man went unto his own house.

Upon being questioned, the officers responded that "never man spake like this man." Apparently, their hearts had been touched by Jesus's message, much to the chagrin of the chief priests. To the officers' credit, they were more afraid of condemnation by the Messiah than condemnation by the chief priests, who were in effect the officers' religious leaders and employers. The officers risked much by not arresting Jesus and by responding as they did to the question asked by the priests and Pharisees.

In an effort to dissuade the officers, the Pharisees then asked two questions: First, had the officers been deceived regarding Jesus? Second, why

---

35. JST John 7:39.

did none of the rulers or Pharisees believe He was the Messiah? In essence, the Pharisees were indicating that the officers had been deceived because those who sent the officers—those who were supposed to know of religious matters—did not believe. Further, the Pharisees in effect declared that the common people, who did not have the religious training the Pharisees had, were cursed because of their ignorance.[36] One can only wonder what these officers must have thought. Did they subsequently follow Jesus? If so, at what cost? Or did they also choose to reject or ignore Him?

Nicodemus, a member of the Sanhedrin, came to the defense of Jesus and the Jews' system of laws, which the chief priests were ignoring. Rather than directly defending Jesus and risking condemnation himself, Nicodemus reminded the Pharisees and chief priests of their laws. He reminded them that their system required an accusation; a formal hearing of the Sanhedrin, with witnesses testifying; and an opportunity for the accused to be heard.

Because of Nicodemus's response, the chief priests turned on him. They accused him of also being from Galilee—in other words, one who believed in Jesus as the Messiah. They also challenged Nicodemus to search the scriptures, for the Messiah was to be born in Bethlehem, not Galilee.

While teaching at the temple during the feast, Jesus had boldly and at great risk testified of His divinity and of His Father. Jesus was setting an example for the Apostles, who were presumably with Jesus at the festival, for soon they would be called upon to boldly testify of Christ, even though their lives would be in peril for so doing. Jesus was also setting an example for all others. As the Apostle Paul said, "Be not thou therefore ashamed of the testimony of our Lord."[37]

---

36. See Dummelow, *Bible Commentary*, p. 788.
37. 2 Tim. 1:8; see also 1:12; Rom. 1:16.

Chapter 38

I AM THE LIGHT OF THE WORLD

The Apostle John was the principal Gospel writer who recorded events in Jesus's ministry in Jerusalem and is the sole Apostle to write of the events related to Jesus's attendance at the last Feast of Tabernacles before His death. It is well worth considering why John devoted so much of his Gospel record to these events, including the confrontations with scribes, Pharisees, and other Jews regarding various matters, Jesus's declaration that He is the Light of the World, His witness of His divine mission and of the Father, and His teaching that the truth makes people free.

Scribes and Pharisees Accuse a Woman of Adultery (John 8:1–11)[1]

For several days during the Feast of Tabernacles, Jesus had taught people His gospel and had witnessed of Himself, even at the peril of His life. Then, according to John's record, "Jesus went unto the mount of Olives."[2] The record is silent as to whether Jesus took some or all of His Apostles with Him or whether He went alone. The record is also silent as to whether He went to the house of a friend in or near the Mount of Olives or whether He sought relief by being alone outdoors. He may have even gone the short distance to Bethany and stayed with His friends Mary, Martha, and Lazarus for the night.[3] However, it is reasonable to assume that Jesus went alone. He may have wanted to leave the city for a few hours to be free from the city's carnival atmosphere, crowded bazaars, and foulness,[4] as well as from the press of the multitudes ever wanting to see and hear Him. He may

---

1. See note 1 at the end of this chapter.
2. John 1:8.
3. See McConkie, *Mortal Messiah*, vol. 3, p. 140.
4. See Farrar, *Life of Christ*, p. 383.

have wanted to be alone and rest under the ancient trees in a grassy area and to commune with and receive strength and direction from His Father. Whatever His purpose, Jesus left the walled city, went down the steep ravine, and climbed the hillside of the Mount of Olives.

The next day, Jesus returned to the temple, as John's record states:

> **John 8:2–11.** And early in the morning he came again into the temple, and all the people came unto him; and he sat down, and taught them. And the scribes and Pharisees brought unto him a woman taken in adultery; and when they had set her in the midst, they say unto him, Master, this woman was taken in adultery, in the very act. Now Moses in the law commanded us, that such should be stoned: but what sayest thou? This they said, tempting him, that they might have to accuse him. But Jesus stooped down, and with his finger wrote on the ground, as though he heard them not. So when they continued asking him, he lifted up himself, and said unto them, He that is without sin among you, let him first cast a stone at her. And again he stooped down, and wrote on the ground. And they which heard it, being convicted by their own conscience, went out one by one, beginning at the eldest, even unto the last: and Jesus was left alone, and the woman standing in the midst. When Jesus had lifted up himself, and saw none but the woman, he said unto her, Woman, where are those thine accusers? hath no man condemned thee? She said, No man, Lord. And Jesus said unto her, Neither do I condemn thee: go, and sin no more.

Presumably, Jesus initially went to the Court of the Women to teach. As always, many came to see Him and hear His words of eternal life. According to John's record, while Jesus was teaching, scribes and Pharisees came to Him with a woman they claimed they had caught "in the very act" of committing adultery. Farrar provided a possible context for the situation: "It is probable that the hilarity and abandonment of the Feast of Tabernacles, which had grown to be a kind of vintage festival, would often degenerate into acts of license and immorality; and these would find more numerous opportunities in the general disturbance of ordinary life caused by the dwelling of the whole people in their little leafy booths."[5]

---

5. See Farrar, *Life of Christ*, p. 383.

Those attending the feast stayed in booths made of branches, and it may have been easy to see what was transpiring in the booths. The scribes and Pharisees who came to Jesus were likely chief priests,[6] and they were presumably gleeful at having found an opportunity to present a dilemma to snare Him in His words and doctrine.

Imagine this woman's horror at having the scribes and Pharisees catch her committing adultery.[7] They must have known she was married or have had a firsthand report from someone who knew her and knew that she was committing sin. They may or may not have known her partner; they only needed to know that he was not her husband. It is even possible that her husband, feeling humiliation and rage, desired to see his wife punished and was the one who made the report.

The scribes and Pharisees acted with total disregard for the feelings of this woman. There was no compassion. Their focus was on trapping Jesus, and they did not care at all about this woman. This intent is buttressed by the fact that they did not bring her male partner so they could also accuse him, as required by the law.

Since this woman was brought before Jesus while He was in the temple courts, this woman was presumably brought from somewhere else in the city. Imagine the utter humiliation this woman may have felt at presumably being publicly dragged from a booth or house, then through part of the city and into the temple court, and then to Jesus and those who had been listening to Him teach. She now likely felt horror, humiliation, and worry at what was transpiring and what would be her fate.

It was not uncommon to bring difficult cases before a learned rabbi for guidance concerning how to proceed. Though the law of Moses declared that those who commit adultery should be killed, the morality of Israel had decayed to the point that adultery and fornication were common and no punishment was exacted. Disregard for the law was especially common

6. See Farrar, *Life of Christ*, p. 383n2.
7. Leviticus 20:10 states: "And the man that committeth adultery with another man's wife, even he that committeth adultery with his neighbour's wife, the adulterer and the adulteress shall surely be put to death." However, according to Dummelow: "The woman was only betrothed, not married, otherwise her punishment would not have been stoning, but strangulation, for so the rabbis interpreted Lev. 20:10 Dt. 22:22" (Dummelow, *Bible Commentary*, p. 788).

during a festival such as the Feast of Tabernacles. Stoning for adultery had long since been abandoned.[8] Moreover, only Roman officials could condemn someone to death. Even the Sanhedrin could not take a person's life without Rome's permission. The actions of these scribes and Pharisees were a mere pretext in their attempt to bring offense against Jesus, whom they abhorred.

If they could get Jesus to condemn this woman, they could claim that He was too harsh, that He lacked Rome's authority, and that He could therefore be charged with sedition. If Jesus would not condemn this woman despite proof of her act, then the scribes and Pharisees could claim that Jesus disregarded the law of Moses. They thought Jesus was trapped, no matter how He answered.

Therefore, the scribes and Pharisees asked Jesus, "Now Moses in the law commanded us, that such should be stoned: but what sayest thou?" Jesus was fully aware of what was transpiring and of the accusers' true motivation. Rather than answer their question or even acknowledge their presence, Jesus stooped down and wrote in the sand and dirt, which the wind and the feet of many people had brought onto the floor of the temple court. What He wrote is unknown, and speculation is to no avail, for the real lesson was not in what He wrote but that He could blot out sin through His infinite atoning sacrifice, just as the winds of time would blot out what He wrote.[9]

Jesus then stood up and, likely while looking into the eyes, hearts, and souls of the accusers, said the now-oft-quoted words "he that is without sin among you, let him first cast a stone at her." Jesus then stooped down again and wrote in the sand. Jesus's statement was not an abrogation of the penalty required by the law of Moses but a recognition that for the present, the law of Moses was fully in force. Jesus's words must have sounded like a death warrant to this woman. The woman presumably felt horror about the possibility of death. Jesus, however, knew the accusers had no intention of carrying out the prescribed penalty. The tables had been turned: Jesus made it clear that the accusers must be the ones to act on the requirements of the law of Moses or to abrogate those requirements. The scribes and Pharisees' trap had completely failed.

---

8. See Farrar, *Life of Christ*, p. 384.

9. According to apocryphal stories, Jesus wrote the names of the accusers, their sins, or the names of those with whom they sinned.

The accusers were "convicted by their own conscience" and consequently left, one by one. The sting of sin made public can cause anyone to retreat in shame. Further, as Jesus had taught on a hillside in Galilee: "Judge not, that ye be not judged."[10] Jesus's action of writing in the earth is all the more poignant when considering the words Jeremiah recorded centuries earlier: "O Lord, the hope of Israel, all that forsake thee shall be ashamed, and they that depart from me shall be written in the earth, because they have forsaken the Lord, the fountain of living waters."[11]

There is no way to know each of the accusers' sins, which caused the accusers to shrink when they reflected on the words of Jesus and His absolute purity. Some scholars have stated that the accusers were guilty of adultery,[12] but all that is known is that their unworthiness caused them to depart from the presence of the Lord.

Certainly, unrepentant sin can cause sinners to experience deep guilt and leave the presence of those who are righteous. As King Benjamin said in the Book of Mormon: "Therefore if that man repenteth not, and remaineth and dieth an enemy to God, the demands of divine justice do awaken his immortal soul to a lively sense of his own guilt, which doth cause him to shrink from the presence of the Lord, and doth fill his breast with guilt, and pain, and anguish, which is like an unquenchable fire, whose flame ascendeth up forever and ever."[13] If some among the woman's accusers were also guilty of adultery, deciding to cast stones at the woman would have indicated that they too should be stoned.

Perhaps the reason the eldest accuser left first is because he had the longest life and the most cumulative sin on which to reflect. In addition, more years typically lead to a greater understanding of human nature and, presumably, to greater empathy.

After the accusers had slunk away in shame, Jesus asked the woman where her accusers were. "Hath no man condemned thee? She said, No man, Lord. And Jesus said unto her, Neither do I condemn thee: go, and sin no more."

---

10. Matt. 7:1.
11. Jer. 17:13.
12. See McConkie, *Mortal Messiah*, vol. 3, pp. 142–143.
13. Mosiah 2:38; see also 2 Ne. 9:46; Mosiah 3:25.

Jesus's ministry was one of condemning the sin but accepting those who had sinned or were perceived to have sinned and had then come to Him, believed in Him, and followed Him. His ministry was to lift, not to condemn. For example, a few days before, Jesus had taught James and John in an unnamed Samaritan city that He "had not come to destroy men's lives, but to save them."[14] And to Nicodemus He said that He had not been sent into the world to condemn it but to save it.[15] Further, He called Matthew as an Apostle, though he was despised by many Jews because he was a publican.[16] Jesus had also eaten with publicans and sinners.[17] Jesus forgave a "woman of the city"—a sinner who had washed Jesus's feet with her tears, wiped them with her hair, and anointed them with ointment.[18] To a Samaritan woman guilty of adultery, Jesus taught that He was the Living Water.[19] On all these occasions, Jesus demonstrated that His mission and the purpose of His atoning sacrifice were to save, bring hope, lift, inspire belief, and enable repentance. And there was no clearer example than in His lack of condemnation of the woman who now stood before Him.

Jesus told the woman that even those who had previously condemned her no longer sought her life and that He did not condemn her either. Even for this woman, there was hope. Jesus had shown her that her sins could be wiped away by His Atonement, just as the writing on the sand could be wiped away by the wind. On another occasion, the Lord said that when a sinner repents, "I, the Lord, remember them no more."[20] And the prophet Isaiah wrote, "Come now, and let us reason together, though your sins be as scarlet, they shall be as white as snow; though they be red like crimson they shall be as wool."[21]

Importantly, Jesus then told the woman to go and "sin no more." He knew the repentant intent of her heart, but for her repentance to be complete and

<hr/>

14. Luke 9:56.
15. See John 3:17. These teachings are consistent with the Father's work and glory to "bring to pass the immortality and eternal life of man" (Moses 1:39).
16. See Matt. 10:3.
17. See Matt. 9:10–11; 11:19; Mark 2:15–16; Luke 5:30; 7:34; 15:1.
18. Luke 7:37; see also vv. 36, 38–50.
19. See John 4:13–14.
20. D&C 58:42; see also Jer. 3:16.
21. Isa. 1:18.

lasting, she must not sin again. As Alma said to his son Corianton after he had sinned, "I desire that ye should let these things trouble you no more, and only let your sins trouble you, with that trouble which shall bring you down unto repentance."[22] Presumably, the woman then went her way to ponder what she had both done and learned and to change her life.

Those who came to hear the words of Jesus in the temple that morning witnessed an even greater lesson than they might have heard in Jesus's earlier teachings. He came not to condemn but to give hope, mercy, and eternal life. Their lives could be forever changed because of this singular incident, and so can the lives of all others who study it.

"I Am the Light of the World" (John 8:12)

Either later the same day or shortly thereafter, Jesus was again teaching at the treasury in the temple.[23] Jesus publicly declared His divinity. The following is John's account:

John 8:12. Then spake Jesus again unto them, saying, I am the light of the world: he that followeth me shall not walk in darkness, but shall have the light of life.

While speaking, Jesus may have pointed to the two giant, "sumptuously gilded" candelabra that were nearby and that were lit each night of the Feast of Tabernacles.[24] Jesus frequently chose common physical items as metaphors for the concepts He was teaching. For example, He turned water into wine to illustrate how He could make ordinary people extraordinary. He used soil, rocks, thorns, and seeds to illustrate how people receive the gospel. He used a mustard seed to illustrate faith. He used water from the well in Sychar to illustrate that He is the Water of Life. He used a corn being plucked to illustrate the true meaning of the Sabbath day. He used clay to anoint the eyes of the blind so that they could see. He used bread and fish to teach that He is the Bread of Life and that His gospel message can be

22. Alma 42:29.
23. See John 8:20. The treasury "contained thirteen chests with trumpet-shaped openings—called *shopherô*—into which the people, and especially the Pharisees, used to cast their gifts" (Farrar, *Life of Christ*, pp. 390–391).
24. Farrar, *Life of Christ*, p. 391.

multiplied many times over by those who believe. He taught that birds of the air have nests and that foxes have holes but that He had nowhere to lay His head. He used the pounding and tumultuous waves and wind on the Sea of Galilee to demonstrate that He was the master of earth and sky. Now He may have pointed to the giant candelabra in the Court of the Women to illustrate to the Jews in Jerusalem that He was the Light of the World.

The Feast of Tabernacles included a great ceremony called the Illumination of the Temple, which involved the ritual lighting of three or four golden oil candelabra in the Court of the Women. These lamps were approximately seventy-five feet high and were lit each night of the feast to remind the people of the pillar of fire the Lord provided to guide the ancient Israelites in their wilderness journey. Just as the candelabra illuminated the temple and a large portion of the city all night long, the pillar of fire illuminated the desert wilderness at night for the ancient Israelites.

According to Farrar, "Round these lamps the people, in their joyful enthusiasm, and even the stateliest Priests and Pharisees, joined in festal dances, while, to the sound of flutes and other music, the Levites, drawn up in array on the fifteen steps which led to the court, chanted the beautiful Psalms which early received the title of 'Songs of Degrees.'"[25] During this ceremony, the priests and some other Levites would use their own worn out clothing for wicks for the giant lamps. Some Jews believed that the light represented God's *Shecaniah*, or glory, that once filled the temple.[26] Edersheim pointed out that window openings in the temple were narrower on the inside and wider on the outside to allow more light (symbolizing the glory of the Lord) to shine from inside the temple sanctuary to its surroundings.[27]

Now Jesus declared at His and His Father's house that He was the Light of the World. How fitting a place for this public declaration to be made. Christ's declaration was not the first time He or others had stated that He was the Light of the World. For example, shortly after His birth, He was brought to the temple, and Simeon declared that Jesus would be a "light to

25. Farrar, *Life of Christ*, p. 391.
26. See Farrar, *Life of Christ*, p. 391n1.
27. In contrast, window openings in typical Jewish buildings were frequently narrower on the outside and wider on the inside to allow more light to enter the buildings (see Edersheim, *Life and Teachings of Jesus the Messiah*, p. 589).

lighten the Gentiles, and the glory of thy people Israel."[28] Additionally, near the beginning of Christ's mortal ministry, He taught Nicodemus that He was the Light of the World.[29] Jesus also taught Nicodemus the difference between light and darkness, good and evil, as follows: "And this is the condemnation, that light is come into the world, and men loved darkness rather than light, because their deeds were evil. For every one that doeth evil hateth the light, neither cometh to the light, lest his deeds should be reproved. But he that doeth truth cometh to the light, that his deeds may be made manifest, that they are wrought in God."[30] Further, the Apostle John testified in the introductory verses of his Gospel that Christ was the Light of the World: "That [Christ] was the true Light, which lighteth every man that cometh into the world."[31]

However, to many of the Jews, especially the rabbis and Jewish leaders, light was more ritualistic than it was representative of faith and goodness or of belief in the Messiah. Therefore, the Jews concluded that faith and goodness were not vital to them; they considered their heritage as Abraham's children[32] and their strict obedience to rabbinical rules to be sufficient for their salvation. Faith and righteousness were, to a degree, foreign to them.[33]

Christ not only bore witness of Himself as the Light of the World but also told the Jews that those who followed Him would not walk in darkness but would walk in the light. In essence, Christ was promising that those who believe in Him and follow Him can overcome the darkness that Satan brings into the world and can therefore become the sons and daughters of God[34] and obtain eternal life. Further, the Savior was implying that His disciples can be a light to others.[35]

28. Luke 2:32.
29. See John 3:19.
30. John 3:19–21.
31. John 1:9; see also vv. 5–8.
32. See John 8:39.
33. See Edersheim, *Life and Teachings of Jesus the Messiah*, pp. 589–590.
34. See John 1:12.
35. Matt. 5:14; see also JST Matt. 5:14; 3 Ne. 12:14.

Pharisees Challenge Jesus's Witness of Himself (John 8:13–20)

The Pharisees who heard Christ's witness knew full well that He was declaring Himself to be the Son of God and the promised Messiah. They quickly devised another scheme to trap Him: their law required two witnesses in judicial cases, and these Pharisees stated that if Jesus was the only witness of His divinity, then His declaration was not true. The following is John's account:

> **John 8:13–20.** The Pharisees therefore said unto him, Thou bearest record of thyself; thy record is not true. Jesus answered and said unto them, Though I bear record of myself, yet my record is true: for I know whence I came, and whither I go; but ye cannot tell whence I come, and whither I go. Ye judge after the flesh; I judge no man. And yet if I judge, my judgment is true: for I am not alone, but I and the Father that sent me. It is also written in your law, that the testimony of two men is true. I am one that bear witness of myself, and the Father that sent me beareth witness of me. Then said they unto him, Where is thy Father? Jesus answered, Ye neither know me, nor my Father: if ye had known me, ye should have known my Father also. These words spake Jesus in the treasury, as he taught in the temple: and no man laid hands on him; for his hour was not yet come.

The Pharisees' challenge implied that they sat in judgment of Jesus as one suspected of guilt, although no formal judicial proceedings had been instituted and these Pharisees may not have had authority to conduct such proceedings. Regardless of what the Pharisees implied, their challenge was fatally flawed: no mortals aside from Jesus and Mary had firsthand knowledge that Jesus was the Son of God; therefore, Mary was the only other mortal who could give firsthand witness of Jesus's divine conception and birth. These Pharisees must have known that two firsthand mortal witnesses could not be found at that time. Moreover, these Pharisees had totally ignored the witness of Christ's many miracles, including raising the dead. If they had heard the Apostles' witness, these Pharisees must have ignored that witness also. They knew it was unreasonable and even approaching blasphemy to expect God to appear to them and give witness of His Divine Son. It is evident that their real motive was to find a reason to accuse Jesus of blasphemy so they ultimately could justify killing Him. Responding to the Pharisees, Jesus simply but authoritatively said,

"Though I bear record of myself, yet my record is true." Jesus's witness was enough, contrary to what the Pharisees claimed. He then added, "I know whence I came, and whither I go." Jesus knew perfectly who He was in every way, having been taught by His Father. Jesus knew perfectly of His role in the creation of the earth and other worlds. He knew perfectly the eternal concepts of justice and mercy. He knew perfectly the plan of salvation and His role in humbly coming to the earth and completing the Atonement so that justice could give way to mercy. He knew perfectly that He would be crucified and would bring about the resurrection and redemption of all humankind.

Christ then stated that the Father had borne witness of Christ. Presumably, the Father had borne this witness to His Only Begotten Son on many occasions. Further, the Father bore witness to John the Baptist at Jesus's baptism and to Peter, James, and John on the Mount of Transfiguration. If the testimony of two people is sufficient, how much more certain is the testimony of two who are divine![36]

In response to Jesus's words, the Pharisees gave Him a further challenge: "Where is thy Father?" Of course, the Pharisees knew that God was in heaven. Jesus simply responded by telling them that the question they asked indicated they knew neither Him nor His Father. If these Pharisees really knew God, they would also know that Jesus was the Son of God. These Pharisees could not recognize Jesus as the Son even though they stood in the purity and majesty of His presence and heard His words in the temple courts. These Pharisees were spiritually dead. Nevertheless, they did not attempt to take Him into custody at this point. As John explained, the time for Jesus's death had not yet come.

It may be hard for modern believers in Christ to understand why so many of the Jews were spiritually deaf and blind. Perhaps one reason is their unrighteousness, as evidenced by their intent to take Jesus's life, among other wicked acts. These Jews were also blind to the truth because they were bound to their ritualistic, rabbinical rules. Further, none of the Jews had the gift of the Holy Ghost, because Christ was present among them. People today are not in the presence of Christ but do have the witness of the Holy

---

36. See Dummelow, *Bible Commentary*, p. 789.

Ghost, the scriptures, the prophets, and others. People who earnestly seek through faith and prayer can spiritually hear and receive a witness from the Holy Ghost that Christ is the Son of God.

Jesus Further Testifies of the Father (John 8:21–30)

Knowing the murderous thoughts and intents of the Pharisees, Jesus next told them that they would die in their sins and that, because of their murderous intent, they would not be able to return to the presence of the Father (an ominous warning that is applicable to all who reject Jesus). John's account is as follows:

> **John 8:21–30.** Then said Jesus again unto them, I go my way, and ye shall seek me, and shall die in your sins: whither I go, ye cannot come. Then said the Jews, Will he kill himself? because he saith, Whither I go, ye cannot come. And he said unto them, Ye are from beneath; I am from above: ye are of this world; I am not of this world. I said therefore unto you, that ye shall die in your sins: for if ye believe not that I am he, ye shall die in your sins. Then said they unto him, Who art thou? And Jesus saith unto them, Even the same that I said unto you from the beginning. I have many things to say and to judge of you: but he that sent me is true; and I speak to the world those things which I have heard of him. They understood not that he spake to them of the Father. Then said Jesus unto them, When ye have lifted up the Son of man, then shall ye know that I am he, and that I do nothing of myself; but as my Father hath taught me, I speak these things. And he that sent me is with me: the Father hath not left me alone; for I do always those things that please him. As he spake these words, many believed on him.

Jesus knew that the Jews would not arrest Him in the temple courts, and He told them He would go His way unharmed. However, He also stated that He knew they would continue to seek Him and that those who did so would die in their sins.

In response to Jesus's statement that "whither I go, ye cannot come," the Jews asked whether He would take His own life, for they knew He was not speaking about where He might travel in Israel or in other lands. They failed to understand that He was speaking about where the righteous and the wicked would go after dying.

Then Jesus spoke more plainly by saying that if the Jews refused to believe that He was the Son of God, they would die in their sins. These Jews then asked Christ, "Who art thou?" Presumably, they did not ask the question in good faith but rather asked in hopes that He would identify Himself as the Son of God and that they would therefore have a reason to accuse Him of blasphemy. Rather than directly answering their question, Jesus again testified of His Father and said that His Father was the source of what Jesus taught. Further, He told these Jews that after He was "lifted up"—that is, after being crucified on the cross and then being resurrected— they would know who He was.

Jesus also told them of the special relationship that He had with the Father—specifically that all Jesus had done and would yet do had been taught to Him by His Father and that Jesus desired to please the Father by doing the Father's will. There could be no mistake or misunderstanding regarding Jesus's witness of the Father and of being the Son of God.

Jesus's witness of Himself as the Light of the World and His witness of His Father apparently touched the hearts of many who heard, for "many believed on him." Such was the power of Jesus's testimony. This power can likewise accompany all people's testimonies. Jesus's response to the Pharisees is a further scriptural witness that He and His Father are two separate persons, though one in purpose. That purpose is to bring about the salvation of humankind.

Jesus Declares That "the Truth Shall Make You Free" (John 8:31–36)

Jesus next directed His instruction to those who believed Him. He told them that if they would continue to exercise faith and to be obedient to His teachings, they would be His disciples and would know the truth, which would make them free:

> **John 8:31–36.** Then said Jesus to those Jews which believed on him, If ye continue in my word, then are ye my disciples indeed; and ye shall know the truth, and the truth shall make you free. They answered him, We be Abraham's seed, and were never in bondage to any man: how sayest thou, Ye shall be made free? Jesus answered them, Verily, verily, I say unto you, Whosoever committeth sin is the servant of sin. And the servant abideth

not in the house for ever: but the Son abideth ever. If the Son therefore shall make you free, ye shall be free indeed.

What Truth Is

Understanding what the word *truth* means is important in understanding Jesus's teachings. The Lord has said that "truth is knowledge of things as they are, and as they were, and as they are to come."[37] Truth transcends time. Truth is therefore absolute, complete, and eternal. It is "the state of being the case"; "the body of real things, events, and facts"; and "a transcendent fundamental or spiritual reality."[38]

The Lord has equated truth with light,[39] and He is the light of truth.[40] Light and truth are also equated with intelligence, for the Lord has said that "the glory of God is intelligence, or, in other words, light and truth."[41]

Spiritual truth is based on correct, righteous principles. These principles, coupled with truth and light, shine throughout all creation, the immensity of space, and all eternity. Truth is the opposite of error and of incorrect and unrighteous ideas. Truth and light are the opposite of evil and darkness. Though these concepts are difficult to fully understand, they are worth continual contemplation.

God and Christ: The Embodiment of Truth

God and Christ know and embody all truth. It is part of their character. Christ comprehends all things; for example, under the direction of His Father, He exercised truth by creating this world and others.[42] By virtue of His mortal experience, Christ has "descended below all things" and has "ascended up on high."[43] Heavenly Father and Christ are omniscient; there is nothing They do not comprehend.

---

37. D&C 93:24.
38. *Merriam-Webster*, s.v. "truth," accessed November 27, 2019, https://www.merriam-webster.com/dictionary/truth.
39. See D&C 88:6–13; D&C 84:45.
40. See D&C 88:6.
41. D&C 93:36.
42. See Moses 1:32–33.
43. D&C 88:6.

Mere knowledge of spiritual truths is insufficient to gain eternal life. For example, individuals must know that God and Jesus exist and are good,[44] holy,[45] full of infinite charity, just,[46] and merciful[47] and must also follow and obey Their teachings and commandments. As James wrote, "Thou believest that there is one God; thou doest well: the devils also believe and tremble. But wilt thou know, O vain man, that faith without works is dead"?[48]

Moreover, because of Their complete knowledge of truth and Their infinite light, goodness, holiness, love, and power, their righteous creations recognize, obey, and glorify Them.[49] Further, Their dominion is an everlasting dominion, which flows to Them without "compulsory means."[50] Thus, the Savior said to the wind and waves, "Peace, be still," and the wind and waves obeyed.[51] All people who follow the Father and the Son may one day obtain this same everlasting authority.[52]

Because the Father and the Son have all knowledge and are filled with infinite goodness, holiness, and love, all people can trust Them and what They say and do. All can have confidence that Their commandments are for the good of all people and will enable eternal progression. All people can have confidence in the Father's plan of salvation, including Christ's Atonement and Resurrection. Likewise, those who have the Light of Christ in them can be trusted because they carry with them truth. They can, with Christ, hallow the name of the Father.[53]

How People Learn Truth

Christ told the Jews that to learn and know truth, they needed to "continue in my word." Similarly, in the latter days the Lord has said, "He that keepeth his commandments receiveth truth and light, until he is glorified

---

44. See 2 Ne. 9:10.
45. See 2 Ne. 9:20.
46. See 2 Ne. 9:17.
47. See 2 Ne. 9:19.
48. James 2:19–20.
49. See Smith, *Teachings*, p. 291; Rev. 5:13.
50. D&C 121:46.
51. See Mark 4:39.
52. See D&C 121:45–46.
53. See Matt. 6:9; Luke 11:2; 3 Ne. 13:9.

in truth and knoweth all things."[54] Therefore, remaining obedient is essential
to obtaining spiritual truth.

Obedience can help people feel more confident when praying to God
and be more receptive to the whisperings of the Holy Spirit. The Lord has
said that if people will pray "with a sincere heart, with real intent, having
faith in Christ," the Holy Ghost will reveal to them the truth of all things.[55]

An additional way to discern truth is evident in the words of the prophet
Moroni: "And whatsoever thing is good is just and true; wherefore, nothing
that is good denieth the Christ, but acknowledgeth that he is."[56] In other
words, a characteristic of truth is that it is good.

Learning truth in its fullness and thus gaining the ultimate freedom Jesus
promised is not an event but a long-term process. As the Lord has said,
"Behold, ye are little children and ye cannot bear all things now; ye must
grow in grace and in the knowledge of the truth."[57]

How Knowing the Truth Makes People Free

It is important to recognize that something can be true but not lead
to eternal life. For example, two plus two equals four, but knowledge of
this truth does not affect a person's eternal inheritance. In contrast, the
truth of which Jesus spoke—spiritually important truth—makes people
free in multiple ways. For example, knowledge of truth enables humankind
to discern good from evil. Truth also frees people from the bondage of
error, heresy, and false doctrine. Jesus was implying that these Jews were in
bondage. Truth also enables people to break the chains of sin and to forsake
the evil one and the darkness he brings into the world.[58] Knowledge of truth
enables people to meaningfully exercise agency. Proper actions based on
meaningful eternal truth lead to eternal life and enable people to feel the
influence of the Holy Ghost, who provides guidance to avoid sin and error
and who brings peace and hope.

---

54. D&C 93:28.
55. Moro. 10:4; see also v. 5.
56. Moro. 10:6.
57. D&C 50:40.
58. See D&C 93:37.

Truth also brings freedom because truth enables people to do things that might not otherwise be possible. For instance, knowing truth enables people to discern light from darkness and good from evil. Understanding truth enables people to see areas in which they need to repent and improve. By confronting the truth, the woman accused of adultery during the Feast of Tabernacles recognized her error and began the repentance process and thereby the process to be set free from the bondage of sin. She was then able to go her way and begin to experience peace, made available to her through the merciful atoning sacrifice of the Savior. Just as truth enables repentance, repentance brings freedom from sin and its effects. Those who repent will be forgiven and will ultimately be enabled to stand with confidence in the presence of God and Christ.

Truth enables people to see the larger picture as they encounter various events in life. Truth enables people to learn their duty and discern what the Lord would have them do throughout the changing circumstances of their lives, thus enabling them to be free from sins of omission. Truth, therefore, gives people wisdom. Truth and wisdom enable people to better navigate life's trials and tribulations. Truth enables people to avoid always dwelling on problems and difficulties and enables people to focus on the positive and to walk through life with hope. Truth enables people to rise above the mortal world to a more spiritual plane, and properly acting on revealed truth gives those who heed the truth the freedom to progress eternally.

As the Psalmist said, "O send out thy light and thy truth: let them lead me; let them bring me unto thy holy hill, and to thy tabernacles."[59] That message was central to what Christ taught the Jews in the temple during the Feast of Tabernacles. His witness of Himself was truth, as was His witness of His Father.

Jesus also reminded the Jews at the temple that those who fail to properly act on knowledge of truth and sin are the servants of sin. Their actions lead to darkness and bondage. Today, darkness and bondage are certainly the result of addictions, such as to alcohol, tobacco, narcotics, and pornography. Sin can also lower self-esteem and drive away hope, binding people down.

---

59. Ps. 43:3.

Some of those who heard Christ in the temple failed to believe; in response to His teachings about being free, these individuals said they were Abraham's seed and never in bondage to anyone.[60] They also failed to understand that their heritage would not qualify them for eternal life. In the latter days, the equivalent of the Jew's reliance on their ancestry could be a Church member's view that having pioneer heritage is enough to receive exaltation. Or that being baptized is enough. Or that attending church is enough. Christ said that more is required. People need to truly believe and to act on that belief by keeping the commandments and any covenants the individuals have made.

Christ explained that those who sin are servants of sin and that since servants do not own the houses they reside in, they cannot abide in these houses forever. Christ added that if the Jews would believe in Him, they would be His disciples and He would make them free. True freedom, then, is a result of Christ's infinite Atonement. Unfortunately, the Jews failed to comprehend that Christ spoke of moral freedom, not physical or political freedom.

Jesus Declares That Descending from Abraham Does Not Guarantee Salvation (John 8:37–59)

After Jesus declared that His disciples would be free, He and the accusing Jews engaged in a rather lengthy dialogue. He expanded on His response to the Jews' statement that they were Abraham's posterity and addressed their lack of faith in Him. The following is John's account:

> **John 8:37–59.** I know that ye are Abraham's seed; but ye seek to kill me, because my word hath no place in you. I speak that which I have seen with my Father: and ye do that which ye have seen with your father. They answered and said unto him, Abraham is our father. Jesus saith unto them, If ye were Abraham's children, ye would do the works of Abraham. But now ye seek to kill me, a man that hath told you the truth, which I have heard of God: this did not Abraham. Ye do the deeds of your father. Then said they to him, We be not born of fornication; we have one Father, even God. Jesus said unto them, If God were your Father, ye would love me: for I proceeded

---

60. Even then, they had forgotten the bondage of Egypt and the captivity of Babylon, and they were oblivious to their present subjection to Rome.

forth and came from God; neither came I of myself, but he sent me. Why do ye not understand my speech? even because ye cannot hear my word. Ye are of your father the devil, and the lusts of your father ye will do. He was a murderer from the beginning, and abode not in the truth, because there is no truth in him. When he speaketh a lie, he speaketh of his own: for he is a liar, and the father of it. And because I tell you the truth, ye believe me not. Which of you convinceth me of sin? And if I say the truth, why do ye not believe me? He that is of God heareth God's words: ye therefore hear them not, because ye are not of God. Then answered the Jews, and said unto him, Say we not well that thou art a Samaritan, and hast a devil? Jesus answered, I have not a devil; but I honour my Father, and ye do dishonour me. And I seek not mine own glory: there is one that seeketh and judgeth. Verily, verily, I say unto you, If a man keep my saying, he shall never see death. Then said the Jews unto him, Now we know that thou hast a devil. Abraham is dead, and the prophets; and thou sayest, If a man keep my saying, he shall never taste of death. Art thou greater than our father Abraham, which is dead? and the prophets are dead: whom makest thou thyself? Jesus answered, If I honour myself, my honour is nothing: it is my Father that honoureth me; of whom ye say, that he is your God: Yet ye have not known him; but I know him: and if I should say, I know him not, I shall be a liar like unto you: but I know him, and keep his saying. Your father Abraham rejoiced to see my day: and he saw it, and was glad. Then said the Jews unto him, Thou art not yet fifty years old, and hast thou seen Abraham? Jesus said unto them, Verily, verily, I say unto you, Before Abraham was, I am. Then took they up stones to cast at him: but Jesus hid himself, and went out of the temple, going through the midst of them, and so passed by.

Jesus acknowledged that the Jews were descendants of Abraham but stated that they did not follow Abraham's example because they rejected Jesus and sought to kill Him. They were incapable of recognizing His divinity because of their sinful nature and their dead law. They followed Satan, not God. They had murder in their hearts, which contradicted the sixth commandment: "Thou shalt not kill."[61]

Jesus implicitly told the Jews that they could not hear His word because they were spiritually dull of hearing—they failed to hear the truth.

---

61. Ex. 20:13.

Boldly, He then told the Jews that their "father"—that is, the one they followed—was the devil. Imagine their ire at Jesus's castigation of them being children of Satan, particularly since certain of the Jews had previously claimed that Jesus performed miracles through the power of Beelzebub.[62] Now, Jesus used against them their accusations of Him working by the power of Beelzebub.

When Jesus stated that their father was a murderer from the beginning, He may have been referring to Satan enticing Cain to murder Able and also to Satan enticing these Jews to desire to murder Jesus. He also said that their father was devoid of truth and was the father of lies, implying that they were also devoid of truth and honesty. This reproach was especially pointed, given His previous discussion about truth. Jesus had openly criticized their moral condition and told them that they did not accept His words because these Jews were "not of God" but instead followed Satan.

Rather than directly addressing Jesus's condemnation of them, the Jews slanderously attacked Him, claiming that He was a Samaritan and was possessed by a devil, implying that He had no right to teach or condemn them. Many of the Jews detested the Samaritans. Of course, these Jews knew that Jesus was not politically, geographically, or ethnically a Samaritan. The word translated into Greek as *Samaritan* "would have been either *Kuthi* . . ., which, while literally meaning a Samaritan, is almost as often used in the sense of 'heritic,' or else *Shomroni* . . . [which] is also sometimes used as the equivalent of *Ashmedai*, the Prince of the demons."[63] Therefore, the Jews were slanderously calling Jesus a heretic and were bringing forth their old argument that He was the prince of Satan and performed miracles through Satan's power.

Jesus responded by stating that He honored God and that they dishonored Jesus; by implication, Jesus was indicating that they also dishonored God. Jesus then told them that He did not seek His own glory; this statement had meaning far beyond their present understanding. Indeed, in the premortal life He had told His Father that "the glory be thine forever."[64]

---

62. See Matt. 12:24; Luke 11:15.
63. Edersheim, *Life and Teachings of Jesus the Messiah*, p. 595.
64. Moses 4:2.

Jesus then told the Jews that if a person followed His teachings, the person would "never see death." That is, the person would never be bound by death because, for the righteous, death is only a stepping stone to eternal life. Those who followed Jesus would not be consigned to spirit prison— what the Jews considered hades—and then to hell.[65]

In response, the Jews said that they knew Jesus was possessed by a devil because their father Abraham and other prophets of old had died, even though Jesus had said the righteous would not. These Jews failed to understand Jesus's meaning. They then scorned Jesus by asking if He were greater than Abraham and the other prophets.

Jesus replied that He did not seek to honor Himself. He did not claim to be greater than Abraham or other prophets; rather, His Father declared Jesus's divinity. Then, Jesus further condemned the Jews by stating that they did not know God, whom they claimed to worship, but that Jesus knew God and was obedient to Him.

Turning attention back to Abraham, Jesus said that Abraham rejoiced to see Jesus's day. Then the Jews asked, in essence, how Jesus, a man not yet fifty years old, could know what Abraham saw and rejoiced in.

Jesus replied, "Verily, verily, I say unto you, Before Abraham was, I am." Jesus was stating that He was not only the Son of God but also the Jehovah of the Old Testament and the one known to Moses—and, thus, other Israelites—as I Am. As Talmage explained, I Am "is the equivalent of 'Yahveh,' or 'Jahveh' now rendered 'Jehovah,' and signifies 'The Self-existent One' 'the Eternal' 'The First and the Last.' Jewish traditionalism forbade the utterance of the sacred Name; yet Jesus claimed it as His own."[66]

To these self-righteous and spiritually dead Jews, Christ's statement was heresy, and they grabbed stones with which to kill Him, despite the absence of a trial or approval from the Roman government. But His time to die had not come, and He passed through the crowd and left.

Jesus had given a clear witness of the Father and of Himself as the Divine Son of God. If the scribes, Pharisees, members of the Sanhedrin,

---

65. See *HarperCollins Bible Dictionary*, s.v. "hades" and "hell."
66. Talmage, *Jesus the Christ*, p. 387.

and other Jews in Jerusalem did not ultimately accept this witness, it would forever condemn them.

Imagine for a moment how marvelous it would be to stand in the temple courts in Jerusalem and listen to the Savior of the world teach. Hopefully, those present would spiritually hear and deeply feel and covenant to follow Him, keep His commandments, and live the way He taught that people should live.

John Testifies of Christ

As mentioned at the start of this chapter, it is worth asking why John devoted the majority of two of his twenty-one chapters to Jesus's time at the Feast of Tabernacles. John's central purpose in writing his Gospel was to give his witness of the divinity of Christ. Near the end of his record, John stated: "But these are written, that ye might believe that Jesus is the Christ, the Son of God; and that believing ye might have life through his name."[67] Indeed, John's Gospel repeatedly testifies of Jesus, starting with the first verses of the book: "In the beginning was the Word, and the Word was with God, and the Word was God. The same was in the beginning with God. All things were made by him; and without him was not anything made that was made. In him was life; and the life was the light of men. And the light shineth in darkness; and the darkness comprehended it not."[68]

In recording Jesus's words at the Feast of Tabernacles, John documented Jesus's direct witness of Himself and His Father and of His Father sending Jesus into the world. This witness was much the same as His declaration to the woman at the well in Samaria that He was the Living Water[69] and His declaration to the unbelieving Jews near Capernaum that He was the Bread of Life.[70]

In declaring to the Jews at the Feast of Tabernacles that He was the Light of the World, Christ demonstrated His light and mercy to the woman

---

67. John 20:31.
68. John 1:1–5.
69. See John 4:14.
70. See John 6:32–35, 48, 51.

accused of adultery. He was the light that lifted her, and He lifts all others who fall short but desire to change.

These Jews in Jerusalem were left without excuse when they later caused His death, for Jesus had boldly given His witness and testimony of God and of Himself as the Son of God. Providing this testimony was certainly one of the principal reasons Jesus attended the Feast of Tabernacles.

It is reasonable to conclude that this account will be read by Jews in the latter days, that they may read Jesus's witness of Himself and may decide to believe.

Jesus's witness of Himself puts the burden upon all who read John's account to decide for themselves whether Jesus was who He said He was or whether He was a fraud. Having decided, each person should act on that decision. When people say that they do not know and then take no action to find out whether Jesus is the Christ, they are tacitly deciding that Jesus is not who He claims to be or that it is not important enough to find out by asking God.

John's record of what Jesus taught at the Feast of Tabernacles is a witness to the world that Jesus is the Son of God and the Light of the World and that He came to the world to save all people, just as He saved the woman accused of adultery. John's record of these events and of Jesus's teachings can give all people hope.

Notes to Chapter 38

1. Authenticity of the account of the woman taken in adultery. Some modern critics conclude that this account was not written by John or was not written in sequence but was later inserted in John chapter 8 by others.[71] Farrar discussed at length various reasons for and against the story's authenticity and its placement in John's account in the King James Version of the Bible.[72] Talmage, McConkie, and Farrar treated this account in the chronological place it occurs

---

71. See Edersheim, *Life and Times of Jesus the Messiah*, p. 586n17; Dummelow, *Bible Commentary*, p. 788.

72. See Farrar, *Life of Christ*, p. 382n2.

in John's record.[73] Farrar concluded his analysis with this pertinent statement: "Whoever embodied into the Gospels this traditionally-remembered story deserved well of the World."[74]

2. Light of Christ. In seven short verses, the Lord explained the Light of Christ:

> He that ascended up on high, as also he descended below all things, in that he comprehended all things, that he might be in all and through all things, the light of truth; which truth shineth. This is the light of Christ. As also he is in the sun, and the light of the sun, and the power thereof by which it was made. As also he is in the moon, and is the light of the moon, and the power thereof by which it was made; as also the light of the stars, and the power thereof by which they were made; and the earth also, and the power thereof, even the earth upon which you stand. And the light which shineth, which giveth you light, is through him who enlighteneth your eyes, which is the same light that quickeneth your understandings; which light proceedeth forth from the presence of God to fill the immensity of space—the light which is in all things, which giveth life to all things, which is the law by which all things are governed, even the power of God who sitteth upon his throne, who is in the bosom of eternity, who is in the midst of all things.[75]

---

73. See Talmage, *Jesus the Christ*, pp. 381–382; McConkie, *Mortal Messiah*, vol. 3, pp. 140–144; Farrar, *Life of Christ*, pp. 381–390.

74. Farrar, *Life of Christ*, p. 382n2.

75. D&C 88:6–13.

Chapter 39

JESUS HEALS A BLIND MAN AND IS THE GOOD SHEPHERD

Physical sight and hearing are gifts most people have received, without any effort required on their part. In contrast, spiritual sight and hearing require effort. Insight regarding spiritual sight and hearing can come from exploring the account of Jesus healing a blind man on the Sabbath in Jerusalem and the account of Jesus declaring that He is the "door of the sheep" and the "good shepherd." The blind man at first could not see Jesus but heard His voice; after receiving the miracle of physical sight, the man both physically and spiritually saw Jesus and believed. Just as the Good Shepherd knew and loved the blind man, He knows and loves all His other sheep, and they can spiritually hear His voice, whether from His own mouth or from His servants, and choose to believe.

Jesus Heals a Blind Man (John 9:1–41)

On a Sabbath day shortly following the Feast of Tabernacles, Jesus saw a blind man, possibly sitting where he usually did or perhaps at the temple gate or next to a nearby street. Based on the wording of the account, it is likely this man was hoping for generous passersby to give him alms. Although alms were not solicited on the Sabbath, his presence in his usual place may have led to wider notice on the Sabbath and to unsolicited gifts.[1] Likely, Jesus and His disciples momentarily stopped by the man, who had been blind since birth, and the disciples asked Jesus whether the man's blindness was the result of his sins or his parents' sins. It is not known how the disciples

---

1. See Edersheim, *Life and Teachings of Jesus the Messiah*, p. 597.

knew that the man had been blind since birth. It is possible that some of the disciples were familiar with the man, or he may have made his plight known to passersby, or perhaps Jesus or others told the disciples.

Jesus's healing of a blind man is a partial fulfillment of a statement He made near the beginning of His public ministry. While in the synagogue in Nazareth, He read from Isaiah's prophecy of the Messiah and in so doing declared His mission: "The Spirit of the Lord is upon me, because he hath anointed me to preach the gospel to the poor; he hath sent me to heal the brokenhearted, to preach deliverance to the captives, and recovering of sight to the blind, to set at liberty them that are bruised, to preach the acceptable year of the Lord."[2]

With characteristic detail, John provided a lengthy account of Jesus giving precious sight to a blind man. John may have provided so much detail because this incident is significant on many levels.

> **John 9:1–5.** And as Jesus passed by, he saw a man which was blind from his birth. And his disciples asked him, saying, Master, who did sin, this man, or his parents, that he was born blind? Jesus answered, Neither hath this man sinned, nor his parents: but that the works of God should be made manifest in him. I must work the works of him that sent me, while it is day: the night cometh, when no man can work. As long as I am in the world, I am the light of the world.

The disciples' question stemmed from the common Jewish belief that the merits or demerits of parents would appear in their children. Until a child was thirteen years of age, the child was considered to be part of his or her father and liable to suffer for the father's guilt. The rabbis taught that even a mother's thoughts could affect the moral state of her unborn children.[3] The disciples' question also indicates that they had been taught about premortal life, for how could a man sin before his birth if there were no life before birth?

Jesus responded that the man's blindness was not the result of his sins or his parents' sins. Rather, he was blind so "that the works of God should be

---

2. Luke 4:18–19; see also Isa. 61:1–2. For other instances in which Jesus restored sight, see Matt. 9:27–31 (two blind men given sight); Mark 8:22–26 (a blind man at Bethsaida given sight); and Mark 10:46–52, Matt. 20:29–34, and Luke 18:35–43 (a blind man near Jericho given sight).

3. See Edersheim, *Life and Teachings of Jesus the Messiah*, p. 598.

made manifest in him." Christ had turned the discussion from the reason for the man's physical condition to the moral purpose this man's suffering might serve. It seems unreasonable that God would inflict someone with blindness unless there was a higher purpose. In this instance, the man's blindness would give Christ the opportunity to demonstrate His divine authority, which He had so recently testified of in the temple. Jesus's healing of this man was another witness to the Jews at Jerusalem that He was indeed the Light of the World. It is possible that in the premortal life, the man either volunteered for or humbly accepted the opportunity to be born blind so that God and Christ might be glorified. Alternatively, this man's blindness may not have been appointed before his mortality, but when Jesus met the man, He knew that healing him would glorify God. Later that day, even the Pharisees said, "Give God the praise."[4]

The account continues:

> **John 9:6–7.** When he had thus spoken, he spat on the ground, and made clay of the spittle, and he anointed the eyes of the blind man with the clay, and said unto him, Go, wash in the pool of Siloam, (which is by interpretation, Sent.) He went his way therefore, and washed, and came seeing.

With compassion, Jesus spat on the ground, mixed the spit with dirt, and then anointed the man's eyes with the resulting clay. The reason or reasons for Jesus's actions are unknown, although presumably Jesus had a purpose for what He did. Saliva was commonly thought to be a remedy for eye diseases, although not for blindness.[5] Jesus may have chosen to apply the clay to strengthen the faith of the man and others present or those who would later hear of the miracle. Or perhaps Jesus wanted to prepare the man for the miracle, much as an anointing was preparatory to sanctification in ancient Israel.[6] Jesus may have been helping the man learn obedience. Or Jesus may have wanted to demonstrate to this man and all others, including the Pharisees, that "the sabbath was made for man, and not man for the sabbath."[7]

---

4. John 9:24.

5. See Edersheim, *Life and Teachings of Jesus the Messiah*, p. 599.

6. See Lev. 8:12.

7. Mark 2:27.

John's account uses the word *clay* to describe the dirt mixed with Jesus's saliva. The word *clay* was presumably used symbolically to add meaning to the account, for the word is often used in the Bible in reference "to God fashioning humans (Job 10:9; 33:6; Isa. 29:16; 45:9; 64:8; Rom. 9:21). Sometimes clay is used as a symbol for something that is fragile or weak (Job 13:12; Isa. 41:25; 2 Cor. 4:7; Rev. 2:27), [or] malleable (Job 33:14; Jer. 18, 4, 6)."[8] In John's account of Jesus healing the blind man, *clay* may be obliquely pointing to the significant principle that all people are God's children and He is mindful of all of them. God knew of this man's condition and knew what he could become. God knew that the miracle would produce faith and be a witness to others. Additionally, just as Jesus made the clay from the dust of the earth, the man (and all of humankind) was made of the dust of the earth, and to the dust he would he return.[9] Further, this man was certainly weak because he was blind and presumably had to beg for alms to survive. Similarly, all other mortals are weak in some fashion, but all can become strong, as this man did.

Moreover, unlike the condemning Pharisees, this man was malleable. He was receptive to the Spirit and the Light of Christ, and he desired to learn of Christ, believe in Him, and improve. He was like the clay in the potter's hand, as described in Jeremiah. Though the clay was marred, the potter could mold it again and make it perfect. The Lord declared, "O house of Israel, cannot I do with you as this potter? Saith the Lord, Behold, as the clay is in the potter's hand, so are ye in mine hand, O house of Israel."[10] All who believe in the Savior and allow His touch to heal them can be molded and eventually made perfect.

After applying the clay, Jesus directed the man to wash in the pool of Siloam, which means *sent*, according to John. This man was not only sent to wash in Jerusalem but was sent to earth for the purpose of manifesting the works of God and thereby glorifying Him and witnessing of His Son, Jesus Christ. It is likely that the blind man was led to the pool of Siloam by others, perhaps friends or family members, and by helping bring about this miracle they too were instruments in the hands of Christ.

---

8. *HarperCollins Bible Dictionary*, s.v. "clay."

9. See Gen. 3:19.

10. Jer. 18:6; see also vv. 1–5.

Obediently, this man washed his eyes in the pool, and afterward he could see for the first time in his life. What wonder must have filled this man as he saw for the first time the water, those who had helped him travel there, and then the city. Just as the clay had been washed away from the man's eyes and he had received sight, so too can the dirt of sins and spiritual blindness be washed away by the Savior's atoning sacrifice.

John next recorded:

John 9:8–12. The neighbours therefore, and they which before had seen him that he was blind, said, Is not this he that sat and begged? Some said, This is he: others said, He is like him: but he said, I am he. Therefore said they unto him, How were thine eyes opened? He answered and said, A man that is called Jesus made clay, and anointed mine eyes, and said unto me, Go to the pool of Siloam, and wash: and I went and washed, and I received sight. Then said they unto him, Where is he? He said, I know not.

Upon hearing the man confirm who he was, his neighbors and others asked how he had gained sight. After the man explained what had happened, those listening asked the whereabouts of Jesus. The man responded that he did not know.

The people then brought the man to the Pharisees. The motive for so doing is uncertain, although the people may have wanted to prove Jesus's divinity to the Pharisees or may have sought to bring a charge against Jesus for breaking the Sabbath. John's account states:

John 9:13–17. They brought to the Pharisees him that aforetime was blind. And it was the sabbath day when Jesus made the clay, and opened his eyes. Then again the Pharisees also asked him how he had received his sight. He said unto them, He put clay upon mine eyes, and I washed, and do see. Therefore said some of the Pharisees, This man is not of God, because he keepeth not the sabbath day. Others said, How can a man that is a sinner do such miracles? And there was a division among them. They say unto the blind man again, What sayest thou of him, that he hath opened thine eyes? He said, He is a prophet.

After the Pharisees asked the man how he had received his sight, he simply stated the facts of what had happened, without any hint of criticizing Jesus for what He had done on the Sabbath. The Pharisees faced a dilemma, for their rabbinical rules concerning the Sabbath prohibited making clay or putting saliva on one's eyes.[11] The fact of the miracle, however, could not be denied.

The Pharisees needed to either maintain that their fastidious rules were the source of salvation or recognize that Jesus was of God and that believing in Him and following His teachings would lead to salvation. Some chose the former and claimed that Jesus could not be of God because Jesus had not kept the Sabbath according to rabbinical rules. Others countered that Jesus could not have performed such a miracle if He were a sinner. Because the opinions were divided, the Pharisees asked the man for his opinion. He apparently did not yet know that the one who had given him his sight was the promised Messiah, for the man simply and presumably without equivocation said, "He is a prophet."

Unsatisfied, the Pharisees called for his parents to come:

John 9:18–23. But the Jews did not believe concerning him, that he had been blind, and received his sight, until they called the parents of him that had received his sight. And they asked them, saying, Is this your son, who ye say was born blind? how then doth he now see? His parents answered them and said, We know that this is our son, and that he was born blind: but by what means he now seeth, we know not; or who hath opened his eyes, we know not: he is of age; ask him: he shall speak for himself. These words spake his parents, because they feared the Jews: for the Jews had agreed already, that if any man did confess that he was Christ, he should be put out of the synagogue. Therefore said his parents, He is of age; ask him.

The Pharisees wished to transfer their dilemma to the man's parents. His parents were presumably not present when the miracle occurred and therefore did not have firsthand knowledge of how he had received sight; however, the man likely visited his parents after being healed, showing them the great miracle that had been so mercifully wrought upon him.

---

11. Edersheim stated that on the Sabbath, action could be taken to heal someone only in cases of "diseases of the internal organs (from the throat downwards), except when danger to life or the loss of an organ was involved. It was, indeed, declared lawful to apply, for example, wine to the outside of the eyelid, on the ground that this might be treated as washing; but it was sinful to apply it to the inside of the eye. And as regards saliva, its application to the eye is expressly forbidden, on the ground that it was evidently intended as a remedy" (Edersheim, *Life and Teachings of Jesus the Messiah*, p. 600).

Imagine the parents' feelings at being brought before the leaders of the Jews because someone gave their son sight. The Pharisees surely knew that the parents would fear being excommunicated if they testified that Jesus was the Christ. Excommunication was dreadful not only for spiritual reasons but also for social reasons. Moreover, the parents were likely of the poorer class, as suggested by the fact that their son had to beg alms, and would therefore likely be even more inclined to say what the Pharisees wanted to hear so the parents could avoid ecclesiastical punishment. The parents may also have feared what would happen to their son or the one who had healed him.

The Pharisees asked the parents whether the man who could now see was in fact the couple's son and whether he was in fact born blind. They stated what they knew firsthand: the man was their son, and he had been born blind. In answering how their son had gained sight, they directed the Pharisees to ask their son because "he was of age." Given the parents' answer, the Pharisees again spoke to the man:

John 9:24–29. Then again called they the man that was blind, and said unto him, Give God the praise: we know that this man is a sinner. He answered and said, Whether he be a sinner or no, I know not: one thing I know, that, whereas I was blind, now I see. Then said they to him again, What did he to thee? how opened he thine eyes? He answered them, I have told you already, and ye did not hear: wherefore would ye hear it again? will ye also be his disciples? Then they reviled him, and said, Thou art his disciple; but we are Moses' disciples. We know that God spake unto Moses: as for this fellow, we know not from whence he is.

Presumably, the time between the man's first and second appearances before the Jewish leaders was not long. The man probably had enough time to talk with his parents and learn what they had said in response to the Pharisees' questions. As he again spoke to the Jewish leaders, he needed to make a decision. What would he say? Would he risk excommunication simply for receiving his sight and supporting the one who provided this great blessing? Or would he shrink before the learned Jews?

As he stood before the Jews, they told him to "give God the praise." They were attempting to acknowledge that the miracle was from God while at the same time deny that it occurred because of Jesus, who they said was a sinner. Their statement "give God the praise" would be an intellectual millstone around their necks. Even though the man knew that the miracle had occurred on the Sabbath, he did not want to accuse Jesus of being a sinner. The man astutely avoided the Pharisees' trap by responding that he did not know whether Jesus was a sinner but he did know that "whereas I was blind, now I see." The Pharisees again asked him how the miracle occurred, presumably hoping he would provide details that would verify Jesus had violated the rabbinical rules for the Sabbath.

Rather than giving details, the man unabashedly asked the Pharisees a question. If they heard his report again, would they believe and become Jesus's disciples? Through this man's question, the learned leaders of the Jews had been directly challenged. They had been intellectually bettered by one who had presumably never been taught by the rabbis or in their schools but who had begged alms for a meager existence.

Since the man would not denounce Jesus, the Pharisees pronounced him Jesus's disciple, whereas they claimed to be the disciples of Moses, whom Israelites revered as a prophet. With integrity and courage, this man then responded to those who had the power to excommunicate him and thus, in their view, condemn him before God and all the people:

> **John 9:30–34.** The man answered and said unto them, Why herein is a marvellous thing, that ye know not from whence he is, and yet he hath opened mine eyes. Now we know that God heareth not sinners: but if any man be a worshipper of God, and doeth his will, him he heareth. Since the world began was it not heard that any man opened the eyes of one that was born blind. If this man were not of God, he could do nothing. They answered and said unto him, Thou wast altogether born in sins, and dost thou teach us? And they cast him out.

This man, who may have begged alms for many years, likely wore ragged clothes, was a bit dirty, and had unkempt hair as he stood before the Jewish leaders. Nevertheless, he courageously answered the Pharisees by saying, "Why herein is a marvellous thing, that ye know not from whence he is, and yet he hath opened mine eyes." The man was challenging the Pharisees on their own religious grounds. Based on the account, there is little doubt that the man was intelligent and had great spiritual capacity.

The Jewish leaders had already acknowledged that the miracle came from God. If they were as religious as they presented themselves to be, they would know that such a miracle could only have come from God through a righteous man, for they commonly asserted that God did not hear sinners. In fact, no principle was repeated more frequently by the rabbis than that only those who did the will of God would receive answers to their prayers.[12]

Rather than confront the man's irrefutable logic, the Pharisees did what people often do: attack the one delivering the message. The Pharisees stated, "Thou wast altogether born in sins, and dost thou teach us?" They had chosen rabbinical teachings about Sabbath observance instead of evidence of Jesus's miracle. Because they had been stung by the simple logic of this man, whom they considered unlearned, "they cast him out"[13] despite not listening to any other witnesses or conducting the required trial. These Pharisees had become "blind guides." As Jesus had said earlier, they were "blind leaders of the blind." He added that "if the blind lead the blind, both shall fall into the ditch."[14]

After Jesus heard of this man's wrongful excommunication by the self-righteous and intellectually dishonest members of the Sanhedrin, He found the man and asked, "Dost thou believe on the Son of God?" The man responded by asking, "Who is he, Lord, that I might believe on him?" Jesus answered, "Thou hast both seen him, and it is he that talketh with thee." Looking on the Savior with eyes that could now see, the man said "Lord, I believe." And then the man worshipped Jesus.[15]

As the man looked upon the Savior of the world and contemplated the great miracle he had received, he could also spiritually see and discern the truth, something the Jewish leaders chose not to do.

The man believed that the person who gave him sight was indeed the Son of God, the promised Messiah. The man was not wallowing in his former

---

12. See Edersheim, *Life and Teachings of Jesus the Messiah*, p. 603.
13. In this context, *cast out* means excommunication (see Dummelow, *Bible Commentary*, p. 791).
14. Matt. 15:14. Jesus later said to the hypocritical scribes and Pharisees, "Woe unto you, ye blind guides, which say, Whosoever shall swear by the temple, it is nothing; but whosoever shall swear by the gold of the temple, he is a debtor!" (Matt. 23:16). Jesus also referred to them as "ye blind guides, which strain at a gnat, and swallow a camel" (Matt 23:24).
15. See John 9:35–38.

plight of being sightless, in his or his family's poverty, in his need to beg for the necessities of life, or in his wrongful excommunication. He had not let his circumstances canker his soul. He had passed all these mortal tests and valiantly come off conqueror. He now could physically see and could also spiritually see with hope for the future.

It is reasonable to assume that the man began to make changes in his life to further conform to the teachings of Christ and that by so doing he was better able to see who he really was. Thus, the "works of God" that Jesus had referred to earlier were further manifest in the man.

It also seems reasonable to assume that this man became a powerful witness for Christ in the days to come and was ultimately blessed beyond measure.

After the man believed in and worshipped Jesus, He taught the man and others present about what they had seen and heard:[16]

> **John 9:39–41.** And Jesus said, For judgment I am come into this world, that they which see might see; and that they which see might be made blind. And some of the Pharisees which were with him heard these words, and said unto him, Are we blind also? Jesus said unto them, If ye were blind, ye should have no sin: but now ye say, We see; therefore your sin remaineth.

To those who asked whether they were blind also, Jesus responded that if they had not had the opportunity to hear and know, they would not have been guilty of sin. But since they stood in the presence of the Son of God, had heard His words, and had witnessed His miracles and still would not believe, they were guilty of sin.

All People Need to Learn to See

The man who had been blind stood before the self-righteous Pharisees, who were not concerned with the truth but only with preserving their political and religious station, and courageously declared, "One thing I know, that, whereas I was blind, now I see." What does it mean to people today to be able to see?

Through divine authority, Christ gave sight to the blind man and changed his life. Physically seeing requires light.[17] Spiritually seeing requires, in part,

---

16. See John 9:39–41.
17. See note 1 at the end of this chapter.

discerning the spiritual light within. When people are spiritually in tune, they can discern much beyond what their physical eyes can see.

In part, spiritually seeing comes from the Light of Christ, for He is the "light of the world."[18] Jesus Christ explained that He is the "light of truth" because He "ascended up on high, as also he descended below all things, in that he comprehended all things, that he might be in all and through all things. . . . This is the light of Christ. As also he is in the sun, and the light of the sun, and the power thereof by which it was made."[19]

Moroni, the final prophet in the Book of Mormon, wrote that the "Spirit [or Light] of Christ is given to every man, that he may know good from evil; wherefore, I show unto you the way to judge; for every thing which inviteth to do good, and to persuade to believe in Christ, is sent forth by the power and gift of Christ; wherefore ye may know with a perfect knowledge it is of God."[20]

No matter where a person lives or what his or her religious beliefs (if any) are, with the Light of Christ this person can spiritually see, know good from evil, and gain a witness that Jesus is the Christ, the Son of God, just as did the man who had been blind. One way to be touched by the Light of Christ is through reading the testimonies found in the Bible and the Book of Mormon. The Book of Mormon's title page states that the book was written "to the convincing of the Jew and Gentile that Jesus is the Christ."

Light is equated with truth.[21] The Light of Christ helps people to see and to discern truth from error and good from evil. In the Book of Mormon, the missionary Ammon witnessed King Lamoni begin to see: "The dark veil of unbelief was being cast away from his mind, and the light which did light up his mind, which was the light of the glory of God, which was a marvelous light of his goodness—yea, this light had infused such joy into his soul, the cloud of darkness having been dispelled, and that the light of everlasting life was lit up in his soul."[22] Such is the result today as people around the world learn of and accept the gospel.

---

18. John 9:5.
19. D&C 88:6–7.
20. Moroni 7:16; see also vv. 18–19.
21. See D&C 84:45; 93:36.
22. Alma 19:6.

Seeing helps people to know what they should do to further the Lord's work despite their limitations, challenges, and other circumstances. Seeing helps people to know who they can help and lift. Seeing helps people discern "the difference between the holy and profane."[23] Seeing helps people know the path to follow and which decision to make. Seeing helps people better understand the hills, valleys, and rivers of life, just as people see more of the physical landscape as they climb higher up a mountain. Seeing brings wisdom.

The members of the First Presidency and the Council of Twelve Apostles are seers as well as prophets and revelators. "A seer can know of things which are past, and also of things which are to come, and by them shall all things be revealed, or, rather, shall secret things be made manifest, and hidden things shall come to light, and things which are not known shall be made known by them, and also things shall be made known by them which otherwise could not be known."[24] The prophets have had many revelations in which they were permitted to see into the future, helping them know what will be for the benefit of the Church and the world. How grateful members of the Church should be for these leaders.

Similarly, personal revelation and inspiration can help people see clearly what direction they should go, even though the future is unknown. In like manner, spiritually seeing the scriptures by searching and pondering them can fill an individual with greater light and lead to a greater understanding of spiritual things, particularly as they pertain to everyday life. Feasting on the scriptures can also lead to a daily witness and guidance from the Holy Ghost.

Seeing helps people understand and have empathy for others. Similarly, seeing helps people understand the needs of their family members and how best to help when difficulties arise. Seeing enables people to understand and recognize their weaknesses, and with the Lord's help these weaknesses can be turned into strengths.[25] In like manner, seeing enables people to understand their strengths and the good things they have done and can do. Seeing can give people confidence before others and before God, through the cleansing power of the Atonement. Seeing miracles, including healings and a new commitment to Christ, can strengthen testimonies.

---

23. Ezek. 44:23.
24. Mosiah 8:17.
25. See Ether 12:27.

Spiritually seeing can bring faith, hope, comfort, and peace, including during troubled times. Seeing can also give people insight during times of need. As an example, the prophet Elisha was in danger when the king of Syria sent horses, chariots, and a great host to capture Elisha in the city of Dothan. When Elisha's servant saw the army, he asked Elisha what they should do. Elisha told his servant to not be afraid, "for they that be with us are more than they that be with them."[26] Then Elisha prayed that his servant's eyes would be opened, and the Lord consequently enabled the servant to see that "the mountain was full of horses and chariots of fire round about Elisha."[27] The Lord also temporarily blinded the eyes of the Syrian warriors, enabling Elisha to lead them into another land and to avoid being captured by them.[28]

Seeing includes understanding hidden things of the Lord. Numerous scriptures refer to seeing and understanding hidden things. For example, the Lord told the prophet Isaiah, "Thou hast heard, see all this; and will not ye declare it? I have shewed thee new things from this time, even hidden things, and thou didst not know them."[29] In Doctrine and Covenants 89, the Lord promised that living the Word of Wisdom leads to wisdom and "great treasures of knowledge, even hidden treasures."[30] Doctrine and Covenants 101 states that when the Lord comes again to the earth, "He shall reveal all things—things which have passed, and hidden things which no man knew, things of the earth, by which it was made, and the purpose and the end thereof—things most precious, things that are above, and things that are beneath, things that are in the earth, and upon the earth, and in heaven."[31]

Additionally, seeing includes understanding the "mysteries of the kingdom, even the key of the knowledge of God."[32] Those who seek wisdom rather than riches and who keep God's commandments will learn the

---

26. 2 Kgs. 6:16.
27. 2 Kgs. 6:17.
28. See 2 Kgs. 6:8–18.
29. Isa. 48:6.
30. D&C 89:19.
31. D&C 101:32–34.
32. D&C 84:19.

mysteries of God, which "shall be in [them] a well of living water, springing up unto everlasting life."[33]

Perhaps in the next life, people will even see more gloriously, for the Lord has said: "There is no such thing as immaterial matter. All spirit is matter, but it is more fine or pure, and can only be discerned [seen] by purer eyes."[34] The righteous—those who will inherit the celestial kingdom—will receive the mysteries of the kingdom of heaven through revelation from the Holy Ghost.[35] Those who inherit the celestial kingdom will ultimately be able to comprehend all things both physical and spiritual, for all knowledge is of a complete union. As Joseph Smith instructed:

> The place where God resides is a great Urim and Thummim. This earth, in its sanctified and immortal state, will be made like unto crystal and will be a Urim and Thummim to the inhabitants who dwell thereon, whereby all things pertaining to an inferior kingdom, or all kingdoms of a lower order, will be manifest to those who dwell on it; and this earth will be Christ's. Then the white stone mentioned in Revelation 2:17, will become a Urim and Thummim to each individual who receives one, whereby things pertaining to a higher order of kingdoms will be made known.[36]

Christ came into the world to help the blind man and all people see and discern spiritual truths and, as a result, believe in Him. This sight is what enables people to obtain exaltation in the celestial kingdom.

Jesus Is the Good Shepherd (John 10:1–21)

After Jesus taught about the importance of seeing and believing, He spoke of His divine commission as the Good Shepherd. Good refers to His love, service, sacrifice, and care for all people, as well as to the instruction He gave verbally and by example.

In continuing to teach the people, Jesus used an allegory involving sheep and shepherds, both of which the Israelites were familiar with. Israel was a pastoral land with many sheep and shepherds, and in the temple in Jerusalem,

---

33. D&C 63:23; see also D&C 6:7.
34. D&C 131:7.
35. D&C 76:7; 90:14.
36. D&C 130:8–10.

sheep and lambs were regularly sacrificed. Further, most Israelites and certainly the leaders of the Jews were familiar with King David's 23rd Psalm:

> The Lord is my shepherd; I shall not want. He maketh me to lie down in green pastures: he leadeth me beside the still waters. He restoreth my soul: he leadeth me in the paths of righteousness for his name's sake. Yea, though I walk through the valley of the shadow of death, I will fear no evil: for thou art with me; thy rod and thy staff they comfort me. Thou preparest a table before me in the presence of mine enemies: thou anointest my head with oil; my cup runneth over. Surely goodness and mercy shall follow me all the days of my life: and I will dwell in the house of the Lord forever.

The Israelites were also familiar with the prophetic promises of Isaiah and Ezekiel that Christ would be Israel's shepherd[37] and with the Lord's castigation of Israelite leaders who "feed themselves" but "feed not the flock."[38]

Jesus Is the Keeper of the Gate (John 10:1–10)

Jesus began His allegory as follows:

John 10:1–10. Verily, verily, I say unto you, He that entereth not by the door into the sheepfold, but climbeth up some other way, the same is a thief and a robber. But he that entereth in by the door is the shepherd of the sheep. To him the porter openeth; and the sheep hear his voice: and he calleth his own sheep by name, and leadeth them out. And when he putteth forth his own sheep, he goeth before them, and the sheep follow him: for they know his voice. And a stranger will they not follow, but will flee from him: for they know not the voice of strangers. This parable spake Jesus unto them: but they understood not what things they were which he spake unto them. Then said Jesus unto them again, Verily, verily, I say unto you, I am the door of the sheep. All that ever came before me are thieves and robbers: but the sheep did not hear them. I am the door: by me if any man enter in, he shall be saved, and shall go in and out, and find pasture. The thief cometh not, but for to steal, and to kill, and to destroy: I am come that they might have life, and that they might have it more abundantly.

---

37. See Isa. 40:11; 49:9–10; Ezek. 34:12–15, 23–31; 37:24; cf. Jer. 3:15; 23:4; Heb. 13:20; 1 Pet. 2:25; 5:4; Rev. 7:17.
38. Ezek. 34:2–3.

Dummelow provided pertinent background information regarding these verses: "To understand the imagery, it must be remembered that Eastern Folds are large open enclosures into which several flocks are driven at the approach of night. There is only one door, which a single shepherd guards, while the others go home to rest. In the morning the shepherds return, are recognized by the doorkeeper, call their flocks around, and lead them forth to pasture."[39] Note that the shepherds led the sheep and did not drive them.

Jesus stated that a true shepherd was recognized by the porter[40] and was allowed to enter the sheep enclosure through the door; someone who tried to enter the enclosure in another way was a thief. Jesus also explained that the shepherd knew each sheep, called each by name, and led the flock out of the enclosure. The sheep would follow because they recognized the shepherd's voice; they would not follow a stranger but would, instead, flee.

Hearing and recognizing Jesus's voice involves not only physically hearing Him teach but also spiritually recognizing the truthfulness of His message and His status as the Son of God. Hearing and recognizing Him can result from hearing the testimony of others and consequently believing in Him and feeling His love. Hearing His voice is an important companion principle to seeing Him, as Jesus taught by healing the blind man, who, after being healed, not only physically saw Jesus but also spiritually saw Him and believed in Him.

An implication of this parable is that the leaders of the Jews, who claimed to be shepherds in Israel, were false shepherds, did not really know or care about the sheep, were therefore not recognized by the porter, and were thus thieves. These leaders did not believe in the "gatekeeper," who is Christ; rather, they believed that salvation came only through obedience to their laws and rabbinical instructions. Further, as the prophet Ezekiel described, these leaders fed themselves but not the flock.[41] Additionally, they were thieves—thieves break in to steal and may destroy and even take life in the process. Metaphorically, Satan is the thief who steals people's souls, destroys their spiritual sensitivity, and keeps them from eternal life. The

---

39. Dummelow, *Bible Commentary*, p. 791.

40. The Greek word for *porter* is *thurōros*, which means "door" or "gatekeeper" (see Young, *Analytical Concordance*, s.v. "porter").

41. Ezek. 34:2.

Pharisees must have been furious because Christ was telling them that they were thieves and that salvation came only through Him, not through them or obedience to rabbinical rules.

In contrast to the Pharisees who acted as thieves, the Savior explained that "I am come that they [His sheep] might have life, and that they might have it more abundantly." Abundant means "marked by great plenty" and "amply supplied."[42] Christ's use of the word *abundantly* implies peace, joy, richness, and fullness of life on the earth, even in the face of great trials and struggles. Further, because of Christ's Atonement and Resurrection, life will be eternally abundant in that people can continue to progress toward exaltation.

Just as sheep recognize their shepherd, those who are spiritually prepared are able to recognize their True Shepherd and His gospel message. Similarly, the True Shepherd knows all His sheep, even by name.[43] Further, the True Shepherd lovingly cares for His sheep and does not push them. As Isaiah said of the Messiah, "He shall feed his flock like a shepherd: he shall gather the lambs with his arm, and carry them in his bosom, and shall gently lead those that are with young."[44]

Jesus taught how those who believe in Him can be His undershepherds. His undershepherds know each of the shepherd's sheep, especially those for whom the undershepherds have responsibility of some kind. The sheep recognize the undershepherds' righteousness, charity, and care and therefore willingly follow the undershepherds.[45] These attributes are needed by all servants in the Lord's kingdom. Today, as in Jesus's day, good undershepherds are obedient and committed in their daily lives, even when challenges come. These undershepherds are willing to sacrifice for the Lord's kingdom on earth. They also have proper priorities. Though wolves can be found almost everywhere, good undershepherds must never fear nor lose focus and must never forsake the sheep.

Presumably because the Jews failed to fully understand Jesus's allegory, He then directly told them that He was the "door of the sheep"—in other

---

42. *Merriam-Webster*, s.v. "abundant," accessed November 1, 2020, https://www.merriam-webster.com/dictionary/abundant.

43. Isa. 40:26.

44. Isa. 40:11.

45. See D&C 121:45–46.

words, the gatekeeper. Jesus's teaching in this regard is profound: "I am the door: by me if any man enter in, he shall be saved, and shall go in and out, and find pasture." A person enters Christ's sheepfold by believing in Him, becoming a member of His Church, and following His teachings. Those who become His sheep will "find pasture"; that is, as the Book of Mormon states, they will "prosper in the land."[46]

By implication, Jesus was teaching that individuals could not properly serve in God's kingdom unless they believed in Jesus and accepted Him as the Son of God and the gatekeeper to the kingdom of heaven. Upon hearing Jesus's words, those with hardened hearts must have become even more irate.

On another level, Jesus may have been referring to paradise, which the righteous are permitted to enter after dying. Some may have callings and responsibilities to minister to those in this realm, to teach the gospel to those in spirit prison, and on certain occasions to minister to those on the earth. Those in paradise experience peace and rest, becoming renewed after no longer experiencing the trials of mortal life.

Jesus twice declared that He was the door. Similarly, Jacob in the Book of Mormon referred to Christ as the gatekeeper: "Behold, the way for man is narrow, but it lieth in a straight course before him, and the keeper of the gate is the Holy One of Israel; and he employeth no servant there; and there is none other way save it be by the gate; for he cannot be deceived, for the Lord God is his name."[47] It is clear that the Lord will be the one who admits the righteous into the kingdom of heaven, and He cannot be deceived.

In referring to Himself as the door, Jesus may also have been referring to temples in the latter days. To enter, people must be worthy according to the standards set by the Lord. Those who enter and keep the covenants made there will be saved. Those who are worthy are permitted to attend regularly, and when they attend, they typically find peace and spiritual food—"pasture."

All those with open hearts who heard Jesus's merciful, tender, yet pointed words must have been deeply touched. He spoke not as the Pharisees, who focused on obedience to their laws and interpretations thereof; rather, He spoke with divine, unbounding love and hope as the Son of God.

---

46. 1 Ne. 4:14; 2 Ne. 1: 20; Jarom 1:9; Mosiah 2:22; Alma 9:13; 36:1, 30; 37:13; 38:1; 48: 25; 50:20; see also 1 Ne. 2:20; 4:4; Omni 1:6.

47. 2 Ne. 9:41.

Jesus Is the Good Shepherd (John 10:11–13)

After Jesus taught that He is the keeper of the gate, He then explained that He is also the Good Shepherd:

John 10:11–13. I am the good shepherd: the good shepherd giveth his life for the sheep. But he that is an hireling, and not the shepherd, whose own the sheep are not, seeth the wolf coming, and leaveth the sheep, and fleeth: and the wolf catcheth them, and scattereth the sheep. The hireling fleeth, because he is an hireling, and careth not for the sheep.

In Jesus's statement, the word *the* is important. He is not merely one of many caring shepherds; he is the only Good Shepherd, the Son of God. The word *good* also provides insight. Christ is good in that there is no evil in Him. He is good because He is filled with holiness, love, compassion, and justice.[48] He is good in that He diligently cares for His sheep, desires to keep them from danger, and saves them from the wolves of the world. He is good because He can be relied on. He exemplifies the definition of good provided in Merriam-Webster: "Conforming to the moral order of the universe . . . praiseworthy . . . [and advancing] prosperity or well-being."[49] He is good because He is humble; He recognized that "there is none good but one, that is, God."[50] He is good because of His knowledge and omnipotence. As Isaiah said of Jesus, "Who hath measured the waters in the hollow of his hand, and meted out heaven with the span, and comprehended the dust of the earth in a measure, and weighed the mountains in scales, and the hills in a balance?"[51]

Jesus implied that He would give His life for humankind, whereas hirelings would not because they did not deeply care about the sheep and did not know each sheep individually. When wolves came, the hirelings would abandon the sheep in order to avoid danger themselves.

Metaphorically, the Jewish leaders were wolves, though outwardly they were dressed in the robes of sanctity. These leaders were as the prophet Ezekiel described: "Her princes in the midst thereof are like wolves ravening

48. See 2 Ne. 9.
49. *Merriam-Webster*, s.v. "good," accessed January 1, 2020, https://www.merriam -webster.com/dictionary/good.
50. Matt. 19:17.
51. Isa. 40:12.

the prey, to shed blood, and to destroy souls, to get dishonest gain."[52] Though Jesus's words likely cut these Jews to the core, they would not repent or believe. They were utterly unfit as leaders and teachers of the Jewish nation.

The scattered sheep that Jesus referred to symbolize those who are lost because of sin or neglect and who need Christ's rescuing hand. Those who heard Jesus could surely understand the metaphor Jesus used. Among them stood the Good Shepherd, who loved His sheep and would ultimately lay down His life for them all, not only those who would believe His message.

Jesus Knows His Sheep (John 10:14–15)

Jesus then reaffirmed that He is the Good Shepherd and added that He knows His sheep and that His sheep know him:

> **John 10:14–15.** I am the good shepherd, and know my sheep, and am known of mine. As the Father knoweth me, even so know I the Father: and I lay down my life for the sheep.

Christ knows each of God's children by name.[53] He knows who each person was in the premortal life and what each person's ultimate potential is. He knows each person's strengths, weaknesses, deepest yearnings, trials, and disappointments. He understands when there is a lack of family support or basic necessities. In short, the Good Shepherd knows everything about His sheep.

Just as Christ intimately knows each of His sheep, so does Heavenly Father. God is not some distant being who does not care. Thus, people can have confidence that their prayers will be heard and answered. Understanding that Christ and God know Their sheep can provide comfort and hope as people journey through life.

Jesus also stated that His sheep know Him. Often in Jesus's day, multiple shepherds led their sheep into a common enclosure for safety and security at night. While in the enclosure, the sheep from the different flocks would intermingle. When morning came, each shepherd would call to his sheep; these sheep, knowing their shepherd, would respond and follow, while the other sheep would not. Similarly, those who know Christ may recognize the

---

52. Ezek. 22:27.
53. See Isa. 40:26.

Light of Christ[54] and the whisperings of the Holy Ghost and may respond. Some will respond immediately, while others will respond after some time, perhaps after trials and challenges.

Jesus then affirmed His unity with the Father. Jesus knows the Father intimately, and the Father knows Jesus. In the premortal world, He volunteered to come to earth, atone for humankind, be crucified, and bring about the resurrection and redemption of humankind. Certainly, the Pharisees who heard Him speak did not comprehend the full meaning of His words. Even today, people cannot fully comprehend the depth of His goodness, His holiness, His knowledge, His love for all people, His unity with the Father, the anguish He experienced during the Atonement, and His power to be resurrected.

Jesus Has Other Sheep (John 10:16)

Next, Jesus stated that His mission was not limited to those in the nation of Israel. The following is John's account of Jesus's words:

> **John 10:16.** And other sheep I have, which are not of this fold: them also I must bring, and they shall hear my voice; and there shall be one fold, and one shepherd.

Even Jesus's disciples did not understand the scope of what He needed to do, where He needed to go, and what sheep He needed to visit. Following Jesus's death, He appeared to those in the spirit world. From among the righteous spirits, He organized a missionary force to take the gospel to all who had departed this life so that they could have the opportunity to learn of and accept the gospel message and the atoning sacrifice of the Savior.[55] They were among the other sheep that would hear His voice and recognize Him.

Further, following Christ's Resurrection and His appearance to Mary in the garden,[56] He ascended to His Father,[57] then appeared to His Apostles,[58]

---

54. Mormon explained, "For behold, the Spirit of Christ is given to every man, that he may know good from evil; wherefore, I show unto you the way to judge; for every thing which inviteth to do good, and to persuade to believe in Christ, is sent forth by the power and gift of Christ; wherefore ye may know with a perfect knowledge it is of God" (Moroni 7:16).

55. See D&C 138.

56. See John 20:13–16.

57. See John 20:17.

58. See Luke 24:36–40.

and thereafter appeared to the Nephites. He declared to the Nephites that "ye are they of whom I said: Other sheep I have which are not of this fold; them also I must bring, and they shall hear my voice; and there shall be one fold, and one shepherd."[59]

Jesus also told the Nephites: "I have other sheep, which are not of this land, neither of the land of Jerusalem, neither in any parts of that land round about whither I have been to minister. For they of whom I speak are they who have not as yet heard my voice; neither have I at any time manifested myself unto them. But I have received a commandment of the Father that I shall go unto them, and that they shall hear my voice, and shall be numbered among my sheep, that there may be one fold and one shepherd; therefore I go to show myself unto them."[60] Jesus was referring to the lost tribes of the house of Israel.

Other sheep may also include Joseph Smith and other modern-day prophets. For example, Christ and the Father appeared to Joseph Smith to usher in the restoration of the gospel in the latter days,[61] and Jesus gave numerous revelations to Joseph Smith in order to reestablish the foundation of His Church.

Other sheep may also include additional groups of people. Doctrine and Covenants 88:46–61 suggests that the scope of who is included is beyond present comprehension, perhaps because there are worlds without number[62] and there is no end to the works of the Father and Jesus Christ.[63] Doctrine and Covenants 88 refers to many kingdoms and infers that Jesus will visit each in its own time.

Jesus Has Power to Lay Down and Take Up His Life (John 10:17–18)

Jesus then spoke of His death and Resurrection:

John 10:17–18. Therefore doth my Father love me, because I lay down my life, that I might take it again. No man taketh it from me, but I lay it down of

---

59. 3 Ne. 15:21.
60. 3 Ne. 16:1–3.
61. See JS–H 1:13–20.
62. See Moses 1:33.
63. See Moses 1:35.

myself. I have power to lay it down, and I have power to take it again. This commandment have I received of my Father.

Jesus was indicating that though the Jewish leaders sought to take His life, they would not be able to do so unless He allowed it. He alone had the power, given by His Father, to lay down His life. Jesus was willing to follow the commandment of the Father by submitting Himself to the cruel cross.

Christ also made it clear that He received the glorious power of the resurrection from the Father. Because Jesus was resurrected, all other people will receive the glorious blessing of having a body for eternity.

The Jews Are Divided (John 10:19–21)[64]

Many of the Jews who heard Jesus's words continued to reject Him, claiming that He was working through Beelzebub or that He was mad. As Jesus had previously said, "For this people's heart is waxed gross, and their ears are dull of hearing, and their eyes they have closed."[65] In contrast, others recognized that Jesus's miracle of giving sight to the blind man was a witness that He was the Son of God. The differing responses resulted in another division among the Jews. The following is John's account:

> **John 10:19–21.** There was a division therefore again among the Jews for these sayings. And many of them said, He hath a devil, and is mad; why hear ye him? Others said, These are not the words of him that hath a devil. Can a devil open the eyes of the blind?

Just as there was a division among the Jews in Jesus's time, there is a division among people today as to whether there really was a Christ and, if so, what His role is in people's lives today. Like the Jews in Jesus's day, all people today must decide whether to believe in Christ. There is no real middle ground. Either Christ is the divine Son of God or He is not.

Christ's words as recorded in John 10 are a beautiful witness of Himself. They are a witness of His divinity and His mission on earth. They are a

---

64. Jesus likely delivered the latter part of the parable of the good Shepherd (John 10:22–30) after returning to Jerusalem two to three months later for the Feast of Dedication, and this portion will be more fully discussed in chapter 46 of this volume.

65. Matt. 13:15.

witness of His unbounding goodness, of His limitless love for and knowledge of each person, and of His death and the significance of His Resurrection.

As the prophet Alma said in the Book of Mormon: "And he shall go forth, suffering pains and afflictions and temptations of every kind; and this that the word might be fulfilled which saith he will take upon him the pains and the sicknesses of his people. And he will take upon him death, that he may loose the bands of death which bind his people; and he will take upon him their infirmities, that his bowels may be filled with mercy, according to the flesh, that he may know according to the flesh how to succor his people according to their infirmities."[66]

Christ's words as recorded in the Gospel of John can motivate people to be obedient undershepherds. Good undershepherds diligently serve so that people can spiritually see Christ and hear His voice, leading to the day that there will indeed be "one fold, and one shepherd."[67]

Note to Chapter 39

1.   **Parallelism.** There is interesting poetic contrast between the hireling and Christ in His teachings about the Good Shepherd. The following are examples:

Hireling	Christ
Is an employee	Owns the sheep
Tends the sheep	Is the Good Shepherd
Does not love the sheep	Knows and loves His sheep
Flees from danger	Lays down His life for the sheep
Allows a wolf to kill the sheep	Protects the sheep
Allows the sheep to be scattered	Rescues lost sheep

66.   Alma 7:11–12.
67.   John 10:16.

Chapter 40

JESUS TEACHES ABOUT HOW TO INHERIT ETERNAL LIFE

How long Jesus remained in Jerusalem after the Feast of Tabernacles is not known. Sometime after the feast, Jesus and His disciples left Jerusalem and traveled to other areas in Judea and to places in Perea.[1] John records that Jesus went to Bethabara[2] and that He "walked no more openly among the Jews." This chapter focuses on Jesus's teachings and other recorded activities during this time, which spanned approximately three months.[3] Because the scriptures referring to His activities during this period often do not include specific times or locations, the order in which these events are discussed here may not be completely chronological. However, the precise chronology is not important; the important information regards what Jesus said and did.

---

1. Bethabara is located in Judea, which is a region in Israel. At the time of Christ, the region spanned from the Jordan River and the Dead Sea on the east to the Mediterranean Sea on the west and as far north as Samaria to almost as far south as the southern end of the Dead Sea. In Christ's day, Judea was governed by the Roman governor Pontius Pilate. (See *HarperCollins Bible Dictionary*, s.v. "Judea," and "Pilate, Pontius.") Perea is also a region in Israel. During Christ's life, Perea was bounded on the west by the Jordan River and the Dead Sea, was bounded on the north by the Decapolis region, and extended to the south to about halfway down the Dead Sea. In Christ's day, Perea was governed by Herod Antipas.

2. See John 10:40; John 1:28. Bethabara is likely where Jesus was baptized (see 1 Ne. 10:9). Bethabara was likely on the west side of the Jordan River near Jericho (see *HarperCollins Bible Dictionary*, s.v. "Bethabara").

3. Jesus briefly visited Jerusalem for the Feast of Dedication (see John 10:22–39) and returned again the last week of His life. Talmage suggested the possibility that Jesus also traveled to Galilee at some point by taking a short detour across the border into Samaria (see Talmage, *Jesus the Christ*, p. 397). Jesus began His ministry in Judea and Perea approximately six months before His death.

The Seventy Return and Report on Their Missions (Luke 10:17–20)

At some point, likely soon after Jesus attended the Feast of Tabernacles, the Seventy returned from their missions. Jesus had sent them "into every city and place, wither he himself would come."[4] Therefore, they presumably taught in the various cities of Perea and Judea.

Likely, the Seventy did not all return at the same time but, rather, over a period of several days. Luke records that the Seventy returned with "joy." It is reasonable to assume that Jesus and at least some of His Apostles listened to the individual reports of the Seventy. They likely performed miracles of healing in the name of Christ as they served. The Seventy likely also experienced joy as they shared the gospel message and consequently saw people's hearts change. The Seventy also felt joy because, through Christ's name, they had power even over evil spirits. Jesus surely rejoiced in the joy of the Seventy, for each was important to Him.

The following is Luke's record:

> **Luke 10:17–20.** And the seventy returned again with joy, saying, Lord, even the devils are subject unto us through thy name. And he said unto them, I beheld Satan as lightning fall from heaven. Behold, I give unto you power to tread on serpents and scorpions, and over all the power of the enemy: and nothing shall by any means hurt you. Notwithstanding in this rejoice not, that the spirits are subject unto you; but rather rejoice, because your names are written in heaven.

Hearing the Seventy's report that they felt joy because they had power over evil spirits, Jesus may have wanted them to fully understand that their power to overcome evil spirits was real, not imagined, and that this authority came through their ordination by Christ as members of the Seventy.

Jesus also used this occasion to teach further about Satan, declaring that He had "beheld Satan as lightning fall from heaven." This statement implies that Jesus remembered witnessing the War in Heaven.[5] It is also possible that the mortal Jesus was reminded by His Father about the details of the premortal war, Jesus's role in honoring the will of the Father, and Satan and his followers being cast from heaven to the earth for rebellion. Whatever the

---

4. Luke 10:1.
5. See Moses 4:1–4; Rev. 12:7–9.

case, Jesus was now confirming the reality of the influence of Satan and his followers on humankind.

Isaiah stated that in the premortal world, Satan was a "son of the morning";[6] this phrase signifies his brilliance. This brilliance ended in an instant, like lightning, as he and his followers were cast out of heaven. It is possible that Satan was cast down to the earth rapidly and that this casting out was visible, like lightning, to all in heaven.

Lightning also has other symbolism. It appears and strikes suddenly, just as Satan's temptations can come at any time. Further, lightning sometimes strikes at the highest places, and people who are in or close to those places can be vulnerable to the destructive power of lightning. Similarly, if people place themselves in temptation's path through being lifted up with pride, they can be especially vulnerable to Satan's destructive power. Like sin and temptation, lightning can often be fascinating and enticing to watch but deadly when in its path. Further, a lightning flash begins and ends in an instant[7] and, unlike the Savior's light, does not lead to eternal life.

Jesus may have taught the Seventy and His Apostles much more than is recorded about the fall of Satan and his followers. Teaching this information may have helped the Seventy better understand the evil influence that Satan and his followers have on God's children.

Jesus might have taught the Seventy and the Apostles of Satan's rebellion so that they would more fully comprehend the large number of evil spirits on the earth and why they are here. The exact number of evil spirits is unknown. Abraham stated that when Satan rebelled in heaven, "many followed after him."[8] In Doctrine and Covenants 29:36, the Lord defined the number of Satan's followers as a "third part of the hosts of heaven."

Jesus may also have also wanted to help His disciples better understand the necessity of avoiding pride lest they boast of their actions and fall as Satan did. As Moses's account states, Satan was cast out in part because he rebelled against God and wanted God's power. Isaiah described Satan's intentions as follows: "For thou hast said in thine heart, I will ascend into

---

6. Isa. 14:12; see also D&C 76:26.
7. In contrast, the Light of Christ enlightens the soul, can endure, and leads to eternal life.
8. Abr. 3:28.

heaven, I will exalt my throne above the stars of God: I will sit also upon the mount of the congregation, in the sides of the north: I will ascend above the heights of the clouds; I will be like the most High."[9]

Christ may also have taught the Seventy and His Apostles that Satan and his followers were tempting humankind because Satan and his followers had been cursed with eternal misery and therefore "sought also the misery of all mankind."[10] In teaching the Seventy and the Apostles, Jesus may have reminded them of Satan's temptation of Adam and Eve and their resulting fall, which would prevent them and their posterity from obtaining salvation if Christ did not atone for humankind and rise from the grave.

Jesus then gave the Seventy power to "tread on serpents and scorpions, and over all the power of the enemy: and nothing shall by any means hurt you." The Seventy would not only be protected from venomous creatures[11] but would also have power over Satan and his followers, who are often depicted as serpents, scorpions,[12] and other mortal enemies.

Jesus's central message to the Seventy was to focus on things that really matter—that is, the Seventy's standing before God and their attainment of eternal life. Jesus told the Seventy that their real joy and rejoicing should come not because they had power over evil spirits but because their names were "written in heaven," which is the Lamb's Book of Life.[13] The Book of Life is a record that is kept in heaven and that contains the names of the faithful and their righteous deeds.[14] As John said in the book of Revelation: "And I saw the dead, small and great, stand before God; and the books were opened: and another book was opened, which is the book of life: and the dead were judged out of those things which were written in the books, according to their works."[15] The names of those who

---

9.　Isa. 14:13–14.

10.　2 Ne. 2:18.

11.　See Mark 16:18; Acts 28:5.

12.　See Rev. 12:9; 20:2; cf. Gen. 3:1–4, 14–15.

13.　See Rev. 21:27; D&C 132:19.

14.　See D&C 128:6–7; Ps. 69:28; Rev. 3:5.

15.　Rev. 20:12.

will inherit eternal life are "written in heaven, where God and Christ are the judge of all."[16]

Jesus Gives Thanks to the Father (Luke 10:21–24)

After contemplating the Seventy's joy and then teaching them, Jesus addressed the Father in a humble prayer of thanksgiving. The following is Luke's account:

> **Luke 10:21–24.** In that hour Jesus rejoiced in spirit, and said, I thank thee, O Father, Lord of heaven and earth, that thou hast hid these things from the wise and prudent, and hast revealed them unto babes: even so, Father; for so it seemed good in thy sight. All things are delivered to me of my Father: and no man knoweth who the Son is, but the Father; and who the Father is, but the Son, and he to whom the Son will reveal him. And he turned him unto his disciples, and said privately, Blessed are the eyes which see the things that ye see: for I tell you, that many prophets and kings have desired to see those things which ye see, and have not seen them; and to hear those things which ye hear, and have not heard them.

Jesus was thankful for the faithfulness of the Seventy and for the Father's protection of them. Jesus also expressed gratitude for the joy He felt in the Seventy's success, their righteous exercise of priesthood authority, and their understanding that they had power over evil spirits. He also expressed gratitude to His Father that spiritual truths were revealed to His disciples, who were "babes" in their gospel knowledge, and that these truths were withheld from Jews who were of the world and who professed to be wise and knowledgeable.

In His prayer of thanksgiving, Jesus expressed his profound gratitude that He had received all things from His Father. Presumably, many of the Seventy and at least some of the Apostles heard Jesus's prayer and acknowledgment that He is the Son of God.

Jesus then acknowledged in His prayer that no mortal at that time could fully comprehend who He was. Likewise, no one could fully comprehend God except Jesus and those to whom Jesus revealed this knowledge. Though the Seventy could not fully comprehend Jesus and Heavenly Father, the

---

16. D&C 76:68; see also D&C 88:2; 132:19.

Seventy could—and needed to—understand the relationship between Jesus and His Father, as well as the Seventy's relationship with God and their dependence on Him for all they had.

Jesus then turned to His "disciples"—presumably His Apostles[17]—and told them privately that they were blessed even above the prophets and kings of old because of the opportunity to be in the presence of the Son of God and to be taught by Him things pertaining to the kingdom of heaven, including the nature of God and the reality of Satan and his followers.

What does the account of Jesus's teachings to the Seventy and the Apostles mean for people today? Just as Jesus revealed truth to the Seventy and His Apostles, much has been revealed in the latter days. In this dispensation of the fulness of times,[18] knowledge of God and Jesus Christ has been restored to the earth,[19] and the Lord will yet "reveal unto my church things which have been kept hid from before the foundation of the world."[20] During this dispensation, Christ will "gather together in one all things in [Him], both which are in heaven, and which are on earth"[21] and will "bring salvation unto men."[22]

Christ's Church and the priesthood authority of God have been restored to the earth. The fulness of the gospel has been revealed. Latter-day Saints have the privilege of participating in sacred ordinances of salvation and in making sacred covenants for themselves and for those who have died, that all may be one with Christ. This dispensation is a time of preparation for the Lord's return to the earth.

The Lord said of the Seventy that their "names are written in heaven." All people should regularly ask themselves, "What must I do in order for my name to be written in heaven? Given my circumstances and talents, how can I help build the kingdom of God on the earth in preparation for Christ's

---

17. Often in the New Testament, the term *disciples* is used to refer to the Apostles (see *HarperCollins Bible Dictionary*, s.v. "apostle," and "disciple"; see also, for example, Matt. 10:1–2; Luke 6:13).

18. See D&C 112:30; 128:18, 20; 138:48.

19. See JS–H 1:16–18.

20. D&C 124:41; see also D&C 121:26–32.

21. Eph. 1:10; see also D&C 27:13.

22. 2 Ne. 2:3; see also 2:26.

return?" One answer is found in the parable of the good Samaritan, which is presented next in Luke's account.

Jesus Gives the Parable of the Good Samaritan (Luke 10:25–37)

The parable of the good Samaritan is only in Luke's record, but the message of the parable is vital. Jesus gave the parable in response to a "certain lawyer" who asked a question that all should ask regularly: "Master, what shall I do to inherit eternal life?" The following is Luke's account:

> **Luke 10:25–28.** And, behold, a certain lawyer stood up, and tempted him [Jesus], saying, Master, what shall I do to inherit eternal life? He said unto him, What is written in the law? how readest thou? And he answering said, Thou shalt love the Lord thy God with all thy heart, and with all thy soul, and with all thy strength, and with all thy mind; and thy neighbour as thyself. And he said unto him, Thou hast answered right: this do, and thou shalt live.

The Greek word for *lawyer* as used in Luke is *nomikos*, which means "belonging to the law."[23] The man who asked the question may not have been a lawyer but a rabbi, since rabbis are the ones who dealt with interpretations of the law. Luke also used the word *tempted*. The Greek word for *tempt* is *ekpeirazō*, which means "to try, prove exceedingly."[24] Unlike the Jews in Jerusalem, this lawyer did not seek to accuse Jesus of violating the law but, instead, sought to use his skills, training, and knowledge of the law to best Jesus and perhaps thereby enhance his standing with the people.

Jesus was not willing to debate the law with this man; rather, as always, He taught the gospel message. Jesus asked this lawyer what was written in the law, presumably desiring to help the man deepen his understanding and gain even greater truth. The man responded correctly: "Thou shalt love the Lord thy God with all thy heart, and with all thy soul, and with all thy strength, and with all thy mind; and thy neighbour as thyself."[25]

The response was based on the Lord's commands to the ancient Israelites that "thou shalt love the Lord thy God with all thine heart, and with all thy

---

23. Young, *Analytical Concordance*, s.v. "lawyer."
24. Young, *Analytical Concordance*, s.v. "tempt."
25. Jesus said almost the same thing to a questioning Pharisee, as recorded in Matt. 22:36–40.

soul, and with all thy might"[26] and that "thou shalt not avenge, nor bear any grudge against the children of thy people, but thou shalt love thy neighbour as thyself."[27] Because the man tied these two passages of scripture together, it is reasonable to conclude that he not only was learned but also had spent much time trying to understand and apply the law. Luke's account is silent as to what this man did after his encounter with Jesus. This account states that the man's motive was to tempt Jesus, and many Jews tried to trap Jesus in order to find cause to take His life. Therefore, it may be easy to conclude that the man simply would not see, hear, or believe. However, this man's question and response suggest that he may have gained an understanding of the greatness of the Master and his own shortcomings and sins, and he may have desired to believe.

Jesus's response was simple and direct: "This do, and thou shalt live." These words may have penetrated the man's soul, causing deeper introspection. Seeking to justify himself, the lawyer then asked a thought-provoking question very applicable today: "And who is my neighbour?" Jesus answered with the parable of the good Samaritan. The following is Luke's account:

Luke 10:29–37. But he, willing to justify himself, said unto Jesus, And who is my neighbour? And Jesus answering said, A certain man went down from Jerusalem to Jericho, and fell among thieves, which stripped him of his raiment, and wounded him, and departed, leaving him half dead. And by chance there came down a certain priest that way: and when he saw him, he passed by on the other side. And likewise a Levite, when he was at the place, came and looked on him, and passed by on the other side. But a certain Samaritan, as he journeyed, came where he was: and when he saw him, he had compassion on him, and went to him, and bound up his wounds, pouring in oil and wine, and set him on his own beast, and brought him to an inn, and took care of him. And on the morrow when he departed, he took out two pence, and gave them to the host, and said unto him, Take care of him; and whatsoever thou spendest more, when I come again, I will repay thee. Which now of these three, thinkest thou, was neighbour unto him that fell among the thieves? And he said, He that shewed mercy on him. Then said Jesus unto him, Go, and do thou likewise.

---

26. Deut. 6:5.
27. Lev. 19:18.

As the setting of the parable, Jesus selected the road from Jerusalem to Jericho, which the man was presumably familiar with and which was perhaps close by. The road is approximately eighteen miles long and is in a desolate and rocky region.[28] A traveler would descend from Jerusalem, which is at approximately twenty-three to twenty-five hundred feet above sea level in the Judean Mountains,[29] and travel along this road to Jericho, which is at approximately eight hundred feet below sea level.[30] In Jesus's day, the road was dirt and perhaps somewhat rutted, and it was notoriously insecure.[31] According to St. Jerome, "a certain part of this road was called the red or the bloody way, so much blood had there been shed by robbers."[32]

Though the man attacked in the parable was not identified by name or nationality, those listening to Jesus tell the parable likely assumed that the man was a Jew since he came from Jerusalem and that the aid was provided by a Samaritan, who presumably would be less likely than a priest or Levite to assist a Jew. However, the fact that the man's identity was not disclosed provides an important lesson: all people, regardless of who they are, should be offered help when they are in need.

Jesus noted in the parable that the man was stripped of his clothes, wounded, and left half dead. The man's dire condition made the priest's and the Levite's failure to act more condemnable and the Samaritan's mercy and aid more notable. The contrast between the inaction and the action made the parable more poignant.

The Master Teacher carefully wove the threads of different men's lives into a shared event and lesson. Jesus indicated in the parable that the priest's and the Levite's encounters with the man were by "chance." As the priest and the Levite traveled, they were apparently not looking for someone who had been robbed and beaten and needed aid. In the parable, both the priest and the Levite failed to see that the man lying beside the road was a child of God, and they failed to see that they were missing an opportunity to serve and to grow personally and that they were being tested to see if their outward piousness

28. See Trench, *Notes on the Parables*, p. 110.
29. See *HarperCollins Bible Dictionary*, s.v. "Jerusalem."
30. See Smith, *Bible Dictionary*, s.v. "Jericho."
31. See Edersheim, *Life and Times of Jesus the Messiah*, p. 639.
32. As qtd. in Trench, *Notes on the Parables*, p. 110.

was matched with inward morality. By virtue of their lineage and priesthood responsibilities, the priest and Levite were called upon to serve others. Both the priest and the Levite were under the Lord's command to render aid, even to a fallen ox: "Thou shalt not see thy brother's ass or his ox fall down by the way, and hide thyself from them: thou shalt surely help him to lift them up again."[33] How much more important is a man's life than an ox's? Nevertheless, the priest and the Levite chose not to help the wounded man.

Upon seeing the man, the priest went to the other side of the road, perhaps thinking that he could justify not helping since he did not know the true condition of the man. The priest may have been in a hurry, may have feared that he would suffer the same fate as the wounded man, or may simply not have wanted to be bothered with another man's plight. Whatever the reason, the priest chose to ignore the man in need. The Levite's conduct was perhaps even worse than the priest's, for the Levite took a closer look at the man and would have seen his dire condition but still did not provide assistance.

The Samaritan may have been tempted to make excuses for not helping the wounded man. He may have been in a hurry. He may have thought that the wounded man was beyond help or that the robbers were nearby. Since he was a Samaritan, he may have even thought he could be accused of being the one who had wounded the man and stolen his belongings, and if the man died, he may have been accused of murder. But the Samaritan made no such excuses.

Samaritans and Jews despised and heaped indignities upon each other; nevertheless, this Samaritan's heart was not hardened against helping a Jew in need. The Samaritan stopped, thereby delaying his journey, to pour soothing oil and presumably cleansing wine on the man's wounds and then to bandage them, likely with some of the Samaritan's own clothing. He may also have used some of his own garments to clothe the man, who had been stripped by the robbers. The Samaritan gave of both his time and his substance.

When the man could travel, the Samaritan used his own animal to carry the man to an inn and further cared for the man when there. Significantly delaying his own plans, the Samaritan stayed with the man until the next day.

---

33. Deut. 22:4; see also Ex. 23:5.

As the Samaritan left the inn, he gave the host two pence—the equivalent of two days' wages for a laborer[34]—and requested that the host continue caring for the man. The Samaritan assured the innkeeper that he would pay for any additional costs the next time he passed by the inn.

The innkeeper, presumably a Jew, must have recognized the integrity of the Samaritan because of his actions, for the innkeeper was apparently willing to care for the wounded man with only the Samaritan's word that he would return. Or perhaps the innkeeper was willing to provide lodging and render assistance even if he never received compensation.

This parable teaches that in contrast to what Jews typically believed, achieving eternal life requires being loving, nonjudgmental, and compassionate, not just being outwardly obedient. In telling this parable, Jesus presumably wanted to teach that people should show love and compassion regardless of what their callings, positions, needs, resources, or time restraints are. Love and compassion should be at the very core of a person's character.

Upon concluding the parable, Jesus asked the lawyer which of the three men who saw the wounded man responded like a neighbor. Of course, the lawyer identified the Samaritan. Jesus then said to the lawyer, "Go, and do thou likewise." Though Jesus was speaking to the lawyer, His instruction applies to all people, no matter who they are or what their circumstances are. It is evident from the parable that people would do well to ask themselves, "Have I done any good in the world today? Have I helped anyone in need?"[35]

The good Samaritan's character is somewhat a reflection of Christ's character. Christ left heaven to come into mortality, with all its evils, prejudices, and trials. He came with compassion and healing, both physical and spiritual. He came not to obtain worldly wealth or comfort but to serve and lift others. There is never even a hint in the scriptures that He was in too much of a hurry to help someone in need. Christ was good, and so was the Samaritan.

---

34. See Edersheim, *Life and Times of Jesus the Messiah*, p. 640.
35. Will L. Thompson, "Have I Done Any Good?" *Hymns*, no. 223.

Picture Christ healing the infirm at the pool of Bethesda and giving sight to the blind. Envision Him tenderly healing a leper, giving strength to the infirm, restoring hearing to the deaf, and giving speech to the mute. View Him casting out devils; feeding the five thousand and the four thousand; healing the Centurion's servant; and restoring life to the daughter of Jairus, to the son of the widow of Nain, and to Lazarus. Picture Him as He stilled the wind and the waves and brought peace to His disciples on the Sea of Galilee and then reached out a saving hand to Peter. Envision Him bowed with the weight of the world as He atoned for the sins of all, causing Him to bleed from every pore, and then as He suffered and died on the cruel cross. Feel joy because of His Resurrection. All He did, He did for each of God's children. He came to bring salvation to humankind. He paid the awful price Himself. He was scorned by His own people, yet He loved and served them. Who else could truly heal a wounded and sinful soul? Could the rabbinical laws do it? No!

Jesus Speaks with Mary and Martha (Luke 10:38–42)

Luke next recorded that Jesus visited the house of Martha, Mary, and Lazarus in Bethany,[36] less than two miles east of Jerusalem.[37]

> **Luke 10:38–42.** Now it came to pass, as they went, that he entered into a certain village: and a certain woman named Martha received him into her house. And she had a sister called Mary, which also sat at Jesus' feet, and heard his word. But Martha was cumbered about much serving, and came to him, and said, Lord, dost thou not care that my sister hath left me to serve alone? bid her therefore that she help me. And Jesus answered and said unto her, Martha, Martha, thou art careful and troubled about many things: but one thing is needful: and Mary hath chosen that good part, which shall not be taken away from her.

It is unclear from Luke's account whether others accompanied Jesus into Mary and Martha's home. The account states "as they went," implying that Jesus traveled with others, likely including His Apostles. In addition, Martha

---

36. Scholars have differing opinions regarding whether Jesus had previously visited Mary and Martha's home.

37. See John 11:18.

was busy serving during the visit, which suggests that Jesus was not the only guest. On the other hand, the account also states that "he" (Jesus) entered into a certain village and that Martha received "him" into her house, implying that Jesus visited the home by Himself.

Whatever the number present in Martha and Mary's home at the time, it is evident that Martha was weighed down with the responsibility of providing food for those present and otherwise serving them. Mary had apparently been helping Martha before Jesus arrived, but as Jesus began to teach, Mary had stopped to sit by Jesus and listen to Him.

Finally, Martha said to Jesus, possibly within Mary's hearing, "Dost thou not care that my sister hath left me to serve alone? Bid her therefore that she help me." Jesus responded with a mild rebuke: "Martha, Martha, thou art careful and troubled about many things." Then He said that "Mary hath chosen that good part" by listening to what He had been saying. As the Bread of Life, Jesus offered spiritual food that was of far greater value than the physical food the group would eat.

It is easy for people to be like Martha, so consumed with the many details of daily living that they miss the whisperings of the Spirit and the opportunity to learn from the Master.

Jesus Teaches How to Pray (Luke 11:1–4)

Luke then recorded that when Jesus finished praying "in a certain place," one of His disciples asked Him to teach them to pray:

Luke 11:1–4. And it came to pass, that, as he was praying in a certain place, when he ceased, one of his disciples said unto him, Lord, teach us to pray, as John also taught his disciples. And he said unto them, When ye pray, say, Our Father which art in heaven, Hallowed be thy name. Thy kingdom come. Thy will be done, as in heaven, so in earth. Give us day by day our daily bread. And forgive us our sins; for we also forgive every one that is indebted to us. And lead us not into temptation; but deliver us from evil.

It is understandable that Luke included this account after the accounts of the Seventy returning, the parable of the good Samaritan, and Jesus's visit to Mary and Martha. Jesus was now teaching about the need to pray regularly and earnestly. The words of the prayer Jesus gave as an example of how to pray were essentially the same as the words He used in the prayer He gave during the Sermon on the Mount in Galilee.[38]

Although the Gospels seldomly mention Jesus praying, He undoubtedly prayed to His Father frequently. It is essential to pray regularly in order to receive needed help from God. God hears and answers prayers. In fact, He has reserved this role for Himself; He does not delegate this role to Christ or the Holy Ghost, though God has delegated other responsibilities to these members of the Godhead.

It is reasonable to assume that because the disciples asked Jesus how to pray, He taught them not only what to pray for but also how often to pray. He likely taught them that it was good to humbly approach God at least morning and night but that it was even better to let their hearts be continually filled with prayer. He likely taught them to pray in places where they could be alone and also to pray with their families and others. Regarding what to pray for, He likely taught that giving thanks was a central principle of prayer. He likely taught the disciples that they should pray for help and direction in their ministries, including in their future ministries when Jesus would no longer be with them. He presumably also taught them to pray for their and their families' welfare, for help in becoming more like Christ, for forgiveness of their sins, and for everything else they needed. In essence, Jesus taught that regular prayer is another important component in gaining eternal life.

---

38. See Matt. 6:9–13. For a more detailed discussion, see chapter 18 in volume 1 of this series. Some scholars have suggested that Luke 11:2–4 is a record of the prayer Jesus gave during the Sermon on the Mount and not a prayer He gave at a different time. These scholars believe that the chronology of events in Luke's account is more accurate and that Matthew's account is more complete (see Dummelow, *Bible Commentary*, p. 752). However, there is no reason to conclude that Jesus taught the manner of prayer on only one occasion. Further, Matthew's account states that Jesus was in Galilee when giving the prayer, whereas Luke's account states that Jesus was in Judea.

Jesus Gives the Parable of the Friend at Midnight (Luke 11:5–8)

Luke's record then moves to Jesus's parable of the friend at midnight, which in part symbolizes the need for regular prayer:

> **Luke 11:5–8.** And he said unto them, Which of you shall have a friend, and shall go unto him at midnight, and say unto him, Friend, lend me three loaves; for a friend of mine in his journey is come to me, and I have nothing to set before him? And he from within shall answer and say, Trouble me not: the door is now shut, and my children are with me in bed; I cannot rise and give thee. I say unto you, Though he will not rise and give him, because he is his friend, yet because of his importunity he will rise and give him as many as he needeth.

Joseph Smith's inspired translation of the Bible includes the following phrase, which gives added meaning to the parable: "Your heavenly Father will not fail to give unto you whatsoever ye ask of him."[39]

Significantly, in the parable the person who would be hosting took on the needs of the guest. Likewise, disciples of Christ should take on and seek to meet the needs of others. Moreover, in the parable, the request was not fulfilled immediately but, rather, after the man repeatedly asked his friend for assistance. If all prayers were answered immediately and the answers were easy to recognize, people's faith would never be fully tried and spiritual growth would be limited. Heavenly Father understands what people seek and need, including metaphorical food for guests at inconvenient times. Heavenly Father is the ultimate friend. His desire is to help His children gain eternal life. Qualifying for eternal life does not happen in an instant. The refining required for eternal life occurs over time and involves frequently petitioning Heavenly Father for help as life's circumstances change.

Jesus Teaches That If People Will Ask, They Will Receive Answers (Luke 11:9–13)

The Lord then gave the capstone message of His discussion about prayer:

> **Luke 11:9–13.** And I say unto you, Ask, and it shall be given you; seek, and ye shall find; knock, and it shall be opened unto you. For every one that

---

39. JST Luke 11:5.

asketh receiveth; and he that seeketh findeth; and to him that knocketh it shall be opened. If a son shall ask bread of any of you that is a father, will he give him a stone? or if he ask a fish, will he for a fish give him a serpent? Or if he shall ask an egg, will he offer him a scorpion? If ye then, being evil, know how to give good gifts unto your children: how much more shall your heavenly Father give the Holy Spirit to them that ask him?

Jesus used the words *ask*, *seek*, and *knock* to help His disciples better understand their role in communicating with Heavenly Father. Asking, seeking, and knocking are all required.

Those who ask and seek will find answers. Heavenly Father gives liberally to those who ask, just as a mortal father would give his son bread when asked. Of course, a person must exercise faith when asking Heavenly Father for an answer. As James, the Lord's brother, stated: "If any of you lack wisdom, let him ask of God, that giveth to all men liberally, and upbraideth not; and it shall be given him. But let him ask in faith, nothing wavering. For he that wavereth is like a wave of the sea driven with the wind and tossed. For let not that man think that he shall receive any thing of the Lord."[40] God will not chastise anyone for asking Him in prayer, but deep communication with God requires faith.

Exercising faith requires effort, such as through seeking. The Lord explained this principle in a revelation for Oliver Cowdery regarding his desire to help translate the golden plates:

> Behold, you have not understood; you have supposed that I would give it unto you, when you took no thought save it was to ask me. But, behold, I say unto you, that you must study it out in your mind; then you must ask me if it be right, and if it is right I will cause that your bosom shall burn within you; therefore, you shall feel that it is right. But if it be not right you shall have no such feelings, but you shall have a stupor of thought that shall cause you to forget the thing which is wrong; therefore, you cannot write that which is sacred save it be given you from me.[41]

In summary, Luke's grouping of the accounts of the return of the Seventy, the parable of the good Samaritan, Jesus's visit to Mary and Martha,

---

40. James 1:5–7.
41. D&C 9:7–9.

and His instruction on prayer address principles regarding eternal life. The Savior taught the Seventy that they should rejoice in having their names written in heaven. In the parable of the good Samaritan, Jesus answered the question "What shall I do to inherit eternal life?" The answer was to serve. All too often, people are so busy with daily life that they do not hear the Spirit's promptings to help others. When people miss opportunities to serve, they also miss opportunities to develop the character needed to gain eternal life. The account of Jesus in Mary and Martha's house adds dimension to the theme of things that matter most. People who are too busy to listen to and learn His teachings by metaphorically sitting "at Jesus's feet" may miss the opportunity to refine their character and become like Him. Finally, in teaching about prayer, the Savior emphasized that regularly communicating with Heavenly Father is essential in gaining what matters most: eternal life.

Chapter 41

A TIME TO DECIDE

Christ's ministry among the Jews included teaching them of His divine ministry and of the higher law, which leads to eternal life. In contrast, Satan sought to thwart the Father's plan by blinding the hearts and minds of as many as he could so they would not accept Christ's message. The contest between good and evil was continuing. The people needed to choose whether to believe in Jesus.

Jesus Casts Out a Devil (Luke 11:14–26)

According to Luke's record, after Jesus taught His disciples further about prayer, He cast out an evil spirit from a man who had been made dumb by that evil spirit. There is no indication in Luke's record where this event took place, but presumably it was somewhere in Perea. As mentioned in the previous chapter, it is difficult to know the exact chronology of events, including the ones discussed in this chapter.

Luke 11:14–26. And he was casting out a devil, and it was dumb. And it came to pass, when the devil was gone out, the dumb spake; and the people wondered. But some of them said, He casteth out devils through Beelzebub the chief of the devils. And others, tempting him, sought of him a sign from heaven. But he, knowing their thoughts, said unto them, Every kingdom divided against itself is brought to desolation; and a house divided against a house falleth. If Satan also be divided against himself, how shall his kingdom stand? Because ye say that I cast out devils through Beelzebub. And if I by Beelzebub cast out devils, by whom do your sons cast them out? Therefore shall they be your judges. But if I with the finger of God cast out devils, no doubt the kingdom of God is come upon you. When a strong man armed keepeth his palace, his goods are in peace: But when a stronger than he shall come upon him, and overcome him, he taketh from him all his armour wherein he trusted, and divideth his spoils. He that is not with me is against me: and he that gathereth not with me scattereth. When the unclean spirit is gone out of a man, he walketh through dry places, seeking rest; and finding none, he saith, I will return unto my house whence I came out. And when he cometh, he findeth it swept and garnished. Then goeth he, and taketh to him seven other spirits more wicked than himself; and they enter in, and dwell there: and the last state of that man is worse than the first.

Luke states that after Jesus cast out the evil spirit, the "people wondered." Some said that He cast out the evil spirit by the power of Beelzebub—an accusation the Jews had previously made against Jesus. Others sought a heavenly sign of His divinity. Of course, Christ never gave such a sign to satisfy people's requests. Moreover, the people had just witnessed a sign from heaven, in that Jesus cast out the evil spirit, thus enabling a man to speak. This miracle, which these Jews could not perform, should have been more than sufficient evidence. These Jews, however, were filled with pride and blind to the truth.

After Christ was accused of working through Satan, He responded: "Every kingdom divided against itself is brought to desolation; and a house divided against a house falleth."[1] Further, Christ said that if Satan is "divided against himself, how shall his kingdom stand?" Based on Jesus's answer, the only logical response would be to admit the miracle was of God, but these Jews would not do so. Some wondered, while others would not believe. However, the man whom Jesus healed likely left praising Him and likely was an ambassador for Him wherever the man went.

Jesus then metaphorically compared the Israelite nation in Old Testament times, the Jewish nation during His day, and the Jewish nation in the future[2] to a palace overseen by a strong man who protected his palace

---

1. This verse formed the basis of Abraham Lincoln's famous "House Divided" speech, which he delivered at the Illinois Republican State Convention in 1858. Lincoln had just won the nomination to run for US Senate against Stephen A. Douglas. Douglas wanted a compromise on the slavery issue, and Lincoln said there could be no compromise; the country could not endure if half the states allowed slavery and the other half outlawed slavery. (See *Encyclopedia Britannica*, s.v. "Abraham Lincoln, the road to presidency.")

2. See, for comparison, Zenos's allegory of the tame and wild olive tree, recorded in Jacob chapter 5.

and its goods. This man represents the strength of the past Israelite nation. This man is overcome by a stronger man, who represents Jehovah and His prophets who cleaned the Israelite nation of idolatry. However, Israel had once again embraced idolatry and sin, and by the time of Christ, the evil had greatly increased, leading many people to reject Jesus as the Son of God. Jesus also may have been referring to the Jewish nation's shift from focusing on morality to focusing on obeying their interpretations of the law, which obscured the need for Christ.[3]

This short parable may also refer to the latter days. Today, some nations view themselves as relatively strong and protective of their citizens. But the time will come when Christ, the stronger man, will return in glory and destroy the wicked. In that day, the majority of the righteous will be spared— they will be with Christ. Those who accept Christ but then leave Him or His Church may seek others who have also abandoned the gospel, and their state will be worse than if they had not believed in the first place.

Those Who Hear and Follow the Word of God Are Blessed (Luke 11:27–28)

While Jesus was teaching, a woman began praising Jesus's mother for giving birth to Him. In response, Christ remarked that rather than praising His mother, people should listen to His words and follow them. Jesus was not castigating this woman for praising His mother; rather, He was giving the woman and all others with Him vital counsel. The following is Luke's account of this brief incident:

> **Luke 11:27–28.** And it came to pass, as he spake these things, a certain woman of the company lifted up her voice, and said unto him, Blessed is the womb that bare thee, and the paps which thou hast sucked. But he said, Yea rather, blessed are they that hear the word of God, and keep it.

The woman may have recognized that Jesus was the Messiah or a prophet with great authority from God and thus wanted to honor His mother. Although Mary was truly pure, highly favored, and blessed among women,

---

3. See Edersheim, *Life and Teachings of Jesus the Messiah*, p. 614.

as the angel declared,[4] only her Son, His teachings, and His atoning sacrifice could enable people to gain eternal life.

An Evil Generation Seeks a Sign (Luke 11:29–32)

People were now gathered closely together to see and hear Jesus, perhaps out of curiosity if not for other reasons. Neither they, the priests, or members of the Sanhedrin had power to cast a spirit out of a man and thereby restore his speech. They must have known that such a miracle could only come from God; nevertheless, they still would not believe, and they sought for a further sign from God. In response, Jesus explained that the wicked seek a sign but will not receive one. Luke's record is as follows:

> **Luke 11:29–32.** And when the people were gathered thick together, he began to say, This is an evil generation: they seek a sign; and there shall no sign be given it, but the sign of Jonas the prophet. For as Jonas was a sign unto the Ninevites, so shall also the Son of man be to this generation. The queen of the south shall rise up in the judgment with the men of this generation, and condemn them: for she came from the utmost parts of the earth to hear the wisdom of Solomon; and, behold, a greater than Solomon is here. The men of Nineve shall rise up in the judgment with this generation, and shall condemn it: for they repented at the preaching of Jonas; and, behold, a greater than Jonas is here.

After perhaps looking at each one in the multitude, Jesus spoke words that must have pierced all to the core: "This is an evil generation: they seek a sign." The thoughts of those in the crowd were likely varied because they all had unique life experiences and varying opinions of Jesus. Nevertheless, His criticism of them collectively likely either encouraged them to repent or gave them further reason to find cause against him.

Jesus told the multitude that the only sign they would receive would be the sign of Jonah the prophet. Jonah was in the belly of a great fish for three days and nights before preaching to the Ninevites, and Jesus would be in a tomb on three days following His death. Just as Jonah was released from the belly of the fish, Jesus would be released from the darkness of the grave through His Resurrection—the crowning witness of His divinity.

---

4. See Luke 1:28

Following His Resurrection, perhaps some who were now listening to Jesus would remember His words and believe in Him.

After referring to Jonah being a sign, Jesus stated that the Jews would be condemned for unbelief by the Ninevites, who repented upon hearing Jonah preach,[5] and by the Queen of Sheba, who traveled a long distance to hear King Solomon's wisdom.[6]

Once again, each person had to decide whether to believe in and follow Jesus, deny Him, or fail to seriously consider whether He was the Son of God. This account is a powerful warning for people today, for some want an additional marvelous sign from heaven that there is a God, that Christ is His Son, and that They have restored Their Church on the earth.

No One Lights a Candle and Puts It under a Bushel (Luke 11:33–36)

Jesus said the following to those who believed in Him:

Luke 11:33–36. No man, when he hath lighted a candle, putteth it in a secret place, neither under a bushel, but on a candlestick, that they which come in may see the light. The light of the body is the eye: therefore when thine eye is single, thy whole body also is full of light; but when thine eye is evil, thy body also is full of darkness. Take heed therefore that the light which is in thee be not darkness. If thy whole body therefore be full of light, having no part dark, the whole shall be full of light, as when the bright shining of a candle doth give thee light.

Jesus reminded those who believed that the light they saw in Jesus could fill their bodies with light but that if they reverted to sin, they would be full of darkness. It was their choice whether to be filled with the light they were experiencing while with Him. Jesus warned that just as the eye could be filled with light from God, it could also be filled with darkness from the evil one. It was not sufficient to have a testimony of Christ for a moment; disciples should be filled with the Light of Christ continually, and their light would shine to others as does a candle. Their light needed to endure and not be

---

5. See Jonah 3:1–5.
6. See 1 Kgs. 10:1–13.

extinguished because of neglect or sin.[7] The light derived from believing in Christ would shine within them and fill their entire being.

Jesus Eats with a Pharisee and Rebukes the Pharisees for Hypocrisy (Luke 11:37–44)

The enmity the Pharisees in Jerusalem and Galilee had for Jesus was bitter, and they continually sought to find fault in Him in order to take His life. In contrast, apparently not all Pharisees in Perea felt this degree of hatred, for one of them asked Jesus to dine with him and other Pharisees, scribes, and lawyers (rabbis).[8] It is reasonable to assume that the host notified the other guests that he had invited Jesus, whom the people said had performed great miracles. By this time, Jesus's fame had spread throughout the land. It is possible that those who attended the meal did so out of curiosity and a desire to meet Him. On this occasion, Jesus taught of the sins of pride and hypocrisy. The following is the beginning of Luke's account:

> **Luke 11:37–44.** And as he spake, a certain Pharisee besought him to dine with him: and he went in, and sat down to meat. And when the Pharisee saw it, he marvelled that he had not first washed before dinner. And the Lord said unto him, Now do ye Pharisees make clean the outside of the cup and the platter; but your inward part is full of ravening and wickedness. Ye fools, did not he that made that which is without make that which is within also? But rather give alms of such things as ye have; and, behold, all things are clean unto you. But woe unto you, Pharisees! for ye tithe mint and rue and all manner of herbs, and pass over judgment and the love of God: these ought ye to have done, and not to leave the other undone. Woe unto you, Pharisees! for ye love the uppermost seats in the synagogues, and greetings in the markets. Woe unto you, scribes and Pharisees, hypocrites! For ye are as graves which appear not, and the men that walk over them are not aware of them.

Up to this time, many in this area of Perea thought of Jesus as a rabbi or prophet. The Pharisee probably invited Jesus partly out of curiosity; there is

---

7. See Matt. 10:22; 24:13; Mark 13:13; 1 Ne. 13:37; 23:31; 2 Ne. 9:24; 31:16, 20; 33:4; Omni 1:26; 3 Ne. 15:9; Morm. 9:29; D&C 18:22; 20:25.

8. The *HarperCollins Bible Dictionary* states that the "lawyers Jesus engages in conversation are essentially Bible scholars" (*HarperCollins Bible Dictionary*, s.v. "lawyers").

no indication that the Pharisee intended to make an accusation against Jesus. After Jesus arrived and sat down to eat, He did not ceremonially wash His hands, a practice that was required by rabbinical law.

Regarding the ceremonial washing, Edersheim stated the following:

> As the guests enter, they sit down on chairs, and water is brought to them, with which they wash one hand. After this the cup is taken, when each speaks the blessing over the wine partaken of before dinner. Presently they all lie down at table. Water is again brought them, with which they now wash both hands, preparatory to the meal, when the blessing is spoken over the bread, and then over the cup, by the chief person at the feast, or else by one selected by way of distinction. The company responded by *Amen*, always supposing the benediction to have been spoken by an Israelite, not a heathen, slave, nor law-breaker. Nor was it lawful to say it with an unlettered man, although it might be said with a Cuthaean (Ber. 47b—heretic, or else Samaritan), who was learned. After dinner the crumbs, if any, are carefully gathered—hands are again washed, and he who first had done so leads in the prayer of thanksgiving.[9]

The ceremonial washing was fraught with triviality. For example, Jews disputed whether the washing was required before or after the cup was filled with wine and where the towel was to be deposited.[10]

The Pharisee who was hosting the meal and the other guests must have deemed Jesus's failure to ceremonially wash His hands an insult and a defiance of Jewish law and the long-standing traditions of the synagogue.[11]

Presumably, Jesus deliberately did not ceremonially wash his hands. He was the Son of God and entirely free from sin and did not need to ceremonially wash to be clean. Further, as the Son of God, He desired to let all present know that the ritualistic washing would not lead to eternal life. He did not come to placate those He met by following rabbinical customs. He once again pointed out the fastidiousness of the Pharisees' outward purifications in contrast to their inward defilement, which the Pharisees never sought to remove. As always, His object was not to condemn but to motivate individuals to confront their failure to observe the more important

---

9. Edersheim, *Life and Teachings of Jesus the Messiah*, p. 618.
10. See Edersheim, *Life and Teachings of Jesus the Messiah*, p. 620.
11. See Edersheim, *Life and Teachings of Jesus the Messiah*, p. 620.

elements of the law so that they might be saved.[12] They had ignored in their own lives the two great commandments in the law: "Love the Lord thy God with all thy heart, and with all thy soul, and with all thy strength, and with all thy mind; and thy neighbor as thyself."[13]

Apparently, these Jews were more interested in ritualistic customs than in the need for inward purity. Christ had exposed that despite the Jews' outward cleanness, they were inwardly unclean because of their hypocrisy, greed, and failure to feed the flock.[14] They had turned away the needy, had not visited the sick, and had not imparted their substance to aid the poor.[15] Moreover, they could not discern the divinity of the Son of God, who was in their presence, because their focus was on strict adherence to ceremony alone.

Presumably, Jesus knew that He needed to be direct in order to encourage those present to critically examine their lives and repent. Moreover, He may have wanted to leave them no room for excuse. He said to the host, "Now do ye Pharisees make clean the outside of the cup and the platter; but your inward part is full of ravening and wickedness."

Jesus told the Pharisees, "Ye fools, did not he that made that which is without make that which is within also." He was reminding those present that God had made the earth and its elements, had created the spirit of each person, and had made it possible for each to receive a mortal body and that it was much more important for a person to be spiritually clean than physically clean. Jesus then identified one way to begin to become inwardly clean: "Give alms of such things as ye have."

Pointing to the triviality of the Jewish law and the Pharisees' greed, Jesus then stated that those present tithed common garden herbs, such as mint and rue,[16] but failed to judge righteously and love God.

And then Jesus pronounced a woe upon them because they loved the "uppermost seats in the synagogues, and greetings in the markets." He also said that those who were present were hypocrites because they were prideful,

---

12. See John 3:17.
13. Luke 10:27.
14. See Ezek. 34:2.
15. See Alma 34:28.
16. Rue is an herb "used as condiment, medicinal ingredient, and charm component. Paying a tithe on rue (Matt. 23:23) symbolizes scrupulous attention to details of ritual law" (*HarperCollins Bible Dictionary*, s.v. "rue").

especially because they sought high positions in the synagogues and wanted ecclesiastical recognition instead of focusing on serving others. Likewise, when they met others in the marketplace, they sought honor and recognition instead of seeking the welfare of those they met. Figuratively, they were blind, like those who unknowingly walked over unmarked graves[17] and thereby became polluted, according to Jewish tradition. Their hypocritical show of outward purity had become one of their greatest impurities.

Jesus Rebukes the Lawyers and Scribes for Hypocrisy (Luke 11:45–54)

Observing Jesus's rebuke of the Pharisees, one of the rabbis asked Jesus whether He also reproached others present. Jesus responded as follows:

Luke 11:45–54. Then answered one of the lawyers, and said unto him, Master, thus saying thou reproachest us also. And he said, Woe unto you also, ye lawyers! For ye lade men with burdens grievous to be borne, and ye yourselves touch not the burdens with one of your fingers. Woe unto you! For ye build the sepulchres of the prophets, and your fathers killed them. Truly ye bear witness that ye allow the deeds of your fathers: for they indeed killed them, and ye build their sepulchres. Therefore also said the wisdom of God, I will send them prophets and apostles, and some of them they shall slay and persecute: that the blood of all the prophets, which was shed from the foundation of the world, may be required of this generation; from the blood of Abel unto the blood of Zacharias, which perished between the altar and the temple: verily I say unto you, It shall be required of this generation. Woe unto you, lawyers! For ye have taken away the key of knowledge: ye entered not in yourselves, and them that were entering in ye hindered. And as he said these things unto them, the scribes and the Pharisees began to urge him vehemently, and to provoke him to speak of many things: laying wait for him, and seeking to catch something out of his mouth, that they might accuse him.

Jesus responded by harshly criticizing the rabbis' failure to help those in need, especially when the rabbis had in part caused the burden. Regarding their hypocritical actions, Geikie stated: "Ye sit in your chambers and schools,

17. Graves were considered unclean (see *Jewish Encyclopedia*, s.v. "tombs").

and create legal rules, endless, harassing, intolerable, for the people, but not affecting yourselves—shut out as you are from busy life."[18] Moreover, the Lord declared that the rabbis built sepulchers for the prophets whom their ancestors killed. The sepulchers were built to appease the people, not to honor the prophets. Then Christ declared that the blood of all the prophets, from Abel to Zacharias,[19] would stand as a testimony against the Jews of Christ's generation.[20]

Jesus also told the lawyers that because of their wickedness, they had prevented others from recognizing spiritual knowledge. They believed that revelation had ceased. Jesus's criticism of the wicked was sharp and to the point. He left no room for excuse. They no longer even claimed they had a prophet to whom they could look for guidance. In response to Jesus's words, those present urged Him to speak further, hoping they would hear something they could use as the grounds for accusing Him and taking His life.

Without fear, Jesus had denounced the pride and hypocrisy of the Pharisees, scribes, and rabbis and had taught of humble and quiet service. Of course, Jesus knew the hearts of those present. He knew He must boldly speak the truth in hope that some might look inside themselves and repent. Nevertheless, they had been warned—and so has the rest of humankind. Just as opposition increased during Jesus's mortal ministry, opposition will increase as the time of his Second Coming approaches. Just as people in Christ's day needed to decide whether to follow Him, people today must make the same decision.

Beware of the Leaven of the Pharisees (Luke 12:1–12)

Despite the hostility of the rabbis, scribes, and Pharisees toward Jesus, others in Perea thronged to see and hear this performer of miracles from Nazareth. Jesus taught the multitudes important lessons about hypocrisy and being His disciple. The following is Luke's account:

Luke 12:1–12. In the mean time, when there were gathered together an innumerable multitude of people, insomuch that they trode one upon

---

18. Geikie, *Life and Words of Christ*, vol. 2, p. 141.
19. See note 1 at the end of this chapter.
20. See Acts 10:43.

another, he began to say unto his disciples first of all, Beware ye of the leaven of the Pharisees, which is hypocrisy. For there is nothing covered, that shall not be revealed; neither hid, that shall not be known. Therefore whatsoever ye have spoken in darkness shall be heard in the light; and that which ye have spoken in the ear in closets shall be proclaimed upon the housetops. And I say unto you my friends, Be not afraid of them that kill the body, and after that have no more that they can do. But I will forewarn you whom ye shall fear: Fear him, which after he hath killed hath power to cast into hell; yea, I say unto you, Fear him. Are not five sparrows sold for two farthings, and not one of them is forgotten before God? But even the very hairs of your head are all numbered. Fear not therefore: ye are of more value than many sparrows. Also I say unto you, Whosoever shall confess me before men, him shall the Son of man also confess before the angels of God: but he that denieth me before men shall be denied before the angels of God. And whosoever shall speak a word against the Son of man, it shall be forgiven him: but unto him that blasphemeth against the Holy Ghost it shall not be forgiven. And when they bring you unto the synagogues, and unto magistrates, and powers, take ye no thought how or what thing ye shall answer, or what ye shall say: for the Holy Ghost shall teach you in the same hour what ye ought to say.

Presumably, the large multitude that had gathered to see and hear Jesus consisted of both men and women of varying ages and circumstances, and these people likely had mixed motives for gathering and had varying degrees of righteousness.

As Jesus looked upon the multitude, He may have considered how the regulations, actions, and omissions of the Pharisees might influence the people. Jesus wanted to be certain that His disciples and others who heard Him teach did not succumb, at that time or later, to the hypocrisy of the Pharisees.

Jesus began His instruction with a metaphor about leaven. As all in the multitude surely knew, leaven is used in bread to help it rise. Jesus's warning about the leaven, or hypocrisy, of the Pharisees was a reminder to those in the multitude to not be influenced by the Pharisees' prominent position or their rules, no matter what the risk might be. Though Jewish leaders could cause someone's physical death, they could do nothing more. In contrast, God had the power to cast hypocrites into hell.

Jesus also reminded those listening to Him that God was the creator of all and that even sparrows, which had little commercial value, were not forgotten by God. Christ promised that if a person was willing to testify of Him, He would testify in heaven that the person was His disciple. It is hard to fully comprehend the joy that the righteous will feel when hearing Christ telling the angels in heaven about His disciples' goodness and mortal witness of Him. Perhaps parents experience this feeling to a small extent when someone praises their children.

Jesus also warned that if individuals did not believe and witness of Him, then He would tell of their wickedness to the angels in heaven. He added that speaking against Him could be forgiven but that blaspheming against the Holy Ghost could not.

Additionally, Jesus taught that if His disciples were brought before the leaders of synagogues or before magistrates, the Holy Ghost would tell Jesus's disciples in that moment what they should say.[21] The same can happen today. Unfortunately, sometimes Church talks, lessons, and agendas are so planned out that there is little room for the whisperings of the Holy Ghost to help people say or discuss the things that would be of most worth to those being addressed. Similarly, sometimes people are so busy that it is hard for them to hear the still small voice, just as many in the multitude listening to Christ were unable to recognize that He spoke the truth.

The Parable of the Rich Fool (Luke 12:13–21)

While Jesus was with the multitude, one man asked Jesus to convince the man's brother to divide the inheritance with the man. In matters of dispute, it was not uncommon to seek the wisdom and assistance of a respected rabbi. A rabbi's decision, though extrajudicial, had almost the force of law.[22] Luke's account is as follows:

> **Luke 12:13–21.** And one of the company said unto him, Master, speak to my brother, that he divide the inheritance with me. And he said unto him,

---

21. See also D&C 100:5–6, wherein Joseph Smith and Sidney Rigdon were counseled to "lift up your voices unto this people; speak the thoughts that I shall put into your hearts, and you shall not be confounded before men; for it shall be given you in the very hour, yea, in the very moment, what ye shall say."

22. See Geikie, *Life and Words of Christ*, vol. 2, p. 142.

Man, who made me a judge or a divider over you? And he said unto them, Take heed, and beware of covetousness: for a man's life consisteth not in the abundance of the things which he possesseth. And he spake a parable unto them, saying, The ground of a certain rich man brought forth plentifully: and he thought within himself, saying, What shall I do, because I have no room where to bestow my fruits? And he said, This will I do: I will pull down my barns, and build greater; and there will I bestow all my fruits and my goods. And I will say to my soul, Soul, thou hast much goods laid up for many years; take thine ease, eat, drink, and be merry. But God said unto him, Thou fool, this night thy soul shall be required of thee: then whose shall those things be, which thou hast provided? So is he that layeth up treasure for himself, and is not rich toward God.

Jesus repudiated the request that He serve as the judge or arbitrator of worldly affairs. He also gave a warning against greed and selfishness, which are often the root of financial strife. Jesus then told a parable about a rich man whose land produced so much food that he did not have enough room to store it all and he decided to replace his existing barns with larger ones. The man was confident that his farm had produced enough to sustain him for many years, and he decided that he could relax, "eat, drink, and be merry."

In making his farm fruitful, the man had apparently prioritized his labor and desire for wealth and material things and had ignored the kingdom of God and the importance of serving others.

The man thought he would enjoy a life of ease for years to come, but He was informed by God, either personally or through a messenger, that he would die that night and that he could not keep his earthly possessions. Jesus then told the multitude that a similar thing will happen to others who focus on amassing material possessions and enjoying life instead of focusing on the things of God: none will be able to retain worldly wealth after dying.

In thinking about death coming suddenly, some in the multitude may have recalled reading or hearing about the Old Testament account of Daniel interpreting one of King Nebuchadnezzar's dreams. Daniel explained that Nebuchadnezzar's life was being compared to a great tree that was suddenly hewn down and that he would be "driven from men, and [would] . . . eat grass as oxen, and his body [would be] wet with the dew of heaven, till his hairs were grown like eagles' feathers, and his nails like birds' claws."[23] Those listening to Jesus may also have remembered the account of Nebuchadnezzar's son, Belshazzar, seeing a man write Belshazzar's fate on the wall of the palace. Belshazzar could not decipher the writing, so he had Daniel interpret it. Daniel's interpretation indicated that God had halted the expansion of Belshazzar's kingdom, had determined that the kingdom was lacking in righteousness, and had decided to give the kingdom to the Medes and Persians. That night Belshazzar was slain, and Darius the Median took the kingdom.[24]

This man's sin lay in focusing on material things rather than on the things of God, in storing his goods so he could secure personal ease instead of sharing his wealth with others, and in failing to thank God for his prosperity.

This parable is a warning that people need to prioritize the things of God in their daily labors, including during retirement, and to not be consumed with material possessions or pleasure. Individuals need to strengthen their spiritual selves throughout their lives and thereby learn to overcome the world,[25] rather than allowing the world to overcome them.

Death can come at any time. That fact should prompt God's children to ponder over and over what they are doing with their lives and whether they are spiritually prepared to leave this life when the time comes, whether when young or old. Each day, people need to decide who they are and who they will be.

Disciples Should Seek First the Kingdom of God (Luke 12:22–34)

A short time later, Jesus explained the manner in which His disciples should serve. He had previously taught the same principles in Galilee[26] and, although not recorded, possibly when preparing the Apostles for their missions. He reemphasized some of these principles:

Luke 12:22–34. And he said unto his disciples, Therefore I say unto you, Take no thought for your life, what ye shall eat; neither for the body, what

---

23. Dan. 4:33; see 4:10–33 for the entire dream.
24. See Dan. 5.
25. See chapter 24 in the first volume of this series.
26. See Matt. 6:25–34.

ye shall put on. The life is more than meat, and the body is more than raiment. Consider the ravens: for they neither sow nor reap; which neither have storehouse nor barn; and God feedeth them: how much more are ye better than the fowls? And which of you with taking thought can add to his stature one cubit? If ye then be not able to do that thing which is least, why take ye thought for the rest? Consider the lilies how they grow: they toil not, they spin not; and yet I say unto you, that Solomon in all his glory was not arrayed like one of these. If then God so clothe the grass, which is to day in the field, and to morrow is cast into the oven; how much more will he clothe you, O ye of little faith? And seek not ye what ye shall eat, or what ye shall drink, neither be ye of doubtful mind. For all these things do the nations of the world seek after: and your Father knoweth that ye have need of these things. But rather seek ye the kingdom of God; and all these things shall be added unto you. Fear not, little flock; for it is your Father's good pleasure to give you the kingdom. Sell that ye have, and give alms; provide yourselves bags which wax not old, a treasure in the heavens that faileth not, where no thief approacheth, neither moth corrupteth. For where your treasure is, there will your heart be also.

Jesus wanted to erase anxiety from His disciples about obtaining the necessities of life as they followed and served Him. They needed to labor solely for the kingdom of God and trust that He would provide clothing, food, and drink when needed. Jesus taught the Apostles that if they were true to their callings, God would be pleased to give them the kingdom of heaven as an inheritance.

Of significance, Jesus referred to His disciples as His "little flock." They were individual sheep and also united in His work. In addition, flock implies the presence of a shepherd, and Jesus is the Good Shepherd. Like the Good Shepherd, who had no home during His ministry, His Apostles were to sell any possessions that they did not need, give the proceeds as alms, and be prepared to receive the treasures of heaven. Heavenly treasures could not be taken away by the world. Heavenly treasures were the only things that the disciples could take with them beyond the grave.

Jesus had witnessed of His divinity to the people of Judea and Perea by performing miracles. Multitudes followed Him. He presumably taught them His higher law, including the path to the celestial kingdom. He boldly and plainly taught the scribes, Pharisees, and rabbis of their failings. Some of the people undoubtedly were humble, repented, and believed. Others hardened their hearts and therefore could not discern His divinity and the spiritual light within Him. They would not heed His counsel to repent. As a result, they became angry and put their eternal life in jeopardy.

Each had to decide.

Note to Chapter 41

1. **Zacharias.** Some scholars think that the Zacharias whom Jesus spoke of was not John the Baptist's father but rather Zechariah, the son of Jehoiada. On this point, Farrar stated that there is not "any authority for the belief of Origen, that the father of John the Baptist was martyred, or that he too was a son of Barachias. The prophet Zechariah was indeed a son of Berechiah (Zech. 1:1), but there is no reason to believe that he was put to death. We must therefore conclude that our Lord referred to Zechariah, the son of Jehoiada (which is the reading in the Gospel used by the Nazarenes), who was stoned by order of Joash 'in the court of the house of the Lord.'"[27] However, Joseph Smith said:

> Let us come into New Testament times—so many are ever praising the Lord and His apostles. We will commence with John the Baptist. When Herod's edict went forth to destroy the young children, John was about six months older than Jesus, and came under this hellish edict, and Zacharias caused his mother to take him into the mountains, where he was raised on locusts and wild honey. When his father refused to disclose his hiding place, and being the officiating high priest at the Temple that year, he was slain by Herod's order, between the porch and the altar, as Jesus said.[28]

27. Farrar, *Life of Christ*, p. 511n5.
28. Smith, *Teachings*, p. 261.

Chapter 42

BE PREPARED FOR THE LORD'S SECOND COMING

On various occasions, Christ had taught His disciples of His impending death and Resurrection. He now taught them that after His death and Resurrection, He would return to the earth in a glorious Second Coming. The thrust of His teaching was that individuals and the Church always need to be prepared because no one would know the precise timing of this great and glorious event. Jesus's teachings in Perea about His Second Coming are of particular importance in the latter days and should be carefully considered.[1]

Disciples Are to Always Be Prepared for the Second Coming (Luke 12:35–40)[2]

According to Luke's account, Jesus started his instruction about being prepared as follows:

Luke 12:35–40. Let your loins be girded about, and your lights burning; and ye yourselves like unto men that wait for their lord, when he will return from the wedding; that when he cometh and knocketh, they may open unto him immediately. Blessed are those servants, whom the lord when he cometh shall find watching: verily I say unto you, that he shall gird himself, and make them to sit down to meat, and will come forth and serve them. And if he shall come in the second watch, or come in the third watch, and find them so, blessed are those servants. And this know, that if the goodman of the house had known what hour the thief would come, he would have watched,

---

1. This chapter will not discuss the Lord's Second Coming in detail; that topic will be discussed in detail in chapters 55–57 of the fourth volume of this series.
2. See also Luke 17:20–37; 18:1–8; Matt. 24.

and not have suffered his house to be broken through. Be ye therefore ready also: for the Son of man cometh at an hour when ye think not.[3]

Girded Loins and Burning Light

Christ began by telling the disciples to "let your loins be girded about, and your lights burning." He was referring to the robes that people regularly wore. People would tie their robes about their loins to permit freedom of movement so they were prepared for work and for battle.[4]

The disciples needed to be fully prepared to carry on the Lord's work after He died, and they likewise needed to be prepared to fight battles against the powers of darkness and other challenges and trials of mortality. To that end, they also needed to keep their lights burning in order to be lights to the world, just as His disciples today are to be lights.

The Wedding

Jesus then likened the preparation to that of servants waiting for their lord to return from a wedding.[5] Jesus may have chosen to refer to a wedding because it was an event that was familiar to the Jews and they would understand the importance of the servants being prepared for the Lord's return. However, the wedding might have symbolic meaning. A wedding is a uniting, and Jesus may have been referring to the fact that He would be united with His Father after dying, being resurrected, and ascending into heaven.[6] Alternatively, Jesus may have been referring to His Second Coming and His uniting with the Saints at that time. Just as those in a wedding party are ready to greet the bride and groom when they appear, Christ's disciples need to be spiritually ready to receive Him when He returns to the earth, whenever He comes. Since no one knows the timing of His Second Coming,

---

3. See also JST Luke 12:35–40.
4. See Smith, *Bible Dictionary*, s.v. "girdle"; see also Jer. 1:17; 1 Kgs. 18:46; 2 Kgs. 9:1; Job 38:3; 40:7.
5. In Jesus's day, it was common for the groom to travel to the bride's house and then accompany the bride to his house or sometimes to his family's house; the guests would follow with oil lamps or torches.
6. It is also possible that Jesus was referring to a significant wedding ceremony of some type that would occur in heaven after His ascension.

His disciples must always be ready. Their spiritual houses should already be in order. They should have already cleaned the spiritual dishes, vacuumed their spiritual rooms, and made their spiritual beds. Likewise, they should have already purchased additional spiritual oil for their lamps.[7]

Marriage is used as a metaphor for the Second Coming in the book of Revelation: "Let us be glad and rejoice, and give honour to him: for the marriage of the Lamb is come, and his wife hath made herself ready. And to her was granted that she should be arrayed in fine linen, clean and white: for the fine linen is the righteousness of saints."[8] Certainly the bride, who represents the Church and its individual members, must be prepared.

The Need to Watch

The Savior also referred to watching. He said that those who are watching when He comes will be blessed. What should His disciples watch for? Certainly, they should watch for the signs indicating that His return is imminent. Watching for the signs of the Lord's return requires studying the scriptures to know what the signs are. Also, seeing and understanding these signs involves being receptive to the whispering of the Holy Ghost.

Further, watching implies being prepared spiritually and temporally for the tribulations that will come prior to the Second Coming. This preparation can come, in part, by listening to and heeding Church leaders' counsel. Moreover, watching involves being aware of the influence of the evil one and not being deceived, becoming complacent, doubting, or disbelieving. Jesus again taught the importance of watching as Peter, James, and John accompanied Him to the Garden of Gethsemane. First, He asked them to "watch with me."[9] Despite the request, these three fell asleep, and Jesus woke them and warned them to "watch and pray, that [they] enter not into temptation."[10] That counsel is important for all who follow Him in the last days.

---

7. See Matt. 25:1–13.

8. Rev. 19:7–8. John's vision regards not only the Lord's coming but also the temple, including the need to be righteous and clothed in clean white linen.

9. Matt. 26:38.

10. Matt. 26:41.

The Lord's Service at His Supper

Jesus then referred to a time when He would have His servants sit down for a meal and He would serve them.[11] The full import of His statement is uncertain and perhaps is much deeper than appears at first reading.[12] Some understanding may come from considering Jesus's words at other times. For example, He said that if an individual would love Him and keep His words, "my Father will love him, and we will come unto him, and make our abode with him."[13] Similarly, Jesus later said, "Behold, I stand at the door, and knock; if any man hear my voice, and open the door, I will come into him, and will sup with him, and he with me."[14]

In Luke 12, Jesus may have been partly referring to the Last Supper, during which He instituted the sacrament and washed the Apostles' feet. Jesus may also have been referring to a time in the latter days, for He told Joseph Smith in Doctrine and Covenants 27: "The hour cometh that I will drink of the fruit of the vine with you on the earth."[15] The Lord stated that others who will participate in that gathering will include prophets, apostles, and others back to the time of Adam.[16] Among the individuals who will be included are those whom Heavenly Father "hath given me [Jesus] out of the world,"[17] presumably individuals who have forsaken the world.[18] It is reasonable to assume that Jesus will provide the emblems of the sacrament at the time referenced in Doctrine and Covenants 27.

Also in the latter days, the Lord stated: "Prepare ye the way of the Lord, prepare ye the supper of the Lamb, make ready for the Bridegroom."[19] In this instruction, the emphasis is on preparing for the Lord's return and

---

11. Jesus was not likely referring the last Passover meal before His death.
12. For additional insight, see the discussion of the parable of the great supper in chapter 43 of this volume.
13. John 14:23.
14. Rev. 3:20.
15. D&C 27:5.
16. See D&C 27:5–12.
17. D&C 27:14.
18. See D&C 29:4.
19. D&C 65:3.

His uniting with the Saints in the latter days.[20] At this day, the Saints will figuratively sit down to eat and the Lord will "come forth and serve them."

Christ's Appearances in the First, Second, and Third Watches

Jesus then taught His disciples that they did not need to know precisely when He would return. What mattered is that His disciples be prepared for His return. Regarding the word *watch*, *Smith's Bible Dictionary* states the following:

> The Jews, like the Greeks and Romans, divided the night into military watches instead of hours, each watch representing the period for which sentinels remained on duty. The proper Jewish reckoning recognized only three such watches: the first or "beginning of the watches" (Lam. 2:19), the middle watch (Judg. 7:19), and the morning watch (Ex. 14:24; 1 Sam. 11:11). These would last respectively from sunset to 10 p.m., from 10 p.m. to 2 a.m., and from 2 a.m. to sunrise. The Rabbis debated whether there were three or four watches. The Romans had four, and in the NT we read of four. . . . These terminated respectively at 9 p.m., midnight, 3 a.m., and 6 a.m.[21]

Jesus's reference to the second and third watches of the night implies that He will return when the world is spiritually sleeping and not looking for His return. Dummelow stated that the references to these watches "represent the dead of night, and by metaphor the unexpectedness of the Second Advent."[22] Joseph Smith's inspired version of Luke 12:41–42 is instructive:

> For, behold, he cometh in the first watch of the night, and he shall also come in the second watch, and again he shall come in the third watch. And verily I say unto you, He hath already come, as it is written of him; and again when he shall come in the second watch, or come in the third watch, blessed are those servants when he cometh, that he shall find so doing.[23]

The timing of these watches is not clear. He states that He will come during the first, second, and third watches and that He has already come—presumably a reference to Christ's life in mortality. The verbs regarding His

20. For further discussion, see chapter 43 in this volume.
21. Smith, *Bible Dictionary*, s.v. "watch."
22. Dummelow, *Bible Commentary*, p. 765.
23. JST Luke 12:41–42.

appearances during the watches ("cometh," "shall also come," and "shall come") indicate that these appearances had not happened at the time Jesus spoke these words. There are several reasonable interpretations regarding what these watches refer to. The references to watches may mean that Christ will return at night since that is when watches occur. Or the reference to watches may be figurative, meaning that He will return in an "hour as ye think not."[24] Of course, the reference to coming during the watches may have other meanings.

It is possible that His coming in the first watch was His appearance to the Apostles on the day of His Resurrection. Regarding this appearance, John recorded: "Then the same day at evening, being the first day of the week, when the doors were shut where the disciples were assembled for fear of the Jews, came Jesus and stood in the midst, and saith unto them, Peace be unto you."[25] Evening would have been the first watch. That timing is consistent with Luke's record, which indicates Jesus appeared to His Apostles after He had walked with two disciples to Emmaus.[26]

It is possible that Christ's appearance during the second watch[27] occurred when He visited the Nephites, although that visit seems to have occurred during the morning or daytime, when "a great multitude gathered together . . . round about the temple."[28] Of course, there are time differences between various parts of the world. If this interpretation is correct, these verses are another witness of the Book of Mormon.

It is reasonable to assume that Jesus's appearance in the third watch refers to His Second Coming, given His statement that "the Son of man cometh at an hour when ye think not." In light of this statement, one may wonder whether the heavenly sign of Christ's return[29] will appear at night. It is also possible that the first, second, and third watches all refer to His

---

24. JST Matt. 1:48.

25. John 20:19.

26. See Luke 24:13–35.

27. Sometime after Christ first appeared to the Apostles following His Resurrection, He appeared to them one morning at the Sea of Galilee and asked whether they had any food (see John 21:5). The morning hours are not part of a watch, so it is reasonable to assume that Jesus was not referring to this appearance when He spoke of returning during the second watch.

28. 3 Ne. 11:1.

29. See JST Matt. 1:36.

Second Coming and indicate that because of different time zones, people on earth will see the sign in heaven at different times.[30]

There are likely other interpretations that are just as reasonable. Whatever the meaning of Jesus's statements, the overall message is clear: He will come when least expected; therefore, people must watch and be ready.

The Goodman of the House

Jesus also presented a brief parable involving a goodman—that is, the master of a house—whose home was broken into because he was not watching out for a thief. The lesson is that those who have responsibility must always be vigilant because the Savior will return at an unexpected time.

Universal Application

Perhaps the most important fact known about the Lord's Second Coming is that it indeed will occur. And perhaps the most important principle regarding His Second Coming is to watch and be prepared. The Lord's return to earth has been referred to as the "great and dreadful day of the Lord."[31] It will be great because the Lord will come in the clouds of glory and usher in the Millennium and the righteous will greet Him. His return will also be dreadful, especially for the wicked, because it will occur at a time of great tribulation and judgment. The Lord's instruction in Luke 12:35–40 is therefore particularly applicable to the latter days.

Similar instruction may have been given to each person before coming to the earth. All spirits who chose to accept God's plan by entering mortality may have been told to gird up their loins for what they were about to experience in mortality; the valiant may have been further counseled to be lights in the world and to live in such a manner that they would be worthy to receive inspiration from the Holy Spirit. Those who were to come to earth in the final dispensation may have been instructed in particular to watch and be prepared.

---

30. Of course, the date and hour of the Lord's return is unknown (see JST Matt. 1:48).
31. Mal. 4:5.

Peter Asks Whether Christ Was Speaking Just to the Apostles (Luke 12:41–46)

Peter then asked Jesus whether He was speaking to His Apostles only or to everyone. Jesus responded that His instruction applied to all. Luke's account is as follows:

> **Luke 12: 41–46.** Then Peter said unto him, Lord, speakest thou this parable unto us, or even to all? And the Lord said, Who then is that faithful and wise steward, whom his lord shall make ruler over his household, to give them their portion of meat in due season? Blessed is that servant, whom his lord when he cometh shall find so doing. Of a truth I say unto you, that he will make him ruler over all that he hath. But and if that servant say in his heart, My lord delayeth his coming; and shall begin to beat the menservants and maidens, and to eat and drink, and to be drunken; the lord of that servant will come in a day when he looketh not for him, and at an hour when he is not aware, and will cut him in sunder, and will appoint him his portion with the unbelievers.

The full meaning of Peter's question and Jesus's response is to some degree uncertain. Peter may have expected there to be some difference between the Apostles and all others, perhaps believing that the Apostles would accompany Jesus to the "marriage supper" rather than be among those who waited for Him to return afterward.[32] Whatever Peter's intent, the Lord's response was far reaching in scope and time and included the time of His Second Coming.

The Lord spoke of faithful and wise stewards. A steward is someone with a responsibility for other people or things, and the faithful and wise stewards Jesus referred to certainly include prophets, apostles, and others who have stewardship responsibilities in the Church. Others with stewardship include parents. Ultimately, all people should be stewards because they have responsibility for their own lives and should care about and help others. This stewardship does not end at death, for those who have passed on to the next life are to be stewards in their sphere.

Jesus explained that faithful and wise stewards will receive their reward when He returns. Their reward will include being rulers over all that the Lord

---

32. See Edersheim, *Life and Times of Jesus the Messiah*, p. 626.

has. That reward is available to males and females of all races, ethnicities, ages, and circumstances.[33]

Christ stated that He "will come in a day when he [the servant] looketh not for him, and at an hour when he is not aware." Christ was pointing to the importance of always being spiritually prepared for His return. Jesus warned about what will happen to those who are not prepared because they rationalize that He will not come soon. He will "cut [them] in sunder, and will appoint [them their] portion with the unbelievers."

There is no doubt that Christ wanted His Apostles and all others who are willing to follow Him to heed His counsel to watch and be ready.

To Whom Much Is Given, Much Is Required (Luke 12:47–48)

Jesus then warned about what will happen to those who fail to prepare:

Luke 12: 47–48. And that servant, which knew his lord's will, and prepared not himself, neither did according to his will, shall be beaten with many stripes. But he that knew not, and did commit things worthy of stripes, shall be beaten with few stripes. For unto whomsoever much is given, of him shall be much required: and to whom men have committed much, of him they will ask the more.

Jesus differentiated between those who hear His gospel but disregard His commandments and those who do not have knowledge of the gospel. Those who knowingly disregard His commandments will experience greater punishment than those who disregard the commandments unknowingly. As Jesus explained, the more knowledge a person has, the more that is expected of him or her. The difference in expectations and in punishment for sin is evidence of His justice and mercy. Jesus may have been referring to sins of omission and commission in that the servant was not prepared and did not do according to his lord's will. Sins of omission may include failing to magnify a Church calling or to help others in need. Jesus's instruction should encourage everyone to think of the actions and inactions they need to repent of. Through Christ's Atonement, repentant individuals will be forgiven. They

---

33. See 2 Ne. 26:33.

will also be enlightened and refined by the Holy Spirit and strengthened to fulfill that which they are asked to do.

Jesus Refers to a Baptism (Luke 12:49–53)

Next, Jesus made it clear that He did not come to the earth to placate people. Rather, He came to bear witness of Himself and of the truth, even if doing so made people uncomfortable or caused them to be divided. The following is Luke's account:

> **Luke 12:49–53.** I am come to send fire on the earth; and what will I, if it be already kindled? But I have a baptism to be baptized with; and how am I straitened till it be accomplished! Suppose ye that I am come to give peace on earth? I tell you, Nay; but rather division: For from henceforth there shall be five in one house divided, three against two, and two against three. The father shall be divided against the son, and the son against the father; the mother against the daughter, and the daughter against the mother; the mother in law against her daughter in law, and the daughter in law against her mother in law.

As with many of Jesus's other statements, His declaration that He came "to send fire on the earth" has more than one meaning. First, He came so that those who believed in Him would have the fire, or zeal, of the gospel message burn in their hearts and, in turn, would share that message with others. That fire had already been kindled and would eventually spread throughout the land.

Second, the Holy Ghost, sometimes referred to as a fire, would come after Christ's death. On the day of Pentecost, the fire of the Holy Ghost was manifest in a most glorious manner. Luke wrote in the book of Acts, "And suddenly there came a sound from heaven as of a rushing mighty wind, and it filled all the house where they were sitting. And there appeared unto them cloven tongues like as of fire, and it sat upon each of them. And they were all filled with the Holy Ghost, and began to speak with other tongues, as the Spirit gave them utterance."[34]

Third, fire is used as a symbol when referring to the separation between the righteous and the evil prior to Christ's Second Coming. For example,

---

34. Acts 2:2–4.

Jesus explained in the parable of the wheat and the tares that the time will come when the tares will be "gathered and burned in the fire . . . at the end of this world."[35] And as the prophet Nephi recorded, "Wherefore, the righteous need not fear; for thus saith the prophet, they shall be saved, even if it so be as by fire."[36]

Jesus then remarked, "What will I, if it [the fire] be already kindled?" Satan had kindled the fire of hate and rage in the hearts of many Sadducees, Pharisees, and members of the Sanhedrin because of who Christ claimed to be and what He taught. In addition, the fire of Christ's wrath will be further kindled prior to His Second Coming as iniquity among humankind increases,[37] and both the house of Israel and the Gentiles will be called to repent.[38]

Jesus also told His disciples that He had a "baptism to be baptized with" and that His course was straight. In speaking of baptism, Jesus may have been referring to making a covenant with God, for Jesus had made a covenant with God in the premortal world to atone and die a most horrible death that He might draw all people unto Him[39] and then enable the resurrection of all.[40] That covenant was reconfirmed when He was baptized by John and later bled in Gethsemane and died on the cross. Jesus continued His teaching by stating that He had not come to placate people's feelings. He knew that His gospel message would even divide families, for some would believe and some would not.

Jesus Says to Watch for Signs of His Second Coming (Luke 12:54–57)

Next, Jesus said that just as people looked at the sky to determine whether rain was coming, they should look for signs foreshadowing His glorious return to the earth:

Luke 12:54–57. And he said also to the people, When ye see a cloud rise out of the west, straightway ye say, There cometh a shower; and so it is. And when ye see the south wind blow, ye say, There will be heat; and it cometh to

---

35. Matt. 13:40; see also D&C 86:1–7.
36. See 1 Ne. 22:17.
37. See Ether 2:9; 9:20.
38. See D&C 18:6.
39. See 3 Ne. 27:13–16.
40. See 1 Cor. 15:20–21.

pass. Ye hypocrites, ye can discern the face of the sky and of the earth; but how is it that ye do not discern this time? Yea, and why even of yourselves judge ye not what is right?

Because Jesus's glorious Second Coming would not occur for about two millennia, His words must have been recorded partly for people in the latter days. He was teaching that the signs of His Second Coming have not been hidden. They can be studied and identified just as the weather can be. Further, Jesus may have also been commenting on people's inability to discern between good and evil.

Jesus Gives a Final Warning (Luke 12:58–59)

Jesus then gave a final warning about the need to repent of sins:

Luke 12:58–59. When thou goest with thine adversary to the magistrate, as thou art in the way, give diligence that thou mayest be delivered from him; lest he hale thee to the judge, and the judge deliver thee to the officer, and the officer cast thee into prison. I tell thee, thou shalt not depart thence, till thou hast paid the very last mite.

In teaching His disciples, Jesus referred to a common occurrence of the time: those who broke the law were brought before the magistrate; then, if necessary, before a judge; and finally to an officer for application of the prescribed penalty. What Jesus was teaching is that all people need to repent while in this life; otherwise, when they stand before God and Christ at the judgment day, they will be condemned until their suffering is sufficient. Jesus made it clear that those who do not repent before the final judgment will pay "the very last mite." Of this suffering, the Lord stated in Doctrine and Covenants 19:15–19:

Therefore I command you to repent—repent, lest I smite you by the rod of my mouth, and by my wrath, and by my anger, and your sufferings be sore— how sore you know not, how exquisite you know not, yea, how hard to bear you know not. For behold, I, God, have suffered these things for all, that they might not suffer if they would repent; but if they would not repent they must suffer even as I; which suffering caused myself, even God, the greatest of all, to tremble because of pain, and to bleed at every pore, and to suffer both body and spirit—and would that I might not drink the bitter cup, and shrink—nevertheless, glory be to the Father, and I partook and finished my preparations unto the children of men.

Since people do not know when they will die, they should continually repent and strive to improve; doing so requires introspection and the will to change.[41]

Jesus Again Calls for Repentance (Luke 13:1–5)

In the same "season" that Jesus gave the instruction just presented, He again called the people to repent. Luke's account is as follows:

Luke 13:1–5. There were present at that season some that told him of the Galilaeans, whose blood Pilate had mingled with their sacrifices. And Jesus answering said unto them, Suppose ye that these Galilaeans were sinners above all the Galilaeans, because they suffered such things? I tell you, Nay: but, except ye repent, ye shall all likewise perish. Or those eighteen, upon whom the tower in Siloam fell, and slew them, think ye that they were sinners above all men that dwelt in Jerusalem? I tell you, Nay: but, except ye repent, ye shall all likewise perish.

Some background information may be helpful in understanding the context. Josephus recorded two incidents in which Pilate incited the contempt of the Jews. The first occurred when Pilate allowed his soldiers to bring into Jerusalem coins and other items bearing the image of Caesar. This action was a direct affront to the Jewish laws prohibiting idolatrous images from being brought into the city. Many petitioned Pilate to remove the items from the city, but Pilate refused. Consequently, many Jews surrounded his palace, lay on the ground for long periods, and mockingly exposed their necks to the Roman soldiers. This uprising lasted for five days and nights. On the sixth day, Pilate ordered his soldiers to draw their swords. Most protesting Jews exclaimed they would rather die than have the idolatrous items remain in Jerusalem. Finally, Pilate relented.[42]

The second incident occurred when Pilate used money from the temple treasury to build aqueducts, through which water could be brought from the pools of Solomon to Jerusalem, which had long suffered from a deficient supply of water. A multitude of Jews revolted because Pilate was using the

---

41. See Prov. 28:13; D&C 58:42–43.
42. See Josephus, *Antiquities*, 28.3.1; *Wars*, 2.9.2

temple funds without the Jews' permission and for purposes other than the support of the temple and the priests, chief priests, and elders. In response to this insurrection, Pilate ordered his soldiers to beat the Jews, and many died either from the beating or from being trampled.[43]

Luke's record states that a group of people told Jesus that Pilate had mingled the blood of some Galileans with their sacrifices; this action by Pilate was another demonstration of his lack of morality and disdain for the Jews. The informants' purpose for telling Jesus is unstated, but they may have thought there was some hidden sin within those who were killed.[44] Or they may have wanted Jesus to explain why people who were doing good by offering sacrifices had been brutally killed. Or possibly these individuals simply wanted to warn Jesus of the danger since He was from Galilee.

Whatever the reason for the report, Jesus told them that they were not to judge other people and that the Galileans' deaths had not been a punishment from God because they were sinners. Jesus then referred to eighteen people who were killed when the tower of Siloam in south Jerusalem fell, and He explained that their deaths had not been the result of great sins.

Jesus had taught in the Sermon on the Mount that God "maketh his sun to rise on the evil and on the good, and sendeth rain on the just and on the unjust."[45] Certainly, some types of sin, such as excessive drinking and immorality, can bring about physical illness and even death. But here, Jesus made it clear that the sins of the Galileans and those at the tower were not greater than those of others. Those who died were not being punished by God.

Jesus then used this occasion to warn the people that if they did not repent, they too would perish—spiritually. Jesus may also have been referring to the Roman army's impending destruction of Jerusalem if the Jews did not repent—with spiritual death leading to physical death.

These two incidents were also warnings—to people today as well in Jesus's day—that death can come to anyone at any time, even to the good

---

43. See Josephus, *Antiquities*, 28.3.2; *Wars*, 2.9.4; see also *HarperCollins Bible Dictionary*, s.v. "Pilate, Pontius."

44. Many Jews thought that illness, infirmity, and catastrophe were the result of extraordinary sin (see, for example, the book of Job).

45. Matt. 5:45.

while doing good. Thus Jesus was once again teaching that people need to be spiritually prepared at all times, for no one knows what may come.

Jesus Gives the Parable of the Barren Fig Tree (Luke 13:6–9)

Jesus continued His warning about the need to repent by giving the parable of the barren fig tree:

> **Luke 13:6–9.** He spake also this parable; A certain man had a fig tree planted in his vineyard; and he came and sought fruit thereon, and found none. Then said he unto the dresser of his vineyard, Behold, these three years I come seeking fruit on this fig tree, and find none: cut it down; why cumbereth it the ground? And he answering said unto him, Lord, let it alone this year also, till I shall dig about it, and dung it: And if it bear fruit, well: and if not, then after that thou shalt cut it down.

As with other parables, this parable should not be taken too literally; the parable's main message is what is important. In this parable, the man who owns the vineyard represents God. It is reasonable to assume that the vineyard represents the then-known world and that the fig tree represents Israel in general and the Jewish nation in particular. It is also reasonable to assume that the fruit represents righteous Jews during Jesus's time.

The man who owned the vineyard came to the vineyard and looked for fruit on the fig tree but found none. Most of the nations of the world did not know of Christ or believe in Him or follow Him. In addition, ten of the tribes of Israel had been scattered, many had presumably become corrupt, and there was no righteous "fruit." Similarly, the Jewish nation, including the institutionalized church, had also become corrupt and therefore bore no fruit, for most of its leaders were no longer righteous. The Jews in Jesus's time were similar to those immediately before the Babylonian captivity centuries earlier. As Jeremiah said before the Babylonian captivity: "And I brought you into a plentiful country, to eat the fruit thereof and the goodness thereof; but when ye entered, ye defiled my land, and made mine heritage an abomination. The priests said not, Where is the Lord? and they that handle the law knew me not: the pastors also transgressed against me, and the prophets prophesied by Baal, and walked after things that do not profit. . . . For my people have committed two evils; they have forsaken me the fountain of living waters, and hewed them out cisterns, broken cisterns, that can hold no water."[46]

Then the vineyard owner said to the dresser (Jesus) that he had looked for fruit on the fig tree for three years but had found none. Likely, the three years represents the three years of Jesus's mortal ministry, which would be ending soon.[47] Although many believed, the Jewish nation as a whole refused to believe notwithstanding the many miracles Jesus had performed. The vineyard's owner told the dresser to cut down the tree, not only because it did not bear fruit but also because it "cumbereth" the ground. The Greek word for *cumber* is *katargeō*, which means to make useless or to work against.[48] In other words, the Jewish nation not only was useless because it did not bring forth fruit but also worked against Jesus and hindered the spread of the gospel throughout the region.

Just as the tree and its fruit served as a metaphor in this parable, John the Baptist had used the metaphor of a tree and fruit in discussing prophesies about what would happen to those who did not bear good fruit: "And now also the axe is laid unto the root of the trees: therefore every tree which bringeth not forth good fruit is hewn down, and cast into the fire."[49] John the Baptist was warning the Jews that they would be destroyed if they did not repent.

The vineyard's dresser recommended that the owner let the tree remain for another year so that the dresser had time to nurture the vineyard. This statement is evidence of Christ's compassion. Though Christ did not live another year, the Apostles, the Seventy, and other disciples did, and they shared the gospel message with all who would listen. Many more believed because of the witness of these disciples and the witness of the Holy Ghost.

In fact, the Jewish nation, as represented by the fig tree, was not destroyed immediately after one year had passed; this delay is symbolic of God's patience with all His children. Just as the vineyard owner stated that

---

46. Jer. 2:7–8, 13.
47. See Trench, *Notes on the Parables*, p. 123, for other interpretations of what the three-year period refers to, such as Moses, other prophets, and Christ or perhaps the natural law, the written law, and Christ's law.
48. See Young, *Analytical Concordance*, s.v. "cumber."
49. Matt. 3:10; see also Luke 3:9.

the tree should be destroyed if it did not bear fruit, Jerusalem was eventually destroyed because of the wickedness of its residents. This destruction occurred in AD 70 with the Roman empire's siege of Jerusalem. As Trench observed, "Multitudes of the inhabitants of Jerusalem were crushed beneath the ruins of their temple and city; and during the last siege and assault, there were numbers also, who were pierced through with Roman darts in the courts of the temple, in the very act of preparing their sacrifices, so that literally their blood was mingled with their sacrifices."[50]

Jesus Heals a Woman on the Sabbath (Luke 13:10–17)

Luke's record next describes Jesus being in a Jewish synagogue on the Sabbath:

> **Luke 13:10–17.** And he was teaching in one of the synagogues on the sabbath. And, behold, there was a woman which had a spirit of infirmity eighteen years, and was bowed together, and could in no wise lift up herself. And when Jesus saw her, he called her to him, and said unto her, Woman, thou art loosed from thine infirmity. And he laid his hands on her: and immediately she was made straight, and glorified God. And the ruler of the synagogue answered with indignation, because that Jesus had healed on the sabbath day, and said unto the people, There are six days in which men ought to work: in them therefore come and be healed, and not on the sabbath day. The Lord then answered him, and said, Thou hypocrite, doth not each one of you on the sabbath loose his ox or his ass from the stall, and lead him away to watering? And ought not this woman, being a daughter of Abraham, whom Satan hath bound, lo, these eighteen years, be loosed from this bond on the sabbath day? And when he had said these things, all his adversaries were ashamed: and all the people rejoiced for all the glorious things that were done by him.

This account is the only one in which Jesus taught in a synagogue in Perea. Presumably, as was the custom, on the Sabbath the ruler of the synagogue presided and read verses from the Old Testament, and he may have commented on them. Jesus may have then been permitted to teach because He was a noted teacher. In the synagogue was a woman who had

---

50. Trench, *Notes on the Parables*, p. 122.

suffered for eighteen years from an infirmity, perhaps a muscle disorder or severe osteoporosis. Her condition may have consisted of more than just a physical ailment, for Jesus said that "Satan hath bound" her. She may have come to the synagogue on the Sabbath simply because she had faith and desired to be as obedient as she could notwithstanding her infirmity. Or perhaps she had come to the synagogue because she had heard Jesus would be there and had some hope, however small, of receiving a miracle. Likely, most others in the synagogue knew her well.

While teaching, Jesus saw her and invited her to come to Him. It may have been difficult for her to walk. Jesus may have called her to Him rather than gone to her because He wanted to both test and strengthen her faith. He likely knew that healing her would elicit a negative reaction from the leader of the synagogue. Those present may have marveled as Jesus cared for the woman, who so desperately needed His healing hand. She did not ask for a blessing or to be healed; rather, Jesus called out to her. The individual was always important to the Master; it did not matter what else He was doing. Jesus lovingly and mercifully reached out to this infirm woman, just as He does to others.

When she came to Jesus, possibly with the help of others, He said to her: "Woman, thou art loosed from thine infirmity." Jesus then placed His hands on her, and she was immediately healed. Jesus's words and touch can heal all people, no matter whether their infirmity is physical, spiritual, or emotional.

Upon being healed, the woman glorified God. Imagine the gratitude in her eyes as she stood straight and looked at Jesus. All in the synagogue were witnesses of Jesus's merciful and tender act and the woman's subsequent rejoicing. They may have recognized that they too were special in His eyes.

The ruler of the synagogue, however, was filled with indignation, for Jesus had healed on the Sabbath day and in front of the entire congregation. The ruler may have been jealous that he did not have the power to perform a miracle and may have thought many in the congregation would think less of him. The ruler chose to express his disapproval to the congregation, and perhaps particularly to the woman, rather than only to Jesus, possibly because the ruler was somewhat afraid of Jesus's majesty. The ruler told the congregation that the act of healing someone should not occur on the

Sabbath because this action was a form of work. Healing, of course, was not work. Moreover, Jesus could not be accused of performing work other than the healing because He did not even walk to the invalid woman; she came to Him. The ruler ignored the miracle and its significance to the woman and presumably to her family; the ruler also ignored the love and mercy Jesus expressed by healing the woman.

Jesus responded by reminding the ruler and all others present that the Jews considered it acceptable for someone to lead his or her ox or ass to a watering spot on the Sabbath. Then He reasoned that if it was okay to care for the basic needs of an animal on the Sabbath, then it was acceptable to heal a woman from her infirmity on the Sabbath.

Jesus's response caused the ruler of the synagogue and others who opposed Jesus to feel ashamed, whereas the others in the congregation rejoiced because of the wonderful things Jesus had done.

The leader of the synagogue needed to learn that the rabbinical rules regarding the Sabbath were not only inconsistent with the Sabbath but also lacked the true spirit of the Sabbath. He also needed to learn to be humble and to recognize that each member of his congregation had individual worth. Additionally, he needed to learn that the promised Messiah stood in the synagogue that Sabbath day.

The woman who was healed likely gave witness of Christ ever after, and the others present may have likewise learned more of the Master Healer.

Jesus Gives the Parables of the Mustard Seed and the Leaven (Luke 13:18–21)

Jesus then gave two parables, one involving a mustard seed and the other involving leaven:

Luke 13:18–21. Then said he, Unto what is the kingdom of God like? and whereunto shall I resemble it? It is like a grain of mustard seed, which a man took, and cast into his garden; and it grew, and waxed a great tree; and the fowls of the air lodged in the branches of it. And again he said, Whereunto shall I liken the kingdom of God? It is like leaven, which a woman took and hid in three measures of meal, till the whole was leavened.

Jesus had given similar parables while in Galilee.[51] On both occasions, Jesus referred to well-known items—a mustard seed and leaven—to indicate that small things can produce large results. Likewise, Christ's Church, which was small at the time, would grow to become the kingdom of God on earth.

Jesus Admonishes the Jews to Enter through the Strait Gate (Luke 13:22–30)

At some point after speaking in the synagogue, Jesus "went through the cities and villages, teaching and journeying toward Jerusalem."[52] Jesus was going to Jerusalem to attend the Feast of Dedication. It is important to remember that Jesus had previously sent the Seventy into every city and place He would go,[53] and their testimonies presumably prepared the people to hear and accept the Lord's teachings. Many came to see Him and hear His message of love, peace, and righteous living and to hear Him witness that He was indeed the Son of God. The following is Luke's account of one incident that occurred as Jesus traveled:

> **Luke 13:23–30.** Then said one unto him, Lord, are there few that be saved? And he said unto them, Strive to enter in at the strait gate: for many, I say unto you, will seek to enter in, and shall not be able. When once the master of the house is risen up, and hath shut to the door, and ye begin to stand without, and to knock at the door, saying, Lord, Lord, open unto us; and he shall answer and say unto you, I know you not whence ye are: Then shall ye begin to say, We have eaten and drunk in thy presence, and thou hast taught in our streets. But he shall say, I tell you, I know you not whence ye are; depart from me, all ye workers of iniquity. There shall be weeping and gnashing of teeth, when ye shall see Abraham, and Isaac, and Jacob, and all the prophets, in the kingdom of God, and you yourselves thrust out. And they shall come from the east, and from the west, and from the north, and from the south, and shall sit down in the kingdom of God. And, behold, there are last which shall be first, and there are first which shall be last.

---

51. See Matt. 13:31–32; Mark 4:30–32; Matt. 13:33.
52. Luke 13:22.
53. See Luke 10:1.

In this account, a person asked Jesus a reasonable question: Were only a few people going to be saved? The person may have wondered whether only the Jews or the house of Israel would be saved or whether Gentiles would likewise be saved. Or the person may have wondered whether only those who believed in Christ and followed His teachings would be saved. Perhaps the person also wondered about his or her own spiritual condition and ultimate reward.

Rather than answering the question directly, Jesus told the person and all others listening: "Strive to enter in at the strait gate." Jesus did not say that a person must be perfect to be saved; rather, He used the word *strive*, which implies focusing on the kingdom of God and endeavoring to live the gospel despite weaknesses and setbacks. Jesus's use of *strive* can give all people hope that they can achieve exaltation.

Jesus also used the term *strait gate*. The Greek word for *strait* is *stenos*, which means narrow and restrained.[54] The Lord had previously contrasted the strait gate with the wide gate: "Enter ye in at the strait gate: for wide is the gate, and broad is the way, that leadeth to destruction, and many there be which go in thereat: Because strait is the gate, and narrow is the way, which leadeth unto life, and few there be that find it."[55] The Lord was teaching that people should focus on living the gospel and not on pursuing the things of the world.

Then Jesus used a metaphor involving the master of a house shutting the door and no longer letting in guests. The master represents Jesus, and after He has shut the door, it is too late to repent.[56] Expanding on this point, Jesus explained that knowing and being with Him were not enough. Nor was it enough that the Jews were descendants of Abraham, even though some thought that this lineage alone would save them. If they did not believe in Him and live the higher law He taught, at the day of judgment they would not receive eternal life, and this knowledge would lead to "weeping and gnashing of teeth."

Jesus then referred to those from the north, south, east, and west—in other words, Gentiles—and indicated that if they lived the commandments,

---

54. See Young, *Analytical Concordance*, s.v. "strait."
55. Matt. 7:13–14.
56. See Alma 34:32–35; Hel. 13:38.

they would be saved. Similarly, Jesus told the Nephites when He visited them after His Resurrection: "But if the Gentiles will repent and return unto me, saith the Father, behold they shall be numbered among my people, O house of Israel."[57] And so today, missionaries go throughout the world to invite Gentiles and those of the house of Israel to come unto Christ.

Jesus concluded His response to the man's question by stating that "there are last which shall be first, and there are first which shall be last."[58] The meaning of this statement is clearer when considering some context. In 721 BC, most members of the house of Israel except for the Jews and some descendants of Benjamin[59] were taken captive by the Assyrians,[60] and the whereabouts of those taken captive were unknown to the Jews of Jesus's day. Descendants of Benjamin who had not been captured eventually intermixed with the Jews, as did those from the other tribes of Israel who were not taken captive and remained in and around the territory of Judah.[61] The Jews believed that if Israelites intermixed with people of other nationalities, these Israelites became Gentiles. So, to the Jews in Jesus's day, the Gentiles were those who were not Jews. Today, the Gentiles are all those who are not of the house of Israel.

During Jesus's mortal ministry, He taught His gospel—the higher law— to the Jews. In this context, they were the first. After Jesus's death, the Apostles preached the gospel to those whom the Jews referred to as Gentiles. They were, therefore, the second (or last) group of people to receive the gospel during the meridian of time. In the latter days, the Gentiles (including all members of the house of Israel who are not Jews) have been and will continue to be the first to receive the gospel; the Jews will generally be the last to receive the gospel. Jesus's prophesy about the first being last and the last being first is being fulfilled in that members of The Church of Jesus Christ of Latter-day Saints preach the gospel in most nations around the world but are not currently permitted to proselyte in Israel.

---

57. 3 Ne. 16:13.

58. See also Matt. 19:30; 20:16; Mark 10:31; 1 Ne. 13:42; Ether 13:12; D&C 29:30.

59. See Smith, *Answers to Gospel Questions*, vol. 1, pp. 112–115.

60. See vol. 1, pp. 56–57, of this series.

61. For example, Lehi was a descendant of Joseph through Manasseh and initially resided in and around the area of Jerusalem (see 1 Ne. 1:4; 5:14; Alma 10:3).

Jesus later stated that "Jerusalem shall be trodden down of the Gentiles, until the times of the Gentiles be fulfilled,"[62] meaning the period during which the Gentiles are the first to receive the gospel. When Christ returns to the earth, the majority of the Jews in Israel will receive a witness of Christ from Him.[63] Jesus explained that those who witness His return will ask Him: "What are these wounds in thine hands and in thy feet? Then shall they know that I am the Lord; for I will say unto them: These wounds are the wounds with which I was wounded in the house of my friends. I am he who was lifted up. I am Jesus that was crucified. I am the Son of God. And then shall they weep because of their iniquities; then shall they lament because they persecuted their king."[64] In the final dispensation, the Jews will be the last to receive the gospel.

Surely, the man who asked Christ about who would be saved in the kingdom of God learned much more than he thought he would in asking the question. People today should be ever grateful for the man's question, for in response the Lord outlined some of what will take place in this dispensation regarding His gospel going throughout the earth. And much more can be learned by studying and pondering the scriptures with the inspiration of the Holy Ghost.

Jesus Is Warned of Herod's Intent to Kill Him (Luke 13:31–33)

On the same day, Pharisees came to Jesus and told him to leave Perea in order to avoid being killed by Herod, who had jurisdiction over Perea. Jesus replied that His ministry was more important than the risk of death. Luke's account is as follows:

> **Luke 13:31–33.** The same day there came certain of the Pharisees, saying unto him, Get thee out, and depart hence: for Herod will kill thee. And he said unto them, Go ye, and tell that fox, Behold, I cast out devils, and I do cures to day and to morrow, and the third day I shall be perfected. Nevertheless, I must walk to day, and to morrow, and the day following: for it cannot be that a prophet perish out of Jerusalem.

---

62. Luke 21:24; see also JST Luke 21:23; D&C 45:24–30.
63. See McConkie, *Mormon Doctrine*, p. 722.
64. D&C 45:51–53; see also Zech. 12:8–14; 13:6.

Herod Antipas was tetrarch of Perea and Galilee during the majority of Jesus's life. The Pharisees' motive for telling Jesus to depart is uncertain. It is possible that at that time, Antipas did want to kill Jesus; Antipas did not have jurisdiction in Jerusalem, so going there could provide Jesus with safety. However, the Pharisees may have been lying about Antipas wanting to kill Jesus, for while He was in Jerusalem just before His Crucifixion, Antipas found no fault with Jesus[65] and in fact had been "desirous to see him of a long season, because he had heard many things of him; and he hoped to have seen some miracle done by him."[66] The Pharisees may have wanted Jesus to return to Jerusalem, where He would be more directly subject to the Sanhedrin.

In Jesus's response, He referred to Antipas as "that fox." Jesus was asserting that Antipas was not only cunning but also evil. He was prone to condoning indiscriminate violence;[67] he had married Herodias, who was his niece and the wife of his half-brother; and he had imprisoned and then approved the death of John the Baptist.[68] Antipas was the only person Jesus is recorded to have referred to as "that fox."

When Jesus referred to "to day, to morrow, and the day following," He was indicating that He did not fear Antipas at any time. Consequently, He would continue to work when and where He deemed appropriate, until He went to Jerusalem and allowed Himself to be arrested, tried, and crucified. After Jesus indicated He did not fear Antipas, He stated that "it cannot be that a prophet perish out of Jerusalem." Jesus knew He would die in Jerusalem at the insistence of the majority of the Sanhedrin and with Pilate's approval. As Dummelow observed, "According to overwhelming precedent, Jerusalem was the place in which a prophet ought to be put to death."[69] On the third day following Jesus's death, He would be resurrected, witnessing not only to Herod Antipas but to all the Jews and all others throughout time that indeed He was the divine Son of God.

65. See Luke 23:6–15.
66. Luke 23:8.
67. See *HarperCollins Bible Dictionary*, s.v. "Herod, Herod Antipas."
68. See Matt. 14:1–12; Mark 6:14–29; Luke 3:19–20; 9:7–9.
69. Dummelow, *Bible Commentary*, p. 756.

Jesus Laments over Jerusalem (Luke 13:34–35)

Jesus then reflected with great sorrow upon the Jews in Jerusalem:

Luke 13:34–35. O Jerusalem, Jerusalem, which killest the prophets, and stonest them that are sent unto thee; how often would I have gathered thy children together, as a hen doth gather her brood under her wings, and ye would not! Behold, your house is left unto you desolate: and verily I say unto you, Ye shall not see me, until the time come when ye shall say, Blessed is he that cometh in the name of the Lord.[70]

Joseph Smith's inspired translation provides further understanding of the emotion Jesus felt when making His statement: "This he spake, signifying of his death. And in this very hour he began to weep over Jerusalem."[71] In particular, Jesus may have been contemplating the betrayal that would lead to His Crucifixion in just a few months. The intensity and depth of Jesus's sorrow for those of the central city of Israel was apparent. It is possible that Joseph Smith saw through revelation this scene of the Savior of the world weeping over those He cared about so much. To some degree, Joseph Smith may have understood that depth of sorrow when he recognized that he too would be called upon to give his life for the gospel's sake.

One might imagine how Jesus looked as He reflected on how a hen gathers her chicks under her wings to provide protection. And then Jesus reflected on His glorious Second Coming, when Jews will recognize He is the Messiah.

Jesus spoke the same words of lament in the temple shortly before His death, adding that "your house is left unto you desolate" and that "ye shall not see me henceforth, till ye shall say, Blessed is he that cometh in the name of the Lord."[72]

Those who feel deep sorrow because family members or friends will not accept the gospel can feel comfort in knowing that Jesus understands, as does God the Father.

---

70. See also Matt. 23:37–39.
71. JST Luke 13:33–34.
72. See also Matt. 23:39.

Chapter 43

JESUS HEALS, TEACHES OF SACRIFICE, AND GIVES PARABLES

Jesus continued teaching in Perea and Judea. Though only a few incidents during Jesus's time in Perea and Judea are recorded in the Gospels, there is little doubt that He taught and healed the sick and infirm wherever He went. Most of the recorded incidents during Jesus's ministry in Perea and Judea are contained in the Gospel of Luke, and this chapter will explore Luke's account of Jesus healing a man and of teaching various groups of people, particularly through parables.

Jesus Heals a Man with Dropsy (Luke 14:1–6)

In an unnamed city, Jesus was invited to dine with one of the chief Pharisees on the Sabbath, likely for the morning meal.[1] A number of others attended, including Pharisees and lawyers (or scribes or rabbis, who were experts in the scriptures),[2] while others may have watched from a distance.

---

1. The Sabbath was a principal day on which Jews entertained guests (see Farrar, *Life of Christ*, p. 422n1). Trench observed, "This was upon the Sabbath, the day which the Jews ordinarily selected for their festal meals: for the idea of the Sabbath among the Jews was not at all that of a day to be austerely kept, but very much the contrary" (Trench, *Notes on the Miracles*, p. 263).
2. See *HarperCollins Bible Dictionary*, s.v. "lawyers."

The meal may have been served inside the home or may have been served on the porch area, as was common. The following is Luke's account:

> **Luke 14:1–6.** And it came to pass, as he went into the house of one of the chief Pharisees to eat bread on the sabbath day, that they watched him. And, behold, there was a certain man before him which had the dropsy. And Jesus answering spake unto the lawyers and Pharisees, saying, Is it lawful to heal on the sabbath day? And they held their peace. And he took him, and healed him, and let him go; and answered them, saying, Which of you shall have an ass or an ox fallen into a pit, and will not straightway pull him out on the sabbath day? And they could not answer him again to these things.

The host was likely well respected and had a relatively large home because he was a chief Pharisee. Although no cooking occurred on the Sabbath, likely a good deal of labor was required that day to accommodate the invited guests. This work on the Sabbath illustrates the insincerity of the Jews, especially the chief rulers, in honoring the Sabbath day.[3]

Luke's statement that "they watched him [Jesus]" suggests that Jesus was invited not because of respect for Him but because of curiosity or malice, likely with the intent to once again try to trap Him in some perceived violation of rabbinical law, such as violation of the Sabbath, so that the Jews would have cause to take His life. As Farrar pointed out, the Pharisees "performed the duty of religious espionage with exemplary diligence."[4]

Among those present was a man who was afflicted with dropsy. Dropsy is referred to today as edema, which is swelling, often in the legs, feet, and other extremities, as a result of the accumulation of fluid, and this condition is sometimes associated with heart failure. The host may have invited the man in hopes that Jesus would heal him on this Sabbath day and provide the host and other Pharisees with a reason to condemn Him.[5] The afflicted man may have been hoping to receive a miracle at Jesus's hands, though not with ill intentions. Jesus likely looked at the man with compassion. Jesus was acutely aware that the Pharisees present were carefully watching for any reason to accuse Him, especially on this Sabbath day. Presumably, these

---

3. See Farrar, *Life of Christ*, p. 422.
4. Farrar, *Life of Christ*, p. 422n1.
5. See Trench, *Notes on the Miracles*, p. 263.

hypocritical leaders did not truly care about the man or his condition. They likely saw him only as a potential means of accusing Jesus.

Rather than curing the man immediately, Jesus asked the distinguished company a simple question: "Is it lawful to heal on the Sabbath day?" If they said yes, they would be abrogating their interpretation of the law. If they said no, they would be indicating, as Jesus subsequently pointed out, that an ox in the mire is of more importance than a man with a serious infirmity—a view that could cause an uproar among the common people. Because both answers were problematic, those present remained silent, meaning Jesus could heal the man without censure.

Jesus then "took" the man, presumably leading him away from the others, and healed him. Not only were the symptoms removed but so was the underlying cause; otherwise, the healing would not have been complete. After Jesus mercifully healed the man, he went his way.

Then Jesus asked, "Which of you shall have an ass or an ox fallen into a pit, and will not straightway pull him out on the Sabbath day?" He was emphasizing the mercy He had extended to the man and was also pointing to the hypocritical nature of the rabbinical interpretations of the law. Again, there was no answer.

Jesus demonstrated to all present that healing on the Sabbath does not violate the law because the Sabbath is a day for doing good and for remembering and serving God.

Jesus Gives the Parable of the Wedding Feast (Luke 14:7–11)

Jesus continued to teach those present by giving the parable of the wedding feast:

Luke 14:7–11. And he put forth a parable to those which were bidden, when he marked how they chose out the chief rooms; saying unto them, When thou art bidden of any man to a wedding, sit not down in the highest room; lest a more honourable man than thou be bidden of him; and he that bade thee and him come and say to thee, Give this man place; and thou begin with shame to take the lowest room. But when thou art bidden, go and sit down in the lowest room; that when he that bade thee cometh, he may say unto thee, Friend, go up higher: then shalt thou have worship in the presence of them that sit at meat with thee. For whosoever exalteth himself shall be abased; and he that humbleth himself shall be exalted.

In this parable, Jesus was addressing the Jewish hierarchy's habit of seeking out the places of honor when they were guests in a person's home. The place of highest honor "was the middle seat in the central triclinium,"[6] which is "a couch extending around three sides of a table used . . . for reclining at meals."[7]

Unrighteous pride has no place in the kingdom of heaven, and these Jews needed correction. As Jesus taught, "Whosoever exalteth himself shall be abased; and he that humbleth himself shall be exalted." Of course, Jesus's message is applicable to all people: everyone needs to demonstrate social courtesy and, even more importantly, to be humble—a characteristic Jesus demonstrated throughout His life. As one example of applying this principle today, people should not aspire to certain Church positions. Otherwise, if an individual does not receive the desired calling, he or she may become offended or discouraged.

Jesus Gives the Parable of the Great Feast (Luke 14:12–24)[8]

Because the host was a chief Pharisee, the guests he invited to his home may have included prominent Jewish leaders in the area, other rich men, officials, renowned scholars, famous rabbis, and the host's brethren.[9] Presumably, the host had invited them in part because they were his friends and he knew they would return the favor, thereby boosting his own ego. In addition, they would likely be able to find cause against Jesus or at least serve as witnesses against Him. They likely had pride in their hearts because they were invited, and they likely loved being seen by their peers and mingling with them. One can almost envision their costly robes and sandals and can almost hear their conversations, perhaps about recent events or their own homes and wealth and the costly feasts they had either hosted or attended.

---

6. Farrar, *Life of Christ*, p. 424.

7. *Merriam-Webster*, s.v. "triclinium," accessed Feb. 6, 2020, https://www.merriam -webster.com/dictionary/triclinium.

8. See chapter 42 of this volume for additional discussion of Christ's service at a supper.

9. See Talmage, *Jesus the Christ*, p. 422.

Notwithstanding their prominence, Jesus was the one who was teaching. He now taught them of humility and service:

Luke 14:12–14. Then said he also to him that bade him, When thou makest a dinner or a supper, call not thy friends, nor thy brethren, neither thy kinsmen, nor thy rich neighbours; lest they also bid thee again, and a recompence be made thee. But when thou makest a feast, call the poor, the maimed, the lame, the blind: and thou shalt be blessed; for they cannot recompense thee: for thou shalt be recompensed at the resurrection of the just.

Jesus's counsel was to the point. He taught those present that instead of inviting wealthy friends into the home, they should invite the poor and the physically afflicted, even though these individuals did not have the means to return the invitation. The reward for helping those in need would be eternal life.

One of those present replied to Jesus by stating, "Blessed is he that shall eat bread in the kingdom of God." The implication is that the prominent Jewish leaders present would inherit that kingdom in the next life. In response, Jesus gave the parable of the great feast. As with other parables, this parable has more than one meaning and is applicable today. The following is Luke's account:

Luke 14:15–24. And when one of them that sat at meat with him heard these things, he said unto him, Blessed is he that shall eat bread in the kingdom of God. Then said he unto him, A certain man made a great supper, and bade many: and sent his servant at supper time to say to them that were bidden, Come; for all things are now ready. And they all with one consent began to make excuse. The first said unto him, I have bought a piece of ground, and I must needs go and see it: I pray thee have me excused. And another said, I have bought five yoke of oxen, and I go to prove them: I pray thee have me excused. And another said, I have married a wife, and therefore I cannot come. So that servant came, and shewed his lord these things. Then the master of the house being angry said to his servant, Go out quickly into the streets and lanes of the city, and bring in hither the poor, and the maimed, and the halt, and the blind. And the servant said, Lord, it is done as thou hast commanded, and yet there is room. And the lord said unto the servant, Go out into the highways and hedges, and compel them to come in, that my house may be filled. For I say unto you, That none of those men which were bidden shall taste of my supper.

In this parable, the one who held the great supper represents God. It is reasonable to assume that the servant is Christ.[10] Because of the context and the location where this parable was given, those initially invited may represent the Jewish leaders and other prominent Jewish men, particularly those who had responsibility for the spiritual welfare of the people. The invitations to attend may have come during premortality, through ancient prophets whose words these Jews studied, or from Jesus during His mortal ministry. It should be remembered that the initial invitation would presumably endure into the future, including into the postmortal spirit world.

The invitation to attend the great supper was given in advance, presumably so that all who were invited would have time to arrange their schedules and affairs in order to attend. After the great supper was prepared, the host told his servant to tell those invited, "Come; for all things are now ready." This wording suggests that all those invited had accepted the invitation when originally given.

When the time of the meal arrived, all of those originally invited declined to attend for somewhat trivial reasons. The first claimed he needed to inspect a piece of land he had purchased, and the second said he had purchased oxen he needed to "prove." The third had married and claimed he could not leave his wife. Of course, the land and oxen could have been seen to after the supper, and the newly married man could have left his wife for a single meal.[11]

These individuals rationalized their decision not to attend. They were concerned about things of the world and their individual circumstances, not about the great supper prepared for them. Because they prioritized temporal things, these individuals were unwilling to make the effort and sacrifice required to attend. Similarly, the desires of those who do not accept God's invitation may not be in and of themselves immoral; rather, the sin is in prioritizing the things of the world over something of eternal significance.

---

10. The interpretation that God is the "certain man" is supported by the statement that came immediately before the parable ("Blessed is he that shall eat bread in the kingdom of God"). The interpretation that the servant in the parable is Jesus is based on the fact that only one servant is referred to.

11. In contrast to those who chose not to attend the supper, many of the Apostles had left their livelihoods and families to follow Jesus.

The master of the house then told the servant to go into the streets, where he would find the poor and the physically afflicted, and to bring them to the supper. In the context of the parable, these individuals presumably represent ordinary Jews, including those who were humble and more receptive to Jesus's message and some who were perhaps sinners. After these individuals were brought to the supper, there was still room for others, so the host directed his servant to compel people at the highways and hedges to come to the feast. The highways and hedges may represent areas beyond Israel, meaning that those who were invited were Gentiles in other lands.

It is interesting that the master of the house directed his servant to "bring" and "compel" individuals. Symbolically, they were to be brought through Christ or His designated servants. They were to be compelled by the whisperings and witness of the Holy Ghost. God invites sinners, the spiritually sick and needy, and the despised to come and partake of His great feast. All who will accept Christ's invitation will be gathered unto God and will fill His house.

Of this parable, Farrar stated: "The application to all present was obvious. The worldly heart—whether absorbed in the management of property, or the acquisition of riches, or the sensualisms of contented comfort—was incompatible with any desire for the true banquet of the kingdom of heaven. The Gentile and the Pariah, the harlot and the publican, the labourer of the roadside and the beggar of the streets—these might be there in greater multitudes than the Scribe with his boasted learning, and the Pharisee with his broad phylactery."[12]

This parable can give hope to those who are ill or infirm, to those who are not of the elite class, and to those who are Gentiles. The parable can give hope to all who have sinned and who think they are unworthy to come to God's house and partake of His great supper. If they repent, Christ's infinite Atonement will enable them to become clean, be numbered among Christ's disciples, and serve in the kingdom of God. Those who are righteous but do not serve in ecclesiastical or political leadership positions can have hope that they can partake of the blessings and opportunities available in the celestial kingdom. All can have hope that if they are faithful, they may attend God's

---

12. Farrar, *Life of Christ*, p. 425

figurative banquet in His kingdom and will receive the greatest of His gifts: eternal life.[13]

Additionally, this parable illustrates a principle that Jesus later taught more directly: "Many be called, but few chosen."[14] In the latter days, the Lord amplified this principle in connection with the priesthood: "Behold, there are many called, but few are chosen. And why are they not chosen? Because their hearts are set so much upon the things of this world, and aspire to the honors of men, that they do not learn this one lesson—that the rights of the priesthood are inseparably connected with the powers of heaven, and that the powers of heaven cannot be controlled nor handled only upon the principles of righteousness."[15] The high-positioned Jews to whom Jesus told the parable had set their hearts on the things of the world rather than on being righteous and serving those in need.

Additional insight regarding the parable comes from considering Doctrine and Covenants 58:9–11, in which the Lord refers to a supper that will occur after the "marriage of the Lamb"—that is, the Second Coming: "A supper of the house of the Lord, well prepared, unto which all nations shall be invited. First, the rich and the learned, the wise and the noble; and after that cometh the day of my power; then shall the poor, the lame, and the blind, and the deaf, come in unto the marriage of the Lamb [the Lord's Second Coming], and partake of the supper of the Lord, prepared for the great day to come."[16] Jesus will invite to the supper those who have heard and accepted the gospel, whether in this life or the next. Of this supper, the Apostle John wrote: "Blessed are they which are called unto the marriage supper of the Lamb."[17] And it could be added, blessed are those who accept the invitation and then put forth the daily effort to be prepared to attend the Lord's supper.

In Christ's role as the servant, He came to the earth not only in the meridian of time but also in the latter days to restore the Church, the gospel, and priesthood authority. In so doing, Christ gave instruction,

---

13. See D&C 14:7.
14. Matt. 20:16; see also 22:14.
15. D&C 121:34–36.
16. D&C 58:9–11.
17. Rev. 19:9.

commandments, and covenants to help bring all people to the great feast so they can partake of eternal life. In this last dispensation, the fulness of times, more than any other dispensation it might be said, as the host said in the parable: "All things are now ready." Christ is declaring His word Himself and through His servants, including ministering angels, "with power and great glory" and with miracles, some seen and many unseen.[18]

Punctuating the application of this parable, Christ stated that those who reject the invitation to attend the great supper are not thereafter permitted to partake of the feast God has prepared. Their rationalization has cost them eternal life. Those who heard Jesus give the parable surely understood that it was castigating them. Their mortal desires, wealth, and station took precedence over partaking of the spiritual feast they could have had. Moreover, though they were invited to God's feast and declined, they attended the Pharisee's feast of wealth and pride. This parable was a powerful and pointed warning to those who heard it from the lips of the Son of God, whom some rejected and sought to kill.

Jesus Teaches of the Sacrifice Required to Be a Disciple (Luke 14:25–35)

As Jesus continued His ministry in Perea and Judea, great multitudes followed Him, as had multitudes in Galilee. Some who followed Jesus believed that if He was the Messiah, they would receive great temporal blessings and even wealth for being His disciples.[19] On one occasion, Jesus turned to the multitude, corrected them, and taught what was required to be His disciple. The following is Luke's account:

> **Luke 14:25–35.** And there went great multitudes with him: and he turned, and said unto them, If any man come to me, and hate not his father, and mother, and wife, and children, and brethren, and sisters, yea, and his own life also, he cannot be my disciple. And whosoever doth not bear his cross, and come after me, cannot be my disciple. For which of you, intending to build a tower, sitteth not down first, and counteth the cost, whether he have sufficient to finish it? Lest haply, after he hath laid the foundation, and is not

18. Moro. 7:35; see also vv. 29–31, 36.
19. See Dummelow, *Bible Commentary*, p. 757.

able to finish it, all that behold it begin to mock him, saying, This man began to build, and was not able to finish. Or what king, going to make war against another king, sitteth not down first, and consulteth whether he be able with ten thousand to meet him that cometh against him with twenty thousand? Or else, while the other is yet a great way off, he sendeth an ambassage, and desireth conditions of peace. So likewise, whosoever he be of you that forsaketh not all that he hath, he cannot be my disciple. Salt is good: but if the salt have lost his savour, wherewith shall it be seasoned? It is neither fit for the land, nor yet for the dunghill; but men cast it out. He that hath ears to hear, let him hear.

Christ's instruction about the sacrifice required for true discipleship is similar to the instruction He had previously given in His ministry.[20] For example, Jesus had said, "No man, having put his hand to the plough, and looking back, is fit for the kingdom of God."[21] Christ was teaching that discipleship requires complete devotion and sacrifice, notwithstanding worldly or family pressures to do otherwise; it was not sufficient for someone to serve for a day and then desert the cause when difficulties came or the things of the world fought for precedence.

To amplify the teaching about sacrifice, Jesus explained that if a man were to come to Him but "hate not his father, and mother, and wife, and children, and brethren, and sisters, yea, and his own life also, he cannot be my disciple." Certainly, Jesus was not telling people to literally hate their family members. What He meant is that people's priorities should be Christ and service in the kingdom of God. Sometimes, family members who do not accept Christ will encourage other family members to not follow Him. In some instances, family members who join the Church are disowned. When family members oppose Church membership, the question is whether those who believe will prioritize Christ, His gospel, and service in His kingdom. Choosing these priorities does not mean that family responsibilities should be shirked or disregarded. There needs to be a proper balance. But when there is a choice between accepting the gospel or family members' preferences, Jesus taught that choosing to be baptized is the proper choice.

20. See, for example, Matt. 7:18–23.
21. Luke 9:62; see also vv. 57–61.

Jesus next indicated that to be a disciple, individuals needed to bear the crosses of mortality, meaning the individuals should not wallow in their circumstances but should serve however and whenever they can. The importance of taking up one's cross is also addressed in the Book of Mormon: "But, behold, the righteous, the saints of the Holy One of Israel, they who have believed in the Holy One of Israel, they who have endured the crosses of the world, and despised the shame of it, they shall inherit the kingdom of God, which was prepared for them from the foundation of the world, and their joy shall be full forever."[22] To despise "the shame of it" can involve choosing to not let infirmities hold people back; to not use infirmities as excuses for not serving; and to not mope around, feeling low self-esteem.

To further illustrate this teaching, Jesus stated that someone who wanted to build a tower would begin by determining the cost, to ensure there was enough money to complete the tower. Likewise, a king who was contemplating going to battle with an enemy would first compare the strength of his army to the strength of his enemy's army. Similarly, to be a valiant disciple, one must understand the cost of discipleship, including sacrifice of time and material things.

Jesus then presented the capstone of His message by stating that those who wanted to be His disciples needed to be willing to sacrifice all they had to follow Him. Jesus was teaching the principles of sacrifice and consecration. Even if the cost of discipleship does not require all, a disciple should be willing to sacrifice all—particularly sins.[23] Those who are not willing to sacrifice all are as salt that has lost its savor and therefore has no value.

Jesus then gave three parables about redemption and the joy that resulted. These parables will be discussed in the following sections.

Jesus Gives the Parable of the Lost Sheep (Luke 15:1–7)

Among the multitudes that followed Christ were publicans (tax collectors) and sinners. They were generally derided by the Pharisees and scribes, whereas Jesus did not discriminate against anyone but rather invited

22. 2 Ne. 9:18.
23. See Alma 22:15–18.

all people to believe in and follow Him. He even called Matthew, a publican, to be an Apostle.[24] Jesus was the Great Physician sent to spiritually heal sinners. He had previously told the scribes and Pharisees in Galilee, "They that are whole have no need of the physician, but they that are sick: I came not to call the righteous, but sinners to repentance."[25] As with the scribes and Pharisees in Galilee, the scribes and Pharisees in Perea and Judea were angry that Jesus associated with and accepted publicans and sinners. In essence, the Jewish leaders were murmuring against Christ for doing what they ought to be doing. In response to this murmuring, Jesus gave the parable of the lost sheep. The parable's message is similar to the message Jesus had given the Jewish leaders in Galilee.[26] The following is Luke's account:

> **Luke 15:1–7.** Then drew near unto him all the publicans and sinners for to hear him. And the Pharisees and scribes murmured, saying, This man receiveth sinners, and eateth with them. And he spake this parable unto them, saying, What man of you, having an hundred sheep, if he lose one of them, doth not leave the ninety and nine in the wilderness, and go after that which is lost, until he find it? And when he hath found it, he layeth it on his shoulders, rejoicing. And when he cometh home, he calleth together his friends and neighbours, saying unto them, Rejoice with me; for I have found my sheep which was lost. I say unto you, that likewise joy shall be in heaven over one sinner that repenteth, more than over ninety and nine just persons, which need no repentance.

Through this parable, Jesus was teaching of the responsibility to reach out to everyone without discrimination, including "lost sheep." Jesus and previous prophets had warned the leaders of Israel, who were to be shepherds. For example, the Lord instructed Ezekiel to give Israel's ecclesiastical shepherds the following warning:

> Woe be to the shepherds of Israel that do feed themselves! should not the shepherds feed the flocks? Ye eat the fat, and ye clothe you with the wool, ye kill them that are fed: but ye feed not the flock. The diseased have ye not strengthened, neither have ye healed that which was sick, neither have ye bound up that which was broken, neither have ye brought again that which

---

24. See Matt. 9:9; Mark 2:14; Luke 5:27–28.
25. Mark 2:17.
26. See Matt. 18:12–14.

was driven away, neither have ye sought that which was lost; but with force and with cruelty have ye ruled them. And they were scattered, because there is no shepherd: and they became meat to all the beasts of the field, when they were scattered. My sheep wandered through all the mountains, and upon every high hill: yea, my flock was scattered upon all the face of the earth, and none did search or seek after them.[27]

To those who were classified by the Jewish leaders as lost sheep, this parable offered a message of hope. In this parable, the sinner is characterized as a sheep that is lost in the wilderness of the world. As with sheep, sometimes people rebel. Sometimes, sin arises because of ignorance; the sinner simply does not recognize his or her actions as sin. Further, many go astray without recognizing that they have a shepherd or that remaining with the flock provides safety.

In their wanderings, these sheep may travel over hills, through canyons, along rocky crags, through the desert, and through swamps. Being alone may feel terrifying, partly because they lack spiritual strength and fear what they might encounter. At one time, they knew the shepherd and their brothers and sisters in the flock. Now they have wandered afar. Many may have forgotten, disbelieved, lost focus or interest on eternal matters, or experienced myriad other things that distanced them from the Holy Spirit, or they may have concluded that because they have wandered by sinning, there is no hope that they will find the flock or be found by the shepherd.

Yet the Good Shepherd knows and loves all the sheep[28]—those within the safety of the flock and those who have wandered. He can rescue the sheep. And His undershepherds can assist. Before Christ's mortal ministry, Ezekiel had prophesied that the Good Shepherd would seek His sheep, and those listening to Jesus, particularly the scribes, were likely quite familiar with the following message that the Lord declared through Ezekiel:

For thus saith the Lord God; Behold, I, even I, will both search my sheep, and seek them out. As a shepherd seeketh out his flock in the day that he is among his sheep that are scattered; so will I seek out my sheep, and will deliver them out of all places where they have been scattered in the cloudy

---

27. Ezek. 34:2–6; see also Zech. 11:17.
28. See John 10:14.

and dark day. And I will bring them out from the people, and gather them from the countries, and will bring them to their own land, and feed them upon the mountains of Israel by the rivers, and in all the inhabited places of the country. I will feed them in a good pasture, and upon the high mountains of Israel shall their fold be: there shall they lie in a good fold, and in a fat pasture shall they feed upon the mountains of Israel. I will feed my flock, and I will cause them to lie down, saith the Lord God. I will seek that which was lost, and bring again that which was driven away, and will bind up that which was broken, and will strengthen that which was sick: but I will destroy the fat and the strong; I will feed them with judgment.[29]

In the parable of the lost sheep, the shepherd continued to search until he found the wandering sheep. Afterward, the shepherd did not punish or criticize the sheep for its foolish actions and did not drive it back to the fold. Rather, with mercy and love, the shepherd lay the sheep on his shoulders and rejoiced that he had found the sheep. Likewise, Christ always extends His love and mercy to those who seek to return to the fold. There is no need for fear of retribution.

When the shepherd returned home (symbolically referring to the Savior's Church or perhaps heaven), he told his friends and neighbors to rejoice with Him. Similarly, the angels in heaven rejoice when someone who was lost is found and repents; this rejoicing is greater than for the ninety-nine who have not wandered.

Thus, this parable is a lesson not only for the Pharisees and scribes who needed to find and care for their lost sheep but also for all who have stewardship responsibility in the Lord's kingdom. This parable, like the two that follow, also points to Christ as the Good Shepherd and His atoning sacrifice, which can give all people hope of rescue.

Jesus Gives the Parable of the Lost Coin (Luke 15:8–10)

Christ continued teaching the publicans and sinners by giving the parable of the lost coin:

Luke 15:8–10. Either what woman having ten pieces of silver, if she lose one piece, doth not light a candle, and sweep the house, and seek diligently

---

29. Ezek. 34:11–16.

till she find it? And when she hath found it, she calleth her friends and her neighbours together, saying, Rejoice with me; for I have found the piece which I had lost. Likewise, I say unto you, there is joy in the presence of the angels of God over one sinner that repenteth.

As with many of Jesus's other parables, this parable has more than one application. A common interpretation of this parable is that the silver coin[30] was dropped or misplaced as a "result of inattention or culpable carelessness on the part of its owner."[31] Therefore, the coin may symbolize those who are lost through their own neglect or the neglect of others, such as parents and Church leaders. The implication is that all people should examine their lives and improve and that those who have responsibility for others should diligently seek, find, and recover those who are lost because they have lost their testimonies and have left the Church. Those who seek to find the lost need to light their own candles by having the Spirit of the Lord with them to guide them. The scribes and Pharisees who may have heard this parable should have clearly understood Jesus's message: that they should not allow any soul to be lost because of their neglect and failure to humbly follow Christ and that if one is lost, they should first assess their own worthiness and then diligently seek to find the spiritually lost.

This parable also has application to the Church as a whole. Just as the woman's savings and security were diminished by losing a single coin, the Church is diminished when a single person is lost. Christ here taught that the Church should function in such a way that those who are spiritually lost will not only be found but will be lovingly welcomed back. Those who have responsibility for others need to try to discern the underlying reason that led to someone becoming lost. And then these stewards need to help resolve the issue (figuratively lighting a candle and sweeping the floor). And they need to do so with love, for love is the essence of true ministering.

The need to minister applies to both men and women, as is indicated by the fact that in the previous parable, the good shepherd was a man and that in the current parable, the person doing the finding was a woman.

---

30. According to the *HarperCollins Bible Dictionary* (s.v. "money"), the lost coin was a drachma, which is "a silver Greek coin that would have been the usual day's wage for a typical laborer."

31. Talmage, *Jesus the Christ*, p. 427.

In the parable of the lost coin, the coin may also represent a testimony. Symbolically, perhaps the woman's precious testimony of God had diminished. Or perhaps overall her testimony remained, for she still had nine coins, but her testimony on a single issue was weak. The woman desired to find the precious coin, and she lit a candle to increase the light before sweeping her house and diligently looking for the coin. In sweeping the house, the woman was metaphorically repenting and becoming fully spiritually prepared to find and once again hold dear her testimony.

Jesus had previously declared that He is "the light of the world,"[32] and His light helps individuals to find what they have lost. In the parable, the woman lit her candle. Metaphorically, that light came from Christ, and the spirit within this woman recognized the truth of His message and who He was. Through lighting the candle, the woman was allowing the Light of Christ to work through her so she could find the lost coin. Several Old Testament references are pertinent. Psalm 18:28 states, "For thou wilt light my candle: the Lord my God will enlighten my darkness." Further, Psalm 20:27 equates the "candle of the Lord" with "the spirit of man." And as Job declared, the Lord's "candle shined upon my head, and when by his light I walked through darkness."[33] The learned scribes and Pharisees would presumably have known of these scriptures and likely would have recognized that the Lord was the woman's candle as well as their own.

Expanding on this parable, lighting one's candle can also inspire the individual to help others find what they may have spiritually lost. As Jesus said in His Sermon on the Mount in Galilee, "Ye are the light of the world. A city that is set on an hill cannot be hid. Neither do men light a candle, and put it under a bushel, but on a candlestick; and it giveth light unto all that are in the house. Let your light so shine before men, that they may see your good works, and glorify your Father which is in heaven."[34] And to the Nephites, He said, "I give unto you to be the light of this people."[35]

---

32. John 8:12; 9:5.
33. Job 29:3.
34. Matt. 5:14–16.
35. 3 Ne. 12:14.

In this parable, just as in the parable of the lost sheep, Jesus stated that there would be rejoicing when what was lost is found. When a precious testimony is rekindled, there is always rejoicing on the part of the person, others who care, and even the angels in heaven.

Jesus Gives the Parable of the Prodigal Son (Luke 15:11–32)

The third parable Jesus gave was that of the prodigal son.[36] This parable is one of the most well-known of the Lord's parables. It is important to remember that this parable symbolizes Heavenly Father and all His children, each of whom He loves and wants to progress. Rather than quoting the entire parable at the beginning of this section, the parable is divided into parts, with each immediately followed by commentary.

Luke 15:11. A certain man had two sons.

The father in the parable represents God. The two sons represent either individuals or groups of people, such as the house of Israel and the Gentiles. The younger son represents all who have departed from God's gospel and later recognize the divine within themselves and return to Him. The older brother represents those who have kept God's laws but have failed to develop the unconditional love of God.

Luke 15:12. And the younger of them said to his father, Father, give me the portion of goods that falleth to me.

According to Hebrew law, the oldest son would receive a double portion of his father's estate—that is, twice as much as that received by other sons. In this parable, the older son would receive two-thirds of the father's estate, and the younger son would receive one-third.[37] Since a portion of the father's estate likely would have been in real property, it is reasonable to assume that the father or the younger son would have had to sell a portion of the land in order to obtain cash for the son's use during the father's lifetime. Of course, this son had no right to claim a portion of

---

36. For a particularly insightful discussion of this parable, see Trench's *Notes on the Parables*.

37. See Deut. 21:17; see also *HarperCollins Bible Dictionary*, s.v. "inheritance."

his inheritance during his father's life;[38] receiving the inheritance early was, in effect, a gift.

In a spiritual sense, the younger son's request for his portion was a request to be free of Heavenly Father and to do what he wanted, perhaps based on the belief that he could do more alone than he could with the help of God. The son's downfall resulted from, among other things, pride, greed, and a desire to not be bound by his father's rules (symbolic of the Lord's commandments). The son wanted to be on his own and separate from his family.

Luke 15:12. And he divided unto them his living.

The father's willingness to give the son his inheritance symbolizes, among other things, God giving agency to humankind. The father allowed this son to learn through his own experience the difference between good and evil and between joy and misery, just as God allows all His children to do as part of His plan of salvation. As the parable later indicates, the father also allowed his elder son to learn on his own to accept and forgive others. Likewise, God has given all His children agency to make decisions and learn from them. Further, just as the father was there for the younger son when he desired to return, God will lovingly and mercifully welcome back His children when they choose to return to Him.

Luke 15:13. And not many days after.

The younger son's departure from his father was rather rapid. Similarly, sometimes departure from God occurs quickly, though often it is more gradual.

Luke 15:13. The younger son gathered all together, and took his journey into a far country.

Likely filled with pride and confidence in his abilities, the younger son accepted his inheritance, gathered together all else he thought he needed, and journeyed far away, possibly with the desire to gain all he could from the world. The faraway country represents the unforgiving wilderness of the world. Today, this faraway land can be as close as the internet or the home of a friend if a person does not act righteously while there.

---

38. See Edersheim, *Life and Times of Jesus the Messiah*, p. 654.

When the son left his father and mother to pursue pleasure in a distant land, he was in effect forsaking his duty to honor and care for them, as set forth in the fifth commandment Moses received on Mount Sinai: "Honour thy father and thy mother: that thy days may be long upon the land which the Lord thy God giveth thee."[39]

Luke 15:13. And there wasted his substance with riotous living.

Rather than putting his inheritance to work, the younger son spent all his funds on inappropriate activities. Presumably, he placed little value on the inheritance he had received. Similarly, people might ignore the marvelous spiritual gifts bestowed by Father in Heaven and might find temporary pleasure in the lusts of the flesh, such as drinking, gambling, and being immoral.

Luke 15:14. And when he had spent all, there arose a mighty famine in that land; and he began to be in want.

The son was not prepared for the challenges that life brought, and he thus could not sustain himself and he began to feel miserable. Satan had enticed the son to partake of the things of the world, and the son fell even further away from God. All that he had inherited had been spent, and because Satan does not support his own, the son began to be in want.

A famine is generally caused by drought—a lack of water. A spiritual famine is a lack of the word and presence of the Water of Life—that is, Christ—as well as God and the Holy Spirit. As Amos prophesied, "Behold, the days come, saith the Lord God, that I will send a famine in the land, not a famine of bread, nor a thirst for water, but of hearing the words of the Lord: and they shall wander from sea to sea, and from the north even to the east, they shall run to and fro to seek the word of the Lord, and shall not find it. In that day shall the fair virgins and young men faint for thirst."[40]

This spiritual famine was evident during Christ's mortal ministry, with many of the Jews unwilling to accept His message, and as Amos prophesied, it continued during the Dark Ages and until the gospel was restored in the latter days. Even when the word of the Lord is available through the

---

39. Ex. 20:12.
40. Amos 8:11–13.

teachings of prophets, the famine occurs for individuals who do not read, hear, and heed the words of the Lord.

The symbolic meaning of the famine in the parable may have been understood by the publicans, sinners, Pharisees, and scribes who heard Jesus give the parable. The publicans and sinners who accepted Christ and followed Him may also have felt hope as they heard the merciful words in this parable. On the other hand, the Pharisees and scribes who refused to repent and accept Jesus as the Son of God may have felt further anger.

Luke 15:15. And he went and joined himself to a citizen of that country; and he sent him into his fields to feed swine.

It is reasonable to assume that the younger son had resided only temporarily in this presumably amoral, far-off country. There, he became a servant of one of the country's citizens. Symbolically, this son trusted in the world rather than in God; however, the world had nothing of worth to offer. As Jeremiah had prophetically taught centuries earlier, "Thus saith the Lord; cursed be the man that trusteth in man, and maketh flesh his arm, and whose heart departeth from the Lord. For he shall be like the heath in the desert, and shall not see when good cometh; but shall inhabit the parched places in the wilderness, in a salt land and not inhabited."[41] Further, the son had become ritually unclean according to Jewish law because he fed swine[42] and interacted with a Gentile.

Luke 15:16. And he would fain have filled his belly with the husks that the swine did eat: and no man gave unto him.

So pitiful was this son's state that he was willing to eat the husks that the swine ate. These husks were not corn husks; rather, the husks were likely the pods of the fruit on carob trees, which were common in that region.[43] Though these husks were typically fed to swine, sometimes poor people would eat the husks because they were inexpensive. However, the son could not obtain even this food from others. On a symbolic level, the son's hunger was spiritual, and the world did not supply spiritual nourishment.

---

41. Jer. 17:5–6.
42. See Lev. 11:7; Deut. 14:8; Isa. 65:4; 66:3, 17.
43. See Trench, *Notes on the Parables*, p. 145.

The son had reached the bottom. Symbolically, Satan was at the heart of the son's downward spiral into misery. Just as Satan is miserable, "he [seeks] also the misery of all mankind."[44] The son had a choice: he could stay at the bottom or choose to rise by seeking redemption. The son had experienced the good with his family and had experienced the bad in the faraway country. As Lehi taught in the Book of Mormon, "It must needs be, that there is an opposition in all things. If not so, . . . righteousness could not be brought to pass, neither wickedness, neither holiness nor misery, neither good nor bad."[45]

Luke 15:17. And when he came to himself, he said, How many hired servants of my father's have bread enough and to spare, and I perish with hunger!

Finally, the son began to remember who he really was: a member of a family; symbolically, he remembered he was a child of God. The son also began to remember that many in his father's service had more than enough to eat and presumably had reasonably comfortable places to live. Upon remembering, the son hoped to regain even a small portion of what he used to have. Pride had given way to humility. He began to realize that the happiness that comes from the world is fleeting. It cannot bring the true joy and plenty that are available through living uprightly. As the prophet Jeremiah said, "Thine own wickedness shall correct thee, and thy backslidings shall reprove thee: know therefore and see that it is an evil thing and bitter, that thou hast forsaken the Lord thy God, and that my fear is not in thee, saith the Lord God of hosts."[46]

Remembering is a concept that flows throughout the scriptures. Remembering is a fundamental principle that provides a foundation in life, helps people remain on the correct path, and helps lift and refine people. Remembering helps people to better understand their circumstances and, in some cases, be more grateful for what they have. Remembering helps people to not repeat sin. As Alma taught his son Corianton, "I desire that ye should let these things trouble you no more, and only let your sins trouble you, with that trouble which shall bring you down unto repentance."[47] Just

---

44. 2 Ne. 2:18; see also v. 27.
45. 2 Ne. 2:11.
46. Jer. 2:19.
47. Alma 42:29.

as the prodigal son remembered, all other people need to remember they are children of God.

Luke 15:18–19. I will arise and go to my father, and will say unto him, Father, I have sinned against heaven, and before thee, and am no more worthy to be called thy son: make me as one of thy hired servants.

The son was humbled to the point that he recognized his errors. He found the strength to correct his situation, even though he thought there was no hope for him but to be a hired servant. Similarly, some who have sinned find the spiritual strength to recognize their faults, and though they believe they have forfeited eternal life, they hope to receive whatever kingdom of glory they think they might be worthy of.

Luke 15:20. And he arose, and came to his father.

Deciding to return to his father was not sufficient. He also needed to act. He swallowed his pride and returned to his father. The scripture states that the son "arose." Likewise, all who transgress need to arise and move forward to a new life. As Isaiah said, "Shake thyself from the dust; arise, and sit down, O Jerusalem: loose thyself from the bands of thy neck, O captive daughter of Zion."[48] Similarly, the prophet Lehi pled with his children, "O that ye would awake; awake from a deep sleep, yea, even from the sleep of hell, and shake off the awful chains by which ye are bound, which are the chains which bind the children of men, that they are carried away captive down to the eternal gulf of misery and woe. Awake! And arise from the dust. . . . Shake off the chains with which ye are bound, and come forth out of obscurity, and arise from the dust."[49]

The son's journey back to his father must have been difficult. The son likely wondered what his father would think and say. Would his father tell him to leave? What would be the thoughts of others in the household, including his brother and his father's servants? Despite any fears of what lay ahead, the son continued step by difficult step.

Luke 15:20. But when he was yet a great way off, his father saw him, and had compassion, and ran, and fell on his neck, and kissed him.

---

48. Isa. 52:2.
49. 2 Ne. 1:13–14, 23.

The father saw his son from a distance; this fact suggests that the father was watching for the son's return. The father knew his son would come home. Similarly, Heavenly Father is ever watchful of His children. He can see them wherever they are and even when they are figuratively far away, and He understands their circumstances and needs.

The father had compassion for his returning son. The Greek word for *compassion* means "to have the bowels yearning."[50] In other words, from deep within, the father yearned for his son. This compassion was not superficial or fleeting. Likewise, the Father of all people yearns for them from deep within.

It is also important to note that the father ran to his son; the father did not wait for the son to arrive at the home, nor did the father merely walk to his son. The father showed his love for his son, even though the son had wasted his inheritance. Likewise, Heavenly Father always loves His children, no matter what they have done, and He is always reaching out to them.

Upon reaching the son, the father did not wait for the son to speak but instead "fell on his neck, and kissed him."[51] The father likely knew that his son needed evidence of boundless love, and the father was willing to demonstrate it. Similarly, God demonstrates His love for each of His children and welcomes them back into the fold.

Luke 15:21. And the son said unto him, Father, I have sinned against heaven, and in thy sight, and am no more worthy to be called thy son.

The son now confessed that he had sinned against both heaven and his father. He humbly stated that he was no longer worthy to be called his father's son. However, the son was wrong. Having repented, he could return to his father and receive a banquet of forgiveness and the blessings of being the father's son. Likewise, Christ's Atonement is sufficient for all who forsake God but then return. Christ's atoning sacrifice lifts people from the mire and provides hope!

Luke 15:22–24. But the father said to his servants, Bring forth the best robe, and put it on him; and put a ring on his hand, and shoes on his feet: And

---

50. Young, *Analytical Concordance*, s.v. "compassion."

51. Other scriptures that refer to falling on someone's neck include Gen. 33:4; 45:14; 46:29; and Acts 20. These scriptures suggest that the action is not merely an embrace given out of courtesy but an embrace of true love.

bring hither the fatted calf, and kill it; and let us eat, and be merry: For this my son was dead, and is alive again; he was lost, and is found.

The son's body, hair, and clothes likely needed to be washed, but the father nevertheless recognized the divine nature of his son, just as Heavenly Father knows well the divinity in His children despite their sins. Because this son had humbly returned, he would be made clean. The father did not yell at his son or point out the results of his son's poor decisions.[52] Instead, the father directed that the best robe—perhaps one of the father's—be put on the returning son to replace the son's presumably filthy clothes. Putting clean clothes on the son symbolized acceptance in the family, reconciliation, and position. Centuries earlier, the symbolism of replacing filthy clothes with clean ones was evident when an angel had told those with Joshua to "take away the filthy garments from him [Joshua]. And unto him he said, Behold, I have caused thine iniquity to pass from thee, and I will clothe thee with change of raiment."[53] Symbolically, the prodigal son had become spiritually clean through the Atonement of Christ. Today, this same spiritual cleansing is symbolically represented by the white robes of the priesthood worn in the temple.

The ring signified the father's authority.[54] Symbolically, the ring may be a sign that the Atonement has been sealed upon a repentant person and that his or her blessings have been restored. The shoes, which were likely placed on his feet after they were washed, suggest that the son was no longer a servant in a foreign land but the father's son, for he was home. Figuratively, his feet were now "shod with the gospel of peace."[55]

The father directed that "the fatted calf" be killed and used for a celebratory meal; the use of the word *the* suggests that the father was referring to a specific cow, which implies there was some prior knowledge and preparation. Presumably, the meat would be sufficient for a feast involving many people, not just a simple meal for a few family members. Servants, friends, and neighbors may have been invited, just as friends and neighbors in the parable of the lost sheep were invited to rejoice after the sheep was

---

52. See James 1:5.
53. Zech. 3:4.
54. For other accounts in which rings signify authority, see Gen. 41:42 and Esth. 3:10; 8:2.
55. See Eph. 6:15.

found.[56] The calf killed for the celebration of the returning son is symbolic of Christ's sacrifice, in Gethsemane and on the cross, for all people.[57]

The first reason the father gave for celebrating is that "my son was dead, and is alive again." Obviously, the son had not been physically dead but had been spiritually dead. Later, the Apostle Paul likewise spoke of those who had been spiritually dead but then brought back to life:

> And you hath he quickened, who were dead in trespasses and sins; wherein in time past ye walked according to the course of this world, according to the prince of the power of the air, the spirit that now worketh in the children of disobedience: among whom also we all had our conversation in times past in the lusts of our flesh, fulfilling the desires of the flesh and of the mind; and were by nature the children of wrath, even as others. But God, who is rich in mercy, for his great love wherewith he loved us, even when we were dead in sins, hath quickened us together with Christ, (by grace ye are saved;) and hath raised us up together, and made us sit together in heavenly places in Christ Jesus: that in the ages to come he might shew the exceeding riches of his grace in his kindness toward us through Christ Jesus.[58]

The father's second reason for celebrating was that his son had been found. The son had found himself, the Holy Spirit had found in the son a humble heart, and his father had found him as he approached home, although the son was never lost to the father's heart.

The son's experience of sinning and then returning from sin is somewhat analogous to what will occur in the resurrection. As Paul wrote, in the resurrection, that which is mortal or "sown in corruption" will be raised to a spiritual body.[59] The prodigal son experienced the corruption of the world but eventually corrected his life, returned home, and was joyously welcomed.

Luke 15:24. And they began to be merry.

When considering the symbolism in the parables of the lost sheep, the lost coin, and the prodigal son, there is little room for doubt that when

---

56. See Luke 15:6.
57. The sacramental bread and water are likewise symbolic of Christ's sacrifice.
58. Eph. 2:1–7.
59. 1 Cor. 15:42; see also vv. 43–55.

someone repents and returns to God, those on earth and in heaven rejoice. The parable now turns attention to the elder son:

> **Luke 15:25–30.** Now his elder son was in the field: and as he came and drew nigh to the house, he heard musick and dancing. And he called one of the servants, and asked what these things meant. And he said unto him, Thy brother is come; and thy father hath killed the fatted calf, because he hath received him safe and sound. And he was angry, and would not go in: therefore came his father out, and entreated him. And he answering said to his father, Lo, these many years do I serve thee, neither transgressed I at any time thy commandment: and yet thou never gavest me a kid, that I might make merry with my friends: but as soon as this thy son was come, which hath devoured thy living with harlots, thou hast killed for him the fatted calf.

The fact that the elder son had been working in the field suggests he was obedient and diligent in fulfilling his duties. Apparently, no one had come to the field to tell him of his brother's return, so when the elder son came toward the home and heard music and saw dancing, he asked a servant to explain the reason for the festivities. Upon hearing the reason, the elder son was upset. He knew that his brother had previously disrespected their father and had taken his share of the inheritance. The elder son may not yet have known that the younger son had spent his inheritance. Upon finding out about the loss of the inheritance, the elder son may have even wondered whether his brother would be given some of the elder son's inheritance.

Unlike the father, the elder son had not forgiven his brother and lacked unconditional love. His jealousy and unforgiving, critical attitude were his flaws that needed correction. Both sons needed the atoning sacrifice of the Savior. As with the two sons, none on the earth are immune from sin. Some sin to a greater degree and in different ways than others, but all need refining and perfecting.

The father came to his elder son and invited him to the festivities. The father did not wait for this son to recognize the error of his ways. Instead, the father reached out to help the son because the father loved this son just as the father loved his other son.

The elder son may have thought that obedience and diligence in performing his duties were sufficient to retain his position in the family and ultimately receive his inheritance. He was somewhat like the Pharisees, who believed obedience to the law and rabbinical regulations alone would save them. He had not learned the lesson that Jesus had taught the lawyer: that the first and great commandment was to "love the Lord thy God with all thy heart, and with all thy soul, and with all thy mind. . . . And the second is like unto it, Thou shalt love thy neighbour as thyself."[60]

The son stated that he had served his father for many years and had never failed to do as his father had requested but that he had never been celebrated even with a goat, let alone a fatted calf. This son implied that his father was not grateful for the son's diligent and faithful service. Perhaps there was in the son a little jealousy, the desire for justice, and even a hint of rebellion. Of course, the elder son had worked diligently, but he could not have been obedient to all his father's directions. Further, though the father had never prepared a feast to honor the faithful service of the elder son, the father had given, or promised to give, this son his inheritance, which was presumably double what the younger son had received. The son's pride was manifested differently than that of the younger son but was nevertheless present. Pride and selfishness were the trial of both.

Luke 15:31. And he said unto him, Son, thou art ever with me, and all that I have is thine.

The father gently reassured that he recognized his son's faithfulness. Though the son needed correction, the father told the son that "all that I have is thine." Symbolically, this statement refers to much more than a financial inheritance. For example, those who magnify their priesthood are promised that they will be "sanctified by the Spirit unto the renewing of their bodies. They become the sons of Moses and of Aaron and the seed of Abraham, and the church and kingdom, and the elect of God. And also all they who receive this priesthood receive me, saith the Lord; for he that receiveth my servants receiveth me; and he that receiveth me receiveth my Father; and he that receiveth my Father receiveth my Father's kingdom; therefore all that my Father hath shall be given unto him. And this is according to the oath and

---

60. Matt. 22:37, 39.

covenant which belongeth to the priesthood."[61] A similar promise is most certainly available to faithful women.

Luke 15:32. It was meet that we should make merry, and be glad: for this thy brother was dead, and is alive again; and was lost, and is found.

The father did not castigate the son's thoughts but rather explained an important principle: the younger son's return was a reason to rejoice. In this parable, Christ taught not only about the joy of a returning son but also about how to compassionately correct others.

Presumably, the elder son was inspired and encouraged by his father's teachings, repented of his shortcomings, and participated in the feast. Likewise, Heavenly Father entreats all His children to attend His feast.

In a sense, all people are prodigal sons or daughters who need to repent and feel Heavenly Father's mercy and forgiveness, which are available through that Atonement of Jesus Christ. In particular, people need to guard against pride, however it may be manifest.

In the parable of the prodigal son, the son who is lost finds himself, whereas in the parables of the lost sheep and the lost coin, the shepherd and the woman are the ones who searched for what was lost. All three parables provide hope for all who are lost. When individuals choose to return to God, whether or not with significant help from others, they will feel His love and encouragement and will be cleansed through Christ's Atonement.

These three parables apply not just to those in mortality who are lost but also to those in the postmortal spirit world who are lost. Certainly, missionary service is being rendered in that realm. There is also service that can be rendered on earth for those who have passed on. Ancestors can be searched for by using online tools, such as those provided by The Church of Jesus Christ of Latter-day Saints. Once these individuals are found, essential ordinances can be performed for them.

The parable of the prodigal son can also be seen as a metaphor about God's children leaving the premortal world and entering mortality, with all its trials and challenges. His children have agency to choose between good and evil, and all fall short to one degree or another. He waits with open arms to greet His children when they decide to repent and return to Him, and the

---

61. D&C 84:33–39.

return of a lost son or daughter causes rejoicing in heaven. Even for those who do not stray far, life is not an easy journey. But God will always help and guide His children. His love is unconditional and never ceases. There is always hope.

Note to Chapter 43

1.   The Lord's Supper. The *HarperCollins Bible Dictionary* describes the Lord's Supper as follows:

> An early Christian celebration modeled on the last meal Jesus shared with his disciples prior to his death; it receives this name from Paul's reference in 1 Cor. 11:20. The Synoptic Gospels describe the Last Supper as a Passover meal, but in John it is eaten before Passover. The words "after supper" in the tradition quoted by Paul in 1 Cor. 11:23–25 indicate that the Lord's Supper was originally a full meal, introduced by the blessing and breaking of the bread and concluded by the blessing and passing of the cup. In earliest Christianity the Lord's Supper was pervaded by intense eschatological expectation. Fervent hope for the new age, to be inaugurated by the risen and exalted Jesus upon his return to earth, is obvious in Mark 14:25 and Luke 22:18 and is echoed in 1 Cor. 11:26.[62]

---

62. *Harper Collins Bible Dictionary*, s.v. "Lord's Supper."

Chapter 44

CHRIST CONTINUES TEACHING IN PEREA

After the Savior spoke with the Pharisees in Perea, He once again directed His attention and teachings to His Apostles and disciples. Through using parables, He taught of the importance of humble and faithful diligence in building up the kingdom of God, pointed to the hypocrisy of the Pharisees and others who sought for prominent positions and wealth, and reminded His disciples that those who are faithful and humble will gain eternal life. Jesus also taught His disciples to forgive and to magnify their callings. In all of these teachings, Jesus spoke with authority as the Son of God.

Jesus Gives the Parable of the Unjust Steward (Luke 16:1–13)

As with Christ's other parables, there is much to learn from the parable of the unjust steward, especially for those who are called to serve in the kingdom of God. This parable is somewhat difficult to understand, likely causing Jesus's disciples and Apostles to ponder it over and over again, perhaps both individually and collectively. The following is Luke's account of the parable:

> **Luke 16:1–13.** And he said also unto his disciples, There was a certain rich man, which had a steward; and the same was accused unto him that he had wasted his goods. And he called him, and said unto him, How is it that I hear this of thee? give an account of thy stewardship; for thou mayest be no longer steward. Then the steward said within himself, What shall I do? for my lord taketh away from me the stewardship: I cannot dig; to beg I am ashamed. I am resolved what to do, that, when I am put out of the

stewardship, they may receive me into their houses. So he called every one of his lord's debtors unto him, and said unto the first, How much owest thou unto my lord? And he said, An hundred measures of oil. And he said unto him, Take thy bill, and sit down quickly, and write fifty. Then said he to another, And how much owest thou? And he said, An hundred measures of wheat. And he said unto him, Take thy bill, and write fourscore. And the lord commended the unjust steward, because he had done wisely: for the children of this world are in their generation wiser than the children of light. And I say unto you, Make to yourselves friends of the mammon of unrighteousness; that, when ye fail, they may receive you into everlasting habitations. He that is faithful in that which is least is faithful also in much: and he that is unjust in the least is unjust also in much. If therefore ye have not been faithful in the unrighteous mammon, who will commit to your trust the true riches? And if ye have not been faithful in that which is another man's, who shall give you that which is your own? No servant can serve two masters: for either he will hate the one, and love the other; or else he will hold to the one, and despise the other. Ye cannot serve God and mammon.

The rich man in this parable may represent God and Christ. Therefore, the first fundamental precept taught in this parable is that God is rich. He has dominion over all things in heaven and on the earth, and all who have lived or will ever live on this earth are His children. Jesus Christ is rich in that He is the Son of God, He created this earth and worlds without number under the Father's direction,[1] and He will preside over this earth in its celestial state.[2]

In the parable, the rich man has a steward, who may represent disciples of Christ who have responsibility to teach, guide, and help others. This concept of stewardship is the second fundamental principle taught in the parable. God and Christ give disciples experiences and responsibilities to help disciples spiritually grow.

The rich man had apparently given his steward responsibility over various goods, and the steward was responsible for collecting debts owed for the goods that had been sold. Similar to a power of attorney, the steward apparently had unlimited authority to supervise the goods for the benefit of

---

1. Moses 1:32–35.
2. See D&C 130:9.

the rich man. In a spiritual context, goods represent God's children on the earth. Stewards have responsibility for those in their stewardships and are to magnify their callings,[3] including by serving with all their "heart, might, mind and strength."[4] This teaching is the third important principle in this parable. The fourth principle is that stewards have agency and therefore can choose whether to serve. Some may choose to serve diligently, with the goal of glorifying God and bring His children to Him; others may choose to serve with the goal of receiving their own praise; and yet others may choose to neglect their callings. From the beginning, agency has been one of the most wonderful and important gifts and principles given to humankind.

The steward in the parable chose to neglect his responsibilities, likely to pursue a life of pleasure. When the rich man heard that the steward had not properly managed the goods, the rich man asked the steward to explain his conduct and then stated that the stewardship would be terminated. Given the steward's position, he should have assumed that at some point he would be required to report to the master, and the steward should have been prepared. Likewise, there will come a time when the Master will ask each individual to give a report of his or her actions and omissions. As with the steward, all people should prepare to give this report by diligently serving and fulfilling their responsibilities, whether great or small.

In the parable, the steward was then confronted with a major problem. He had lost his employment, could not "dig," and was "ashamed to beg." Presumably, he lacked the skills to work in any jobs other than that of a steward, including jobs requiring manual labor, such as digging. Faced with the prospect of begging to stay alive, he analyzed the problem and then creatively came up with a solution. He resolved to make friends with those who owed the master money so that "they may receive me into their houses." He had found a solution to a most difficult problem, but this solution was not the best option, particularly since this solution was dishonest and was fraudulent if he no longer had financial authority or was a further breach of his fiduciary duties if his authority had not yet been fully rescinded. Instead of implementing this solution, he could have

---

3. See D&C 84:33.
4. D&C 4:2.

apologized to his employer and attempted to make amends financially. The steward's honesty may have improved his employer's opinion of the steward and also improved the debtors' opinions of him if they were sensitive to the steward's situation.

Having chosen a solution, the steward spent his energies implementing it. This swiftness to act was another important lesson for the disciples. Although they should never serve for their own benefit, they did need to properly and quickly analyze the problems they faced, develop what they determined were the best solutions, and then spend the majority of their efforts implementing those solutions instead of dwelling on or complaining about the problems.

Christ's disciples who had stewardship responsibilities would confront myriad problems. These problems may have included believing in Christ when family members did not, wavering in faith, experiencing marital challenges, and struggling with serious illnesses or the death of loved ones. Christ's disciples would also confront the challenges resulting from the numerical and geographical growth of the Church; these challenges included determining how to provide administrative and financial support. Further, Christ's disciples would face the challenge of Gentile converts wanting to incorporate their own ideas and philosophies into the Church's doctrines, as well as the challenge of deciding whether the traditions of the Jews, including circumcision, should be imposed on Gentile believers. Additionally, the disciples would likely face persecution from Jewish leaders and neighbors who did not believe. The disciples would also face political challenges from Rome. All these challenges and many others needed prompt and thoughtful solutions.

It is important to note that Jesus stated, "When ye fail." He recognized that failures would come. Failure is part of life, and people often learn more from their failures than from their successes. Jesus may also have been referring to the fact that a general apostasy would occur because of challenges such as the loss of an administrative center, the influence of Jews and of Greek philosophers who attempted to incorporate their beliefs into the Church's doctrine, the sins and diminished testimonies of Church members, and limited means of communicating.

In the parable, the steward went to those who owed the rich man money, presumably for goods purchased or money borrowed, and asked the debtors to pay reduced amounts. For example, the steward asked someone who owed a hundred measures of oil to immediately pay fifty measures. The steward then asked someone who owed a hundred measures of wheat to pay for eighty measures. The debtors were more than willing to have their debts reduced. This fact should lead readers to consider whether those who have debts should accept offers for the debts to be reduced simply because the offer is made.

Upon learning what the steward did, the rich man congratulated the steward on his solution to the problem. Of course, the rich man was not commending the steward for his dishonesty but for his prudence.[5] Despite this commendation, the master did not reinstate the steward's position and any rewards that it brought, for the steward's dishonest actions were the reason that the master's goods had been wasted.

After presenting the parable, Jesus counseled His disciples regarding concepts in the parable. He observed that those of the world are often wiser and more diligent in furthering their financial security than are those who believe in Christ and work to build up the kingdom of God. Just as some of those who are of the world diligently look after their finances, those who are "children of light" should zealously strive to further the work of God, prepare for what may come, and be worthy to receive exaltation.

The Lord then directed His disciples to "make to yourselves friends of the mammon of unrighteousness." They needed to be in the world but not of the world. Christ knew that for His Church to move forward after His death, it would need both financial resources and administrative wisdom. The disciples' success in the world might enable them to be more successful in building the kingdom of God. However, mammon should be used appropriately, such as to meet a person's basic needs, to bless others, and to further God's purposes; mammon should not be used to gain excessive possessions and to pursue pleasure, both of which are fleeting and may result in pride.

---

5. See Talmage, *Jesus the Christ*, p. 434.

Moreover, the Lord implied that for His Church to grow, those who believed needed to have friends both in and outside of the Church, to be good examples, and to provide help when necessary. When those not in the Church are given the opportunity to help, they often grow and gain a more favorable view of the Church. The disciples were to respect all people, even if their beliefs were worldly.

The Lord then instructed His disciples that they would have varying positions of responsibility. He stated that if His disciples were faithful in fulfilling smaller responsibilities, they would also be faithful in fulfilling greater responsibilities; conversely, if they were not faithful in fulfilling smaller responsibilities, they would not be faithful in fulfilling greater responsibilities. The disciples needed to learn to be successful in their secular endeavors, which would in turn help them be successful in serving in the Church and in helping others.

Then came the Lord's balancing caution. Though His disciples needed to learn from wise individuals in the world, learn to be successful, and learn to be good examples for and friends with those who did not believe, His disciples also needed to know that they could not "serve two masters: for either [they] will hate the one, and love the other; or else [they] will hold to the one, and despise the other." They could "not serve God and mammon."

Jesus Teaches of Marriage and Divorce (Matt. 19:1–12; Mark 10:1–12; Luke 16:14–18)

A number of Pharisees had heard Jesus's counsel to His disciples and consequently criticized Him. Jesus responded with divine discernment. Luke's record of this account is expanded upon in Joseph Smith's inspired translation, and therefore the latter version is presented here:

> **JST Luke 16:14–23.** And the Pharisees also, who were covetous, heard all these things: and they derided him. And he said unto them, Ye are they which justify yourselves before men; but God knoweth your hearts: for that which is highly esteemed among men is abomination in the sight of God. And they said unto him, we have the law, and the prophets; but as for this man we will not receive him to be our ruler; for he maketh himself to be a judge over us. Then said Jesus unto them, The law and the prophets testify of me; yea, and all the

prophets who have written, even until John, have foretold of these days. Since that time, the kingdom of God is preached, and every man who seeketh truth presseth into it. And it is easier for heaven and earth to pass, than for one tittle of the law to fail. And why teach ye the law, and deny that which is written; and condemn him whom the Father hath sent to fulfill the law, that ye might all be redeemed? O fools! For you have said in your hearts, There is no God. And you pervert the right way; and the kingdom of heaven suffereth violence of you; and you persecute the meek; and in your violence you seek to destroy the kingdom; and ye take the children of the kingdom by force. Woe unto you, ye adulterers! And they reviled him again, being angry for the saying, that they were adulterers. But he continued, saying, Whosoever putteth away his wife, and marrieth another, committeth adultery; and whosoever marrieth her who is put away from her husband, committeth adultery.

The scriptural record indicates that the Pharisees "were covetous" and hypocritical. They were covetous because they loved money more than they loved God and His children, whom the Pharisees were supposed to serve. The Pharisees were covetous in that they sought costly robes and houses as well as the most-important seats during special events. The Pharisees coveted attention in that they openly displayed their obedience to rabbinical laws, prayer, almsgiving, and general piety in order to gain the recognition of others. They also coveted Jesus's ability to attract multitudes and inspire His disciples to be devout, resulting in fewer followers of Judaism, less participation in the synagogues, and fewer people honoring the Pharisees. Because the Pharisees coveted money, the Pharisees who dealt with temple finances required individuals who were making offerings at the temple to exchange their money for temple coins; these Pharisees charged a fee for the currency exchange, thereby lining their pockets and taking advantage of those who made the required sacrifices at the temple.

As the Pharisees heard Jesus teach about mammon, they may have wondered what a man who was dressed in ordinary robes and who owned no property could know about business success. They may also have wondered how someone who was not from Jerusalem or educated in it by rabbis or teachers could fully understand the economics of a corridor nation—that is, a nation that people from other places passed through to get to and from the Mediterranean Sea, Egypt, and other surrounding areas. These thoughts may have been part of the reason the Pharisees derided Jesus at this time.

Jesus then sharply rebuked them for their hypocritical display of piety and their love of money. He told them that God knew their hearts and that what motivated them was abominable to God. Their response was that they had the law that God revealed to Moses and the words of the Old Testament prophets. The Pharisees believed that mere obedience to the law was sufficient to receive salvation.

Jesus then stated that both the law and the prophets, whom the Pharisees professed to revere, testified of Him, as did John the Baptist. Jesus explained that He had come to fulfill the law. Then He told them that they perverted the law and that the "kingdom of heaven suffereth violence" at their hands. Of course, violence was prohibited by the very law the Pharisees claimed to honor. Further, although they professed to be righteous, they perverted what was good and from God. They also persecuted the meek, considering them to be less worthy and important, and sought to excommunicate those who professed belief in Christ.

Knowing the Pharisees' actions and hearts, Jesus then told the Pharisees that they were adulterers. They were angry at His words, presumably because their consciences condemned them. Then He explained that men who divorced their wives for little cause and then married other women had committed adultery, as had men who married previously divorced women.

Some background information may be helpful in understanding Christ's statements concerning divorce and adultery. During Jesus's day, there were two major schools of teaching among the Pharisees: the school of Hillel and the school of Shammai. The school of Hillel was far more liberal than the school of Shammai, which stressed strict observance of religious laws. For example, the school of Shammai held that a man may divorce his wife for serious offenses only, whereas the school of Hillel allowed divorce for almost any reason.[6]

---

6. Regarding these schools of teaching, Geikie observed: "Among the questions of the day fiercely debated between the great rival schools of Hillel and Shammai, no one was more so than that of divorce. The school of Hillel contended that a man had a right to divorce his wife for any cause he might assign; if it were no more than his having ceased to love her, or his having seen one he liked better, or her having cooked a dinner badly. The school of Shammai, on the contrary, held that divorce could be issued only for the crime of adultery and offences against chastity." (Geikie, *Life and Words of Christ*, vol. 2, p. 347). See also Dummelow, *Bible Commentary*, pp. 642–643; Talmage, *Jesus the Christ*, p. 451n4.

Presumably, the Pharisees whom Jesus was speaking to were of the school of Hillel, and He was rebuking their light treatment of the sanctity of marriage. Given Jesus's strong language about divorce and adultery, it is likely that some present had put their wives away, perhaps in order to marry other women. Christ made His position clear concerning such behavior.

The Gospel of Matthew indicates that at this time or at another time that Jesus taught about marriage and divorce,[7] certain Pharisees asked Jesus about divorce, in an attempt to trap Him. They hoped His answer would provide them with a reason to accuse and arrest Him. The following is Matthew's account, as well as a verse from Mark's record, which makes clear that Christ's teaching was applicable to both men and women:

Matthew 19:3–9. The Pharisees also came unto him, tempting him, and saying unto him, Is it lawful for a man to put away his wife for every cause? And he answered and said unto them, Have ye not read, that he which made them at the beginning made them male and female, and said, For this cause shall a man leave father and mother, and shall cleave to his wife: and they twain shall be one flesh? Wherefore they are no more twain, but one flesh. What therefore God hath joined together, let not man put asunder. They say unto him, Why did Moses then command to give a writing of divorcement, and to put her away? He saith unto them, Moses because of the hardness of your hearts suffered you to put away your wives: but from the beginning it was not so. And I say unto you, Whosoever shall put away his wife, except it be for fornication, and shall marry another, committeth adultery: and whoso marrieth her which is put away doth commit adultery.

Mark 10:12. And if a woman shall put away her husband, and be married to another, she committeth adultery.

The Pharisees may have chosen the topic of divorce because Jesus was from Galilee, where Herod Antipas was tetrarch and had divorced his wife so he could marry Herodias, who was not yet divorced from her husband.

---

7. Luke indicates that Jesus taught about marriage and divorce during His Perean ministry. Matthew indicates that Jesus taught about these topics after He had left Perea, had visited Galilee, and was on his way to Jerusalem for the Festival of Dedication. Biblical scholars are somewhat divided as to whether Luke and Matthew provided accounts of the same event or whether each recounted a different instance of Jesus teaching about marriage and divorce. Because the subject matter in both accounts is much the same, they are treated together in this chapter.

If Jesus condemned divorce, then the Pharisees could ensure that Herod Antipas heard of it, in hopes that the tetrarch would put Jesus to death.

The Savior's declaration regarding divorce and adultery may have also pointed to the Pharisees' hypocritical decision to overlook the law of Moses where Antipas was concerned. The Pharisees listening to Jesus likely wanted to find favor with Antipas and therefore did not want to challenge Antipas's marriage to Herodias. Christ's rebuke of the Pharisees was likely another motivation for Jewish leaders to seek His death a few months later.

Ever standing for truth and purity, Jesus responded by pointing to the Pharisees' apparent lack of understanding of or deliberate choice not to believe in the sanctity of marriage. Jesus then reminded the Pharisees of the statement in the account of the Creation that "a man [shall] leave his father and his mother, and shall cleave unto his wife: and they shall be one flesh."[8] Next, Jesus boldly stated: "Wherefore they are no more twain, but one flesh. What therefore God hath joined together, let not man put asunder." Christ unequivocally affirmed that from the beginning, the marriage of a man and woman was instituted by God.

The Pharisees could not refute Jesus's statement that when man and woman are joined together in marriage, they become as one flesh. The Pharisees were caught in their own snare by divine truth and the scriptures they claimed to revere.

Their only way out was to point to the law that the Lord gave to Moses:[9] "Why did Moses then command to give a writing of divorcement, and to put her away?" They failed to realize that the one standing before them was the Jehovah of the Old Testament, the one who gave Moses the law. Of course, Jehovah did not tell Moses that God approved divorce for any cause, as the Pharisees had implied.

Jesus answered the Pharisees' question by telling them that the only acceptable reasons for divorce were adultery and fornication and that a person who divorced a spouse for any other cause and who then remarried

---

8. Gen. 2:24.

9. Deut. 24:1 states that the Lord directed Moses as follows: "When a man hath taken a wife, and married her, and it come to pass that she find no favour in his eyes, because he hath found some uncleanness in her: then let him write her a bill of divorcement, and give it in her hand, and send her out of his house."

was committing adultery. Jesus also explained that Moses spoke of additional reasons for divorce because the children of Israel had hard hearts. Jesus's teaching about the only acceptable reason for divorce was similar to that in the school of Shammai but contradicted the view of the Pharisees and certainly the actions of Herod Antipas.

Jesus was teaching not only about divorce but also about the eternal importance of marriage and fidelity, something these Jews seem to have forgotten about. Dummelow observed, "The rabbis regarded the liberty of divorce as a special privilege conferred by God upon the chosen people."[10] Further, marriage in Israel had deteriorated to the point that women were property of their husbands and in effect were their slaves.[11] Unfortunately, the Pharisees were not willing to accept Christ's teaching of the higher law concerning marriage.[12] Jesus's response contributed to the ever-increasing opposition to Him.

Upon hearing Jesus's words, His disciples asked whether marriage should be avoided, given the risks associated with divorce and subsequent remarriage. Matthew's account is as follows:

Matthew 19:10–12. His disciples say unto him, If the case of the man be so with his wife, it is not good to marry. But he said unto them, All men cannot receive this saying, save they to whom it is given. For there are some eunuchs, which were so born from their mother's womb: and there are some eunuchs, which were made eunuchs of men: and there be eunuchs, which have made themselves eunuchs for the kingdom of heaven's sake. He that is able to receive it, let him receive it.

In response to the disciples' concerns, Jesus explained that people might remain single for various reasons, such as because of physical

---

10. Dummelow, *Bible Commentary*, p. 688.

11. See Talmage, *Jesus the Christ*, p. 443.

12. Bruce R. McConkie wrote, "It is clear that the high standards of marriage and divorce of which Jesus speaks were for those only to whom they were given by revelation. Needless to say they have not been given to us in our day in their eternal fulness, and marriages to divorced persons do not of themselves constitute adultery." (McConkie, *Mortal Messiah*, vol. 3, p. 296.)

conditions or service in the kingdom of God when the service takes one away from home.[13]

From the beginning, the foundational unit of society has been the family, with a husband and wife and usually children. Adam and Eve were the first eternal family, and they set the pattern for all humankind. A husband and wife legally wedded and sealed together for time and eternity also form the foundational social unit in the celestial kingdom. No contradictory societal trends can change this fact.[14]

Although marital challenges may lead to bitterness, depression, low self-esteem, feelings of unworthiness, insecurity, and financial concerns, a vital truth to remember is that all wounds can be healed through Christ's merciful and loving Atonement. It can lift people out of a dark abyss and into the light. Christ's Atonement enables forgiveness and brings peace and hope, even when they seem unlikely to come.

The lessons that can be gleaned from this incident with the Pharisees are simple and direct. People should avoid covetousness, hypocrisy, and pride in all their conduct. People should focus on eternally important things, such as loving God and others, building up His kingdom, being devoted to family members (including by honoring the marriage covenant), and developing moral character.

Jesus Gives the Parable of the Rich Man and Lazarus (Luke 16:19–31)

Jesus continued teaching the Pharisees by giving the parable of the rich man and Lazarus. Of course, this parable, as with others, has more than one application; however, the meaning of this parable should not be extended beyond the point that Jesus intended regarding the final judgment and the condition of people in the spirit world.

Luke 16:19–31. There was a certain rich man, which was clothed in purple and fine linen, and fared sumptuously every day: and there was a certain beggar named Lazarus, which was laid at his gate, full of sores, and desiring

---

13. There is no scriptural reference to Jesus being married, and He may have remained single during His mortal life so He could fully overcome the world, atone for the sins of humankind, and bring about the resurrection of all. Jesus did not command anyone to remain single; He left the decision to individuals based on their circumstances.

14. See "The Family: A Proclamation to the World."

to be fed with the crumbs which fell from the rich man's table: moreover the dogs came and licked his sores. And it came to pass, that the beggar died, and was carried by the angels into Abraham's bosom: the rich man also died, and was buried; and in hell he lift up his eyes, being in torments, and seeth Abraham afar off, and Lazarus in his bosom. And he cried and said, Father Abraham, have mercy on me, and send Lazarus, that he may dip the tip of his finger in water, and cool my tongue; for I am tormented in this flame. But Abraham said, Son, remember that thou in thy lifetime receivedst thy good things, and likewise Lazarus evil things: but now he is comforted, and thou art tormented. And beside all this, between us and you there is a great gulf fixed: so that they which would pass from hence to you cannot; neither can they pass to us, that would come from thence. Then he said, I pray thee therefore, father, that thou wouldest send him to my father's house: for I have five brethren; that he may testify unto them, lest they also come into this place of torment. Abraham saith unto him, They have Moses and the prophets; let them hear them. And he said, Nay, father Abraham: but if one went unto them from the dead, they will repent. And he said unto him, If they hear not Moses and the prophets, neither will they be persuaded, though one rose from the dead.

The counterpositions in this parable are striking. The rich man wore expensive purple[15] clothes and ate sumptuous meals, whereas Lazarus[16] was very poor, was covered in sores, and begged at the rich man's gate for sustenance. Lazarus was so destitute that he desired to eat the rich man's crumbs, or garbage, which may have been discarded outside the gate of the rich man's house. The rich man likely had many servants to attend to his wants, whereas Lazarus was presumably alone except for the dogs that licked his sores and possibly some people who helped him.

---

15. Purple was "associated with royalty and wealth . . . and prized for priestly vestments in Israel's tradition" (*HarperCollins Bible Dictionary*, s.v. "purple").

16. This parable is the only one in which Jesus gave a character a name, and the name is that of an individual He loved. Lazarus was the brother of Mary and Martha, and Jesus restored him to life shortly before Jesus was betrayed and killed.

Lazarus presumably represents those who are humble and commit to follow Jesus's teachings. The rich man[17] may represent Pharisees, who focused on themselves and not on loving and serving God and others. The Pharisees favored the rich and looked down on the poor because of the belief that prosperity was a sign of God's approval and that poverty was a sign of the curse of God. Therefore, the Pharisees listening to the parable may have assumed that Lazarus's sores were a consequence of his sins.

In the parable, Lazarus died and was carried by angels into Abraham's bosom. The Jews revered Abraham as their father and the source of their spiritual and national heritage,[18] and the term *Abraham's bosom* refers to a place of comfort where the righteous dead await Judgment Day.[19] In Jesus's time, when people ate meals together, the individual who was physically closest to the host was said to be lying on the chest (bosom) of the host and was considered to be in a place of prominence. Thus, being in Abraham's bosom meant that Lazarus was given a place of preeminence in the next life, presumably because he had been righteous during mortality.[20]

The rich man also died and was buried. Presumably, he was wrapped in costly burial robes, friends and hired mourners attended his funeral, and he was placed in an expensive carved tomb. But rather than angels escorting him to heaven, he was consigned to hell. It seems that, as used in the parable, *hell* refers to the rich man's initial abode following his death—the place where he

---

17.   Some traditional writers have given the name of Dives to the rich man; however, *dives* is not actually a person's name but is an adjective that means *rich* (see *Merriam-Webster*, s.v. "dives," https://www.merriam-webster.com/dictionary/Dives; see also Dummelow, *Bible Commentary*, p. 760).

18.   See, for example, John 8:39, 53; Matt. 3:9.

19.   Abraham's bosom is the equivalent of paradise. See note 1 at the end of this chapter. The Hebrew word for *bosom* is *tsallachath*, which means "lap." The Greek word for *bosom* is *kolpos*, which means "hollow thing." (See Young, *Analytical Concordance*, s.v. "bosom.") Both the Hebrew and Greek words came to relate to the Jewish practice of individuals reclining while eating meals together.

20.   See note 1 at the end of this chapter.

would remain until his final judgment.[21] This place is commonly referred to in The Church of Jesus Christ of Latter-day Saints as spirit prison.[22]

Certainly, the rich man was in torment because of his wickedness in mortality. In addition, some of the torment he experienced may have resulted from seeing what he could have inherited if he had been righteous. Further, he may have felt torment because he had previously believed, as the Pharisees did, that being a descendent of Abraham qualified him for exaltation. But as the parable indicates, this heritage did not guarantee exaltation. As Jesus taught at other times, exaltation comes only through believing in Him and living as He taught. The rich man apparently had not done so.

In his torment, the rich man asked Abraham to have Lazarus provide relief by dropping water on the rich man's tongue.[23] However, a drop of water on the tongue does not douse a flame; rather, relief from spiritual pain comes from being baptized by immersion in water, receiving the gift of the Holy Ghost, committing to follow Christ's teachings, continually repenting, and enduring to the end.[24]

When Abraham responded, he referred to the rich man as "son," recognizing that the rich man was indeed of Abraham's lineage. But Abraham then reminded the rich man that he had received the good things of the world during mortality, whereas Lazarus had experienced the challenges of the world. Now the positions were reversed.

Abraham then explained that there was a "great gulf" that prevented Abraham and others from coming to the man and relieving his torment. The

---

21. The use of *hell* may refer to what the *HarperCollins Bible Dictionary* refers to as Sheol and Hades: "The concept of hell is different from Sheol (in the Hebrew Bible) and from Hades (in most Greek literature) in three ways: (1) only the wicked enter hell, whereas good and bad alike occupy Sheol and Hades; (2) the wicked are sent to hell after a final judgment at the end of time, whereas people were thought to enter Sheol or Hades immediately upon death; and (3) hell involves eternal torment, whereas Sheol and Hades were characterized only by absence of life, not enhanced suffering. In NT, however, some references to Hades appear to have been influenced by the concept of hell, so that Hades also can be described as a place of torment reserved only for the wicked or those condemned in the judgment (Matt. 11:23; Luke 16:23)." (*HarperCollins Bible Dictionary*, s.v. "hell.")

22. See McConkie, *Mormon Doctrine*, p. 755. See also note 2 at the end of this chapter.

23. In this regard, Jesus's parable tracks with the Pharisees' belief that those who have died can communicate with each other.

24. See John 3:5. Having a drop of water touch one's tongue may also be a metaphor for standing on the periphery and wondering whether Jesus was the Son of God.

concept of a great gulf dividing paradise and hell in the afterlife was foreign to Jewish thinking.[25] However, the concept was not foreign to the Nephites in the Book of Mormon. For example, Nephi referred to an "awful gulf, which separated the wicked from the tree of life, and also from the saints of God. . . . [And] that awful hell, which the angel said unto me was prepared for the wicked."[26] Mormon wrote of an "everlasting gulf of misery."[27] Similarly, Nephi, the son of Helaman, referred to a "gulf of misery and endless wo."[28]

Only Christ has the keys to bridge the great and awful gulf and to open the doors of missionary work to those who have died and are in spirit prison.[29] As He explained, "I am he that liveth, and was dead; and, behold, I am alive for evermore, Amen; and have the keys of hell and of death."[30] The Pharisees had completely failed to recognize the divine authority of the person before them.

After Abraham said he could not cross the gulf, the rich man asked that Abraham send Lazarus to the home of the rich man's father to tell the rich man's five brothers how to avoid the same fate as the rich man. The rich man thought that his family would believe Lazarus (whom they may have known was a beggar in mortality) even though they had not believed the prophets down through the centuries. The rich man was also implying that during his life, he had not received sufficient warning about how his conduct would affect his eternal fate. It was evident that the rich man had failed to understand the witness of the Old Testament prophets.

Abraham responded that the rich man's brothers could study the writings of the prophets. The rich man replied that they might need a greater witness, such as of one who came to them from the dead. Abraham responded that if they did not accept the words of the prophets, the man's brothers would not be persuaded by one who had died. This statement can be seen as a prophecy that the Jewish leaders would not accept Christ even after His Resurrection,

---

25. See Edersheim, *Life and Times of Jesus the Messiah*, p. 670.
26. 1 Ne. 15:28–29.
27. Hel. 3:29.
28. Hel. 5:12.
29. See D&C 138.
30. Rev. 1:18.

which was the crowning witness that He indeed was the promised Messiah and the Son of God.

When considering this parable, an important point to recognize is that a person's riches or lack of riches does not determine his or her reward in the life to come. The parable implies that the rich man loved material things but did not love God or those in need and would not accept Christ or follow His teachings; for these reasons, the rich man was in torment in the postmortal world. In contrast, Lazarus was presumably humble and moral, had repented of his sins, and believed in Christ, resulting in his reward in paradise.[31] This parable also affirms that there is a postmortal life, a truth that the Sadducees rejected and that some people today reject or ignore.

In a more geographical and political sense, the rich man may represent the Jewish nation arrayed in the purple of a king and the fine linen of a priest, whereas Lazarus represents the gentile nations that surrounded Israel.[32] Throughout history, the Jews have experienced misery and torment at the hands of other peoples.

This parable can give hope to people who do not have wealth or ecclesiastical or political positions or who must rely on help from others. As Jacob in the Book of Mormon taught: "But, behold, the righteous, the saints of the Holy One of Israel, they who have believed in the Holy One of Israel, they who have endured the crosses of the world, and despised the shame of it, they shall inherit the kingdom of God, which was prepared for them from the foundation of the world, and their joy shall be full forever."[33]

Jesus Teaches about Offenses, Forgiveness, and Faith (Luke 17:1–6)

At some point after giving the parables, Jesus gave His disciples further instruction. He first warned that they, like Him, would be subject to persecution:

Luke 17:1–2. Then said he unto the disciples, It is impossible but that offences will come: but woe unto him, through whom they come! It were

---

31. This point is suggested by the fact that Jesus's beloved friend Lazarus had accepted Jesus's message.

32. The sins and sores of the Jews and Gentiles are, in part, enumerated by Paul in Romans 1:21–32.

33. 2 Ne. 9:18.

better for him that a millstone were hanged about his neck, and he cast into the sea, than that he should offend one of these little ones.

Jesus may have given His disciples this instruction in order to encourage them to further prepare. To fully prepare, they needed further strengthening by learning from Him during the remaining months of His mortal ministry; seeing Him after His Resurrection; and receiving the Holy Ghost, which would come to them following Jesus's death. In addition, Jesus indirectly warned those who would cause the offenses, explaining that it would be better for the offenders to drown in the sea than to offend "these little ones." In this context, the term *little ones* refers to those who are young and untried in defending the gospel and Jesus.

Having warned of offenses, Jesus next taught about the need to forgive:

Luke 17:3–4. Take heed to yourselves: If thy brother trespass against thee, rebuke him; and if he repent, forgive him. And if he trespass against thee seven times in a day, and seven times in a day turn again to thee, saying, I repent; thou shalt forgive him.

In referring to forgiving an offender seven times on one day, Jesus was teaching that forgiveness should not be limited to a certain number of offenses. On another occasion, Jesus similarly taught that forgiveness should be granted seven times seventy.[34]

Next, Jesus once again taught about faith, at the Apostles' request:

Luke 17:5–6. And the apostles said unto the Lord, Increase our faith. And the Lord said, If ye had faith as a grain of mustard seed, ye might say unto this sycamine tree, Be thou plucked up by the root, and be thou planted in the sea; and it should obey you.

Instead of directly teaching the Apostles how to increase their faith, Jesus wisely taught them about the results of faith: if they had the faith of a mustard seed,[35] they could cause a sycamore tree to be uprooted and move into the sea. A mustard seed is quite small, and Jesus was indicating that even a small amount of faith could have remarkable results. Further, just as a mustard seed eventually becomes a large plant, a small amount of faith can

---

34. See Matt. 18:21–22.

35. For other references to a mustard seed, see Matt. 6:30; 8:26; 13:31; 14:31; 16:8; 17:20; Mark 4:31; Luke 12:28; 13:19.

grow and mature over time. This teaching may have reminded the Apostles of the divine potential within them and may have reassured them that their young faith would grow.

For a mustard seed to grow and flourish, it needs sunlight, water, and nutrients from proper soil. Likewise, the Apostles needed the proper conditions to spiritually grow and flourish. They needed spiritual light provided by Christ, the water of baptism and other covenants, nutrients provided by faith and the gospel, and strength obtained through obedience. They also needed the enduring witness of the Holy Ghost. They needed to understand that they were the children of God and His chosen vessels to bear His gospel to the world. They needed to allow the Light of Christ and the Holy Spirit to help them understand the mind and will of the Lord so that their desires would be in harmony with His desires.

Further, just as a mustard seed must struggle to sprout, grow up through the soil, and thereafter survive against the elements, the Apostles needed to struggle in order for their faith to grow.

Jesus Gives the Parable of the Unprofitable Servant (Luke 17:7–10)

Jesus then gave the parable of the unprofitable servant:

Luke 17:7–10. But which of you, having a servant plowing or feeding cattle, will say unto him by and by, when he is come from the field, Go and sit down to meat? And will not rather say unto him, Make ready wherewith I may sup, and gird thyself, and serve me, till I have eaten and drunken; and afterward thou shalt eat and drink? Doth he thank that servant because he did the things that were commanded him? I trow not. So likewise ye, when ye shall have done all those things which are commanded you, say, We are unprofitable servants: we have done that which was our duty to do.

A servant who has spent a hard day in the fields may reasonably assume that afterward, he or she is entitled to rest and eat. But in this parable, the servant was required to continue serving the master. Symbolically, the Lord was teaching that even when the initially designated spiritual work is completed, the servants in His kingdom may have other duties to fulfill in the service of the Master. Only when all is completed may the servants eat and rest. The servant represents Christ's Apostles and other disciples,[36] and they needed to continue to serve even after completing their initially prescribed duties and no matter the circumstances, for Christ alone would determine when their work was completed. They needed to labor in the way that the Apostle Paul later described near the end of his life: "For I am now ready to be offered, and the time of my departure is at hand. I have fought a good fight, I have finished my course, I have kept the faith."[37]

The servants also needed to humbly serve without expecting thanks or external reward. Though they had worked hard and had done what was asked, they should consider themselves unprofitable servants, for without Christ, their works would not bring them exaltation. Additionally, as the Apostle Paul stated in his Epistle to the Romans, all need to humbly serve God, "for all have sinned, and come short of the glory of God."[38]

The Apostles in particular also needed to understand that they should consecrate their lives to serving the Lord, including by bringing souls unto Christ. This consecration needed to involve always looking for opportunities to do good. As the Lord instructed Joseph Smith:

> For behold, it is not meet that I should command in all things; for he that is compelled in all things, the same is a slothful and not a wise servant; wherefore he receiveth no reward. Verily I say, men should be anxiously engaged in a good cause, and do many things of their own free will, and bring to pass much righteousness; for the power is in them, wherein they are agents unto themselves. And inasmuch as men do good they shall in nowise lose their reward. But he that doeth not anything until he is commanded, and receiveth a commandment with doubtful heart, and keepeth it with slothfulness, the same is damned.[39]

---

36. See Talmage, *Jesus the Christ*, p. 439.
37. 2 Tim. 4:6–7.
38. Rom. 3:23.
39. D&C 58:26–29.

Notes to Chapter 44

1.   Paradise. McConkie defined *paradise* as "that part of the spirit world inhabited by righteous spirits who are awaiting the day of their resurrection."[40] Alma described paradise as "a state of happiness, . . . a state of rest, a state of peace, where they shall rest from all their troubles and from all care, and sorrow."[41] Joseph Smith said, "The spirits of the just are exalted to a greater and more glorious work: hence they are blessed in their departure to the world of spirits. Enveloped in flaming fire, they are not far from us, and know and understand our thoughts, feelings, and motions, and are often pained therewith."[42]

2.   Spirit prison. Alma described the great sorrow of those in spirit prison as follows:

> And then shall it come to pass, that the spirits of the wicked, yea, who are evil—for behold, they have no part nor portion of the Spirit of the Lord; for behold, they chose evil works rather than good; therefore the spirit of the devil did enter into them, and take possession of their house—and these shall be cast out into outer darkness; there shall be weeping, and wailing, and gnashing of teeth, and this because of their own iniquity, being led captive by the will of the devil. Now this is the state of the souls of the wicked, yea, in darkness, and a state of awful, fearful looking for the fiery indignation of the wrath of God upon them; thus they remain in this state, as well as the righteous in paradise, until the time of their resurrection.[43]

Enoch also described the wicked in spirit prison: "Satan shall be their father, and misery shall be their doom; and the whole heavens shall weep over them, even all the workmanship of mine hands; wherefore should not the heavens weep, seeing these shall suffer?"[44]

---

40. McConkie, *Mormon Doctrine*, p. 554.
41. Alma 40:12; see also Luke 23:43; 4 Ne. 14; Moro. 10:34; D&C 77:2, 5.
42. Smith, *Teachings*, p. 326.
43. Alma 40:13–14.
44. Moses 7:37.

Joseph F. Smith saw in vision how the gospel would be taken to those in spirit prison:

> And as I wondered, my eyes were opened, and my understanding quickened, and I perceived that the Lord went not in person among the wicked and the disobedient who had rejected the truth, to teach them; But behold, from among the righteous, he organized his forces and appointed messengers, clothed with power and authority, and commissioned them to go forth and carry the light of the gospel to them that were in darkness, even to all the spirits of men; and thus was the gospel preached to the dead. And the chosen messengers went forth to declare the acceptable day of the Lord and proclaim liberty to the captives who were bound, even unto all who would repent of their sins and receive the gospel. Thus was the gospel preached to those who had died in their sins, without a knowledge of the truth, or in transgression, having rejected the prophets.[45]

---

45. D&C 138:29–32.

Chapter 45

JESUS HEALS AND TEACHES AS HE TRAVELS TO JERUSALEM FOR THE FESTIVAL OF DEDICATION

As Jesus traveled from Perea toward Jerusalem for the Festival of Dedication,[1] He passed through portions of Galilee and Samaria.[2] The scriptural record is silent on the route He took and which cities and villages He visited along the way. Few events from this period are recorded in the Gospels, and most of those that are recorded are found in Luke's Gospel. The objective of the Gospel writers was not to discuss each incident in Christ's life but, rather, to describe the events that would bear witness that Jesus Christ was the Son of God and also be of most worth to future readers.

---

1. John's account refers to the Feast of Dedication instead of the Festival of Dedication (see John 10:22). Frequently, festivals were times of joy and celebration and often included feasts. Scholars today generally refer to Israelite feasts as festivals. (See *HarperCollins Bible Dictionary*, s.v. "festivals and feasts"; Smith, *Bible Dictionary*, s.v. "feasts"; "festivals.")

2. Biblical scholars are not certain when the incidents discussed in this chapter occurred. Farrar placed these events after Jesus was first rejected at Samaria (see Farrar, *Life of Christ*, p. 415). Edersheim placed these events later, after the Feast of Dedication and Jesus's time in Ephraim but before His final journey to Jerusalem (see Edersheim, *Life and Times of Jesus the Messiah*, p. 701). Talmage observed, "Many writers treat this occurrence as having immediately followed the repulse of Jesus and the apostles in a certain Samaritan village (Luke 9:52–56). We give it place in the order followed by Luke, the sole recorder of the two incidents" (Talmage, *Jesus the Christ*, p. 439). Luke's chronology is followed in this volume's discussion of these events.

Though many details are unknown, while Jesus and some of His disciples traveled through Galilee, they may have paid a brief visit to their families and friends and joined with other disciples who would journey with Jesus to Jerusalem. Further, as Jesus traveled, He was likely followed by multitudes. According to the scriptural record, as He traveled He healed ten lepers, taught of the importance of humble prayer, invited little children to come to Him, taught a rich young ruler, and taught of sacrifice.

Jesus Heals Ten Lepers (Luke 17:11–19)

Luke records that as Jesus traveled, He stopped at an unnamed village. In the village, a group of ten lepers asked Jesus to heal them. The following is Luke's account:

> **Luke 17:11–19.** And it came to pass, as he went to Jerusalem, that he passed through the midst of Samaria and Galilee. And as he entered into a certain village, there met him ten men that were lepers, which stood afar off: and they lifted up their voices, and said, Jesus, Master, have mercy on us. And when he saw them, he said unto them, Go shew yourselves unto the priests. And it came to pass, that, as they went, they were cleansed. And one of them, when he saw that he was healed, turned back, and with a loud voice glorified God, and fell down on his face at his feet, giving him thanks: and he was a Samaritan. And Jesus answering said, Were there not ten cleansed? but where are the nine? There are not found that returned to give glory to God, save this stranger. And he said unto him, Arise, go thy way: thy faith hath made thee whole.

Those with leprosy often congregated because they were outcasts. The ten lepers likely had varying degrees of this serious and dreaded disease. Their limbs and faces likely had the characteristic white ulcers and skin lesions. Some may have lost fingers or toes, and their faces may have become disfigured. Likely, all had covered their bodies with clothing to avoid the embarrassment of the disease. Because of their affliction, they were not permitted to come close to anyone without leprosy. They were also required to wear torn clothes, keep their heads uncovered, and wear a covering on the upper lip. To warn others not to approach, the lepers were required to cry, "Unclean, unclean."[3]

---

3. See Lev. 13:45.

When the ten lepers saw Jesus coming, they asked Him to have mercy on them. They had presumably heard of Him healing others with physical afflictions and hoped for a similar miracle.

In response, He told them to go to the priests. According to Jewish law, priests had the authority to declare that those who had been healed of leprosy were clean. Lepers were required to approach a priest individually, not as a group.[4] Thus, Jesus had directed that the ten lepers report to multiple priests to formally be pronounced clean. As Edersheim explained, "Any priest might declare 'unclean' or 'clean' provided the applicants presented themselves singly, and not in company, for his inspection."[5]

As the lepers obediently and faithfully started toward where they might find priests, the lepers were healed. The scriptural record gives no indication that Jesus gave traditional healing blessings at that time. The healing occurred for all of them as they exercised faith by obediently following the Savior's direction. Dummelow observed, "The Jews probably went to Jerusalem, because of the necessary sacrifices; the Samaritan to Mt. Gerizim, unless we are to suppose that he became a Jewish proselyte. . . . The healing was delayed to test their faith."[6]

Only one of them, a Samaritan, returned to Jesus.[7] The man then praised God and thanked Jesus for the miracle. Addressing the man, Jesus asked where the other nine lepers were. Only the one man, whom Jesus called a stranger—indicating the man was a Samaritan and not of the house of Israel—had returned to thank God for the miraculous healing. There are several possible reasons why the nine other lepers did not return to express thanks for the miracle that changed their lives. Perhaps all ten lepers believed that Jesus could perform such a miracle but only the one believed that Jesus was the promised Messiah. It is also possible that the lepers who were Jews were so accustomed to obeying the letter of the law—in this case, Jesus's instruction to go to the priests—that they simply did not remember to give thanks or they wanted to perfectly follow Jesus's direction. Alternatively,

---

4. See Edersheim, *Life and Times of Jesus the Messiah*, p. 702.

5. Edersheim, *Life and Times of Jesus the Messiah*, p. 702.

6. Dummelow, *Bible Commentary*, p. 762.

7. Based on the wording of the account, most biblical scholars assume that only one of the ten lepers was a Samaritan.

giving thanks may have been inconvenient. Or perhaps the failure to return and express thanks reflected the culture of ingratitude among the Jews at the time.[8] Another reason may be pride. Whatever the reason, they did not take the time and make the effort to return and give thanks for the great miracle that Christ freely gave them.

Much in this account points to the Savior and His atoning sacrifice. The men were cleansed from the loathsome disease of leprosy, just as Christ's Atonement cleanses those who repent from the loathsome disease of sin. At least one of the lepers whom Jesus healed was a Samaritan, signifying that the Savior's atoning sacrifice is for all, regardless of their lineage. Additionally, when the Samaritan returned, he "fell down on his face" before Jesus; similarly, Jesus fell down[9] during the awful agony of the Atonement and prayed to God. Further, the Samaritan worshipped Christ, and Christ had previously taught about the need to worship God in prayer.[10] The Samaritan also demonstrated humility and a contrite spirit as he fell down on his face when thanking Jesus.

The paramount lesson that can be learned from this account is the importance of showing gratitude to God and to Christ for all They have done. In the latter days, the Lord has said: "And in nothing doth man offend God, or against none is his wrath kindled, save those who confess not his hand in all things, and obey not his commandments."[11] Recognizing and appreciating both what God has given and the help that others provide are ways of perceiving the good in life. When gratitude is a core part of a person's character, he or she can more easily avoid pride and arrogance in whatever form they may take. People sometimes wrongfully think that all they have acquired has come solely through their own efforts. Because of pride, they have forgotten that God caused the earth to be created for His children and that all they have and are ultimately come from Him.

The Lord has said, "Thou shalt thank the Lord thy God in all things."[12] Giving thanks to God is more than a routine or hollow exercise; rather,

---

8. It could be similarly said that people today live in a culture of ingratitude.

9. See Matt. 26:39.

10. See Matt. 6:9; Luke 11:2.

11. D&C 59:21.

12. D&C 59:7; see also D&C 46:32; 88:33; 1 Thess. 5:18.

giving thanks is a commandment and should involve deep sincerity. Giving thanks builds character and helps define who one is. For example, consider how important it is for individuals to meaningfully express gratitude daily for the food they have to eat and to remember its ultimate source. Some come to realize they should give thanks for even the adversities that beset them. Facing adversity with faith and with thanksgiving for blessings given helps people increase their spiritual strength. A person's deepest gratitude should be for the Father's plan of salvation, which includes the Atonement and Resurrection of Christ; this plan forms the foundation upon which all gospel truths reside and enables eternal progression.

Sometimes people have a tendency to take good things for granted and to become ungrateful when challenges arise. The importance of being grateful during trials is highlighted in the inspiring hymn "Count Your Many Blessings":[13]

> When upon life's billows you are tempest-tossed,
> When you are discouraged, thinking all is lost,
> Count your many blessings; name them one by one,
> And it will surprise you what the Lord has done.
> Are you ever burdened with a load of care?
> Does the cross seem heavy you are called to bear?
> Count your many blessings; ev'ry doubt will fly,
> And you will be singing as the days go by.

Of the ten lepers healed by the word of Christ, only one paused to give humble thanks. His faith, not in the miracle alone but in Christ as the divine Son of God, made him whole.

Jesus Teaches about the Importance of Praying Humbly (Luke 18:9–14)

During the journey to Jerusalem, Jesus told a parable to individuals who, as Luke records, deemed themselves righteous and looked down upon others. Presumably, the individuals had high opinions of themselves, likely in part

---

13. *Hymns*, no. 241, vv. 1 and 2 (lyrics by Thomas Ken).

because they obeyed the rabbinical law and looked to that law for salvation. The following is Luke's account:

Luke 18:9–14. And he spake this parable unto certain which trusted in themselves that they were righteous, and despised others: Two men went up into the temple to pray; the one a Pharisee, and the other a publican. The Pharisee stood and prayed thus with himself, God, I thank thee, that I am not as other men are, extortioners, unjust, adulterers, or even as this publican. I fast twice in the week, I give tithes of all that I possess. And the publican, standing afar off, would not lift up so much as his eyes unto heaven, but smote upon his breast, saying, God be merciful to me a sinner. I tell you, this man went down to his house justified rather than the other: for every one that exalteth himself shall be abased; and he that humbleth himself shall be exalted.

This parable speaks not of unrighteousness but, rather, of self-righteousness, which manifests as pride and also as contempt for others.[14] The setting presented in the parable was the temple. Generally, the temple was a place to make sacrifices and to privately pray,[15] the latter of which the Pharisee and publican in this parable were doing at the temple.

In the parable, the self-righteous Pharisee stood to pray; he did not kneel. He prayed "with himself," not to God. The Pharisee began his prayer by separating himself from other worshippers, whom he considered less worthy. Presumably, he prayed not to sincerely commune with God but to say to himself and possibly to any others who heard that he was a righteous man. He expressed gratitude that he was not like others, such as extortioners, those who are unjust, adulterers, and publicans.[16] He also said that he fasted twice each week[17] and paid tithes on all that he owned. His prayer was not one of true gratitude but of boastfulness.

---

14. See Edersheim, *Life and Times of Jesus the Messiah*, p. 675.

15. See Edersheim, *Life and Times of Jesus the Messiah*, p. 675.

16. See also Alma 31:17–18.

17. In the Sermon on the Mount, Jesus taught, "And when thou prayest, thou shalt not be as the hypocrites are: for they love to pray standing in the synagogues and in the corners of the streets, that they may be seen of men. Verily I say unto you, They have their reward." (Matt. 6:5.)

Apparently, this prideful Pharisee thought he was doing all that was required—and possibly even more than required—by the rabbinical law to gain eternal life.

Thus, he may have thought that God owed him blessings because he was righteous and did more than the law required. He may have also wanted others to hear him boast about his righteousness.

The Pharisee presumably separated himself from the publican and other similar worshippers. His prayer was really one of boasting and not one of true and humble thanksgiving.

Conversely, the publican, whom the Jews considered unrighteous by virtue of his profession and perhaps his lifestyle, presumably did not come to the temple to be seen of others and did not feel worthy to mingle with those who appeared to be more righteous than he. He was deeply humble, acknowledging his sins, and consequently would not even look toward heaven. Rather, he hit his chest and asked God to be merciful, as was the Jewish custom on the Day of Atonement.[18]

After describing the publican's prayer, Jesus gave the moral of the parable: "This man [the publican] went down to his house justified rather than the other: for every one that exalteth himself shall be abased; and he that humbleth himself shall be exalted."

Jesus Continues toward Jerusalem (Matt. 19:1–2; Mark 10:1)

As Jesus continued on His journey, He stopped in "the coasts of Judaea." Judea is located on the west side of the Jordan River, and the reference to coasts implies that Jesus may have been somewhat close to the river, which divided Perea from Judea. Matthew recorded the following about Christ's activities in this area:

Matthew 19:1–2. And it came to pass, that when Jesus had finished these sayings, he departed from Galilee, and came into the coasts of Judaea beyond Jordan; and great multitudes followed him; and he healed them there.

---

18. It was customary among some Pharisees to fast every Monday and Thursday. These days were also when those who resided outside of the city came to trade goods in the market and to participate in special services in the synagogues, meaning that the Pharisees' fasting would be seen by more people than if the Pharisees had fasted on other days. (See Edersheim, *Life and Times of Jesus the Messiah*, p. 677.)

Wherever Jesus went, multitudes followed Him. Mark's record states that while in Judea, Jesus taught and healed people and that many believed His words.[19] Though the Gospel writers did not describe in detail Jesus's teachings and miracles, they surely touched the lives of those who were present and those who heard accounts afterward.

Jesus Invites Children to Come to Him (Matt. 19:13–15; Mark 10:13–16; Luke 18:15–17)

On a separate occasion, young children were brought to Jesus so they could share a moment with Him and receive a blessing at His hands. Luke's record of this incident states: "And they brought unto him also infants."[20] Presumably, the children were brought by mothers—mothers who wanted the best for their children. What more could mothers hope for than that their children receive blessings from Jesus, an act that might set these children on the proper course for their lives. Those who brought the children likely had previously been in Christ's presence and had felt His divine spirit. They might have then discussed how their children could experience the same. All three synoptic Gospel writers recorded this tender event. The following is Mark's account:

> **Mark 10:13–16.** And they brought young children to him, that he should touch them: and his disciples rebuked those that brought them. But when Jesus saw it, he was much displeased, and said unto them, Suffer the little children to come unto me, and forbid them not: for of such is the kingdom of God. Verily I say unto you, Whosoever shall not receive the kingdom of God as a little child, he shall not enter therein. And he took them up in his arms, put his hands upon them, and blessed them.

Upon seeing the children coming toward Jesus, the disciples rebuked those who brought the children. There may be several reasons for the rebuke. The zealous disciples perhaps believed that the children's visit would disrupt Jesus's travels and His opportunity to teach others. Perhaps the disciples thought, as was common at the time, that children (and women) were of a lower social position than were men. The disciples may also have believed

---

19. See Mark 10:1; see also JST Matt. 19:2.
20. Luke 18:15.

that bringing children to Jesus for blessings was presumptuous. An additional reason is presented in Joseph Smith's inspired translation of Matthew 19:13: "The disciples rebuked them saying, There is no need, for Jesus hath said, Such shall be saved."[21] This addition clarifies that the disciples were not being harsh but were explaining that children did not need to be blessed in order to obtain exaltation. Whatever the reasons for the disciples' rebuke, those who brought the children surely loved them and desired that Jesus bless them. Likewise, Jesus loved the children, and He did bless them.

It is not known what instruction Jesus may have previously given the disciples regarding little children. However, presumably He had taught principles that are recorded in the Book of Mormon. For example, the prophet Abinadi taught that "little children also have eternal life," and the prophet Mormon further explained this precept by stating, "And their little children need no repentance, neither baptism. Behold, baptism is unto repentance to the fulfilling the commandments unto the remission of sins. But little children are alive in Christ, even from the foundation of the world; if not so, God is a partial God, and also a changeable God, and a respecter to persons; for how many little children have died without baptism!"[22]

When Jesus saw the disciples rebuking those who had brought the children to Him, He was "much displeased." He then said that children should not be forbidden from coming to Him, "for of such is the kingdom of God." These little children were pure, and Jesus had taught in His Sermon on the Mount that the pure in heart will "see God."[23] Jesus then affirmed that all must be as little children in order to receive the kingdom of God. Little children are not only pure but also humble. Jesus had taught in the Sermon on the Mount that the humble (i.e., "poor in spirit") will enter the kingdom of heaven.[24]

And then Jesus held and blessed each child. This tender account is not just about children collectively but also about each child. Presumably, Jesus gave each child a blessing tailored to the child's strengths and weaknesses, as well as the opportunities and challenges the child would experience

---

21. Matt. 10:13.
22. Mosiah 15:25; Moro. 8:11–12.
23. Matt. 5:8.
24. See Matt. 5:3.

during life. As Jesus prayed, tears must have filled the eyes of those who had brought the children. Each child who received a blessing and was old enough would likely remember the event for the rest of his or her life. Those too young to remember their blessings were likely reminded of them later by family members. How would parents today feel if they witnessed the Messiah hold their children? How would these parents feel as they heard Him give a blessing to each of their children?

Today, children are blessed in The Church of Jesus Christ of Latter-day Saints. The blessings are not given by Christ but are given in His name by those who hold the proper priesthood authority. Just as Jesus's blessing of the little children was a tender experience, it is likewise a tender experience for a worthy father, grandfather, brother, or other male to bless a little one under inspiration from heaven. And it is just as tender a moment for each mother and others hearing the prayer.

Jesus Teaches a Rich Young Ruler (Matt. 19:16–26; Mark 10:17–27; Luke 18:18–27)

While Jesus and His disciples were leaving the place they had been staying,[25] a young man[26] of great wealth and of high position among the Jews came to Jesus. This young man seems to have realized that if Jesus left before the man could talk with Him, the man might miss an opportunity to gain greater insight regarding what he needed to do to gain eternal life. This event is recorded in all three synoptic Gospels. The following is Mark's account:

> **Mark 10:17–27.** And when he [Jesus] was gone forth into the way, there came one running, and kneeled to him, and asked him, Good Master, what shall I do that I may inherit eternal life? And Jesus said unto him, Why callest thou me good? there is none good but one, that is, God. Thou knowest the commandments, Do not commit adultery, Do not kill, Do not steal, Do not bear false witness, Defraud not, Honour thy father and mother. And he answered and said unto him, Master, all these have I observed from my youth. Then Jesus beholding him loved him, and said unto him, One thing thou lackest: go thy way, sell whatsoever thou hast, and give to the poor, and

---

25. See Edersheim, *Life and Times of Jesus the Messiah*, p. 708.
26. See Matt. 19:20.

thou shalt have treasure in heaven: and come, take up the cross, and follow me. And he was sad at that saying, and went away grieved: for he had great possessions. And Jesus looked round about, and saith unto his disciples, How hardly shall they that have riches enter into the kingdom of God! And the disciples were astonished at his words. But Jesus answereth again, and saith unto them, Children, how hard is it for them that trust in riches to enter into the kingdom of God! It is easier for a camel to go through the eye of a needle, than for a rich man to enter into the kingdom of God. And they were astonished out of measure, saying among themselves, Who then can be saved? And Jesus looking upon them saith, With men it is impossible, but not with God: for with God all things are possible.

The young man ran to Jesus; he did not walk or wait for Jesus to pass by. Presumably he desired to know his standing before God and Christ and what he needed to do to gain eternal life. He was also humble in that he immediately knelt before Jesus. It does not appear that the man was attempting to trap Jesus as the Pharisees had repeatedly tried to do. Rather, it seems that he sincerely wanted to improve and that he respected Jesus as one who might help him in his quest. The question asked, however, may have been born of the Jewish teaching that eternal life is gained solely by obedience to the law of Moses as interpreted by the rabbis, for the young man asked what he should do, not what he lacked in character. Or he may have sincerely wanted to know how he needed to improve his character in order to inherit eternal life.

Whatever the young man's motivation, Christ began by stating that the young man needed to look to and learn from God, who is the embodiment of good. In contrast to philosophers, who have debated what is good and what is bad, Christ simply pointed to His Father as the ultimate embodiment of goodness. The young man could ask the Father in prayer to help him identify what his character lacked. Learning to ask God was important because Jesus would be with the man for only a few minutes, whereas the young man presumably would live for many years to come and certainly would experience many challenges that could help him refine his character. If the young man learned to continually seek help from his Father in Heaven through prayer, the Father would give liberally.[27]

---

27. See James 1:5–7.

Moreover, Jesus may have responded in this manner because He did not want to accept the title of "Good Master" (i.e., good rabbi), which the young man gave Him. Jesus was the divine Son of God and not merely a respected teacher.

Jesus then referred to keeping the Ten Commandments, which had been divinely given. Jesus may have wanted the man to reflect on the level of his obedience so that he would be better prepared to receive what Jesus would next teach. Obedience to some commandments, such as not committing adultery or murder and not bearing false witness or stealing, is clear-cut. Other commandments, such as dealing honestly with others and honoring one's parents, can be obeyed to varying degrees. Despite the degrees of obedience possible, the young man stated that he had observed all of the commandments from the time he was a child. He apparently had tried to keep all of the commandments.

The record states that because of the young man's reply, Jesus loved him. In loving the young man, Jesus was teaching a lesson. This type of love changes hearts and lives; this love is the type needed when ministering in the Lord's kingdom. Jesus presumably saw who this young man really was and what he could become, including a valiant servant in the kingdom of God.

Having heard that the young man diligently kept the commandments, Jesus identified one area in which he could improve—one thing he lacked in character. Jesus directed the young man to sell what he had and give the proceeds to the poor so that he could receive heavenly treasures. Jesus was implicitly teaching of the sacrifice required to be numbered among His disciples. Jesus's direction was for the young man and should not be applied to all; nevertheless, all can learn from this counsel about sacrificing for the kingdom of God rather than focusing on gaining material wealth, political or ecclesiastical station, or public accolades.

In all, Jesus asked the young man to do three things. First, Jesus asked the young man to sell all that he owned. Part of his wealth may have consisted of his home and other assets that may have enabled him not to work. One can only imagine the deep impact Jesus's direction may have had on this young man as he undoubtedly catalogued in his mind the nature and extent of his assets and what his life would be without them, especially if he was married and had children.

Second, Jesus asked the young man to "give to the poor," many of whom may have been in desperate need of food and warm clothing.[28] If the man helped meet the needs of the poor, perhaps by providing a blanket, warm clothes, or money to buy food, his life may have been changed eternally. Third, Jesus asked the young man to take up his cross and follow Jesus. For so doing, this young man would receive eternal treasures in heaven.

The young man may have wondered whether the sacrifices Jesus asked him to make were worth the promised reward. Because he was a wealthy ruler,[29] he likely had high status among the Jews. If he sold all that he had and gave to the poor, he would then be without wealth or material possessions. In addition, if he had a wife and children, he likely considered how difficult it would be to take away their home and other assets and then leave them to follow Jesus, if only for a short while. In addition, taking up his cross involved forsaking all his sins and committing to serve the Lord forever.

For the young man to follow Christ, he needed to do more than just accompany Him from city to city and village to village as He declared His gospel and His witness that He was the Son of God. Following Christ meant learning of His teachings and making them part of the young man's life. It meant learning of Christ's goodness, holiness, unbounding love, mercy, and tenderness and then trying to incorporate these traits in his own life. Following Christ would have also meant that the young man would have to be Jesus's valiant and unwavering witness thereafter.

The young man now had to decide whether he was willing to sacrifice all he had, give to the poor, take up his cross, and follow the Lord. Taking up his cross and following Jesus meant bearing the burden of discipleship even unto death if necessary, just as Jesus would soon voluntarily give up His life.

As the young man considered Jesus's requests, he was sorrowful; he apparently did not want to give up his many possessions. Consequently, he decided to leave, feeling sadness and grief. It is unknown whether he later became a disciple of Jesus or whether he forever foreclosed that opportunity for the sake of riches and high status. Hopefully his encounter with Christ

28. Jesus spoke to the young man at some point shortly before the Feast of Dedication, which was on the twenty-fifth of Chislev. This month corresponds with part of November and December. (See *HarperCollins Bible Dictionary*, s.v. "Dedication, Festival of.")
29. See Luke 18:18.

burned within him and in time he decided to be counted among the valiant followers of Christ.

Deep within, all people know that they are lacking in something—and perhaps many things—in terms of their character. What the young man lacked was a willingness to sacrifice wealth and position in order to follow Christ. Others may lack a willingness to give up certain sins or addictions. Yet others may lack a commitment to attend church or fulfill callings or other responsibilities. Each person can profit by humbly asking God in prayer, "What lack I?" As the Lord told Moroni, "And if men come unto me I will show unto them their weakness. I give unto men weakness that they may be humble; and my grace is sufficient for all men that humble themselves before me; for if they humble themselves before me, and have faith in me, then will I make weak things become strong unto them."[30]

Jesus then turned to His disciples and stated, "How hardly shall they that have riches enter into the kingdom of God!" The disciples were amazed at Jesus's words and may have wondered whether a rich person could ever be good enough to be accepted into the kingdom of heaven. However, Jesus's use of the word *hardly* left room for hope. Jesus then clarified his statement by adding, "How hard is it for them that *trust* in riches to enter into the kingdom of God!" (italics added). Jesus was teaching that no matter a person's wealth or position, his or her trust must always be in God, not in temporal things.

Referencing a common proverb, Jesus then said: "It is easier for a camel to go through the eye of a needle, than for a rich man to enter into the kingdom of God." The phrase "eye of a needle" likely refers to a small side gate for a city.[31] A camel could not pass through this gate without being unburdened of any goods it carried. All people, including the wealthy and those with prominent positions, need to likewise be unburdened of pride and learn to sacrifice all in order to enter the kingdom of God.

The disciples were again amazed and wondered, "Who then can be saved?" Jesus understood their concerns and in effect explained that people cannot by themselves rise above trusting in riches but that with God's

---

30. Ether 12:27; see also D&C 121:34–36.
31. See Farrar, *Life of Christ*, p. 452; Dummelow, *Bible Commentary*, pp. 689–690.

help, nothing is impossible. As part of God's plan for His children, the Atonement of His Only Begotten Son can help people become righteous. As the prophet Moroni said, the Lord's grace is sufficient for all people who humble themselves before Him and have faith in Him.[32]

In the latter days, people may be particularly at risk of prioritizing riches over the kingdom of God because prosperity is greater today than at any time in the history of the world. Therefore, people today would do well to ask themselves and God, over and over again, how they can better serve in the kingdom of God.

Sacrificing for the Kingdom of God Brings Everlasting Life (Matt. 19:27–30; Mark 10:28–31; Luke 18:28–30)

Following the Lord's discussion with the rich young man, Peter asked what reward the Apostles would receive for forsaking all. The following is Matthew's account:

> **Matthew 19:27–30.** Then answered Peter and said unto him, Behold, we have forsaken all, and followed thee; what shall we have therefore? And Jesus said unto them, Verily I say unto you, That ye which have followed me, in the regeneration when the Son of man shall sit in the throne of his glory, ye also shall sit upon twelve thrones, judging the twelve tribes of Israel. And every one that hath forsaken houses, or brethren, or sisters, or father, or mother, or wife, or children, or lands, for my name's sake, shall receive an hundredfold, and shall inherit everlasting life. But many that are first shall be last; and the last shall be first.

The Apostles had given up their employment, had left their families, and had followed Jesus for over two and a half years. He explained that because of their sacrifices, after He was resurrected and sat on a throne of glory, the Apostles would sit on twelve thrones and judge the twelve tribes of Israel. One can only wonder at the thoughts that must have flooded the Apostles' minds as they contemplated both the glory that awaited them in the world to come and the great weight of responsibility involved in being judges of all of Israel. It is one thing to be a judge over matters of a material nature;

---

32. See Ether 12:26–27.

it is an entirely different matter to be the judge of people's lives and help determine their worthiness.

Jesus then added that those who forsake homes, land, or family for His sake will receive blessings "an hundredfold, and shall inherit everlasting life."

Next, Jesus gave the Apostles a larger view of how the gospel would go forth in the latter days, explaining that "many that are first shall be last; and the last shall be first." Jesus was teaching that in the latter days, the gospel would first go to the Gentiles and then would go to the Jews.[33] He presumably wanted His Apostles and disciples to know that His gospel was not just for their time but for all times and that He would reign in heaven with the glory given Him by the Father.

Jesus's teachings discussed in this chapter should prompt all people to seriously consider their standing before God and then ponder their answer to the potentially life-changing question "What lack I?"

---

33. See chapter 42 of this book.

Chapter 46

JESUS TEACHES AT THE TEMPLE AND GIVES THE PARABLE OF LABORERS IN THE VINEYARD

After spending about two months teaching and healing in Perea and Judea and possibly spending a short time in Galilee, Jesus returned to Jerusalem to attend the Festival of Dedication (today known as Hanukkah).[1] After Jesus left this festival, He once again traveled to Perea near where John had baptized followers. Jesus also gave the parable of the laborers in the vineyard in order to further instruct His Apostles and disciples.

Jesus Teaches at the Temple during the Festival of Dedication (John 10:22–42)

As with other Jewish festivals, the Festival of Dedication was a time of rejoicing, celebrating, thanking God for blessings, and asking Him to provide relief for the poor and oppressed. This festival and others were often accompanied by instrumental music, singing, dancing, elaborate meals, and sacrifices.[2] The Festival of Dedication was celebrated each year beginning on the twenty-fifth day of Chislev,[3] which corresponds with November to December.[4] Jesus was not obligated by the law to attend this festival since it

---

1. The Festival of Dedication was established in 164 BC to celebrate the rededication of the temple of Zerubbabel (the second temple) and its altar after Judas Maccabeus had driven out the Syrians (see Smith, *Bible Dictionary*, s.v. "Dedication, Feast of;" see also *HarperCollins Bible Dictionary*, s.v. "festivals and feasts;" notes 1–5 at the end of this chapter).
2. See *HarperCollins Bible Dictionary*, s.v., "festivals and feasts."
3. This month is also called Kislev, Cisleu, and Chisleu (see Zech. 7:1).
4. See *HarperCollins Bible Dictionary*, s.v. "calendar."

was not one of the three great feasts that required Israelite males to go to the temple in Jerusalem.[5] Rather, He went to give the Jews in Jerusalem further witness that He was the Son of God.

The Gospel of John contains the only account of Jesus's attendance at the Festival of Dedication in Jerusalem:[6]

> **John 10:22–42.** And it was at Jerusalem the feast of the dedication, and it was winter. And Jesus walked in the temple in Solomon's porch. Then came the Jews round about him, and said unto him, How long dost thou make us to doubt? If thou be the Christ, tell us plainly. Jesus answered them, I told you, and ye believed not: the works that I do in my Father's name, they bear witness of me. But ye believe not, because ye are not of my sheep, as I said unto you. My sheep hear my voice, and I know them, and they follow me: And I give unto them eternal life; and they shall never perish, neither shall any man pluck them out of my hand. My Father, which gave them me, is greater than all; and no man is able to pluck them out of my Father's hand. I and my Father are one. Then the Jews took up stones again to stone him. Jesus answered them, Many good works have I shewed you from my Father; for which of those works do ye stone me? The Jews answered him, saying, For a good work we stone thee not; but for blasphemy; and because that thou, being a man, makest thyself God. Jesus answered them, Is it not written in your law, I said, Ye are gods? If he called them gods, unto whom the word of God came, and the scripture cannot be broken; say ye of him, whom the Father hath sanctified, and sent into the world, Thou blasphemest; because I said, I am the Son of God? If I do not the works of my Father, believe me not. But if I do, though ye believe not me, believe the works: that ye may know, and believe, that the Father is in me, and I in him. Therefore they sought again to take him: but he escaped out of their hand, and went away again beyond Jordan into the place where John at first baptized; and there he abode. And many resorted unto him, and said, John did no miracle: but all things that John spake of this man were true. And many believed on him there.

---

5. These three great feasts were the Feast of Unleavened Bread (Passover); the Feast of Weeks, also known as the Feast of Ingathering or Pentecost; and the Feast of Tabernacles (see *HarperCollins Bible Dictionary*, s.v. "festivals and feasts"). In addition to these feasts and the Festival of Dedication, the Jews held other feasts, such as the Feast of First Fruits, the Feast of Trumpets, the Feast of Atonement (Yom Kippur), and Purim.

6. John is the Gospel writer who included the most accounts of Jesus while in Jerusalem.

John's record indicates that Jesus was walking in Solomon's Porch in the temple. Because the festival occurred during the winter, it was likely cold in the temple courts. Solomon's Porch is assumed to be a covered area that contained columns and that opened onto the temple's outer court, also known as the Women's Court, and was likely located on the east side, facing the Mount of Olives.[7]

During the festival, many people were likely in the temple courts, including Solomon's Porch. It is unknown whether any of Jesus's disciples accompanied Him; however, because the Apostle John recorded the account, he and possibly other Apostles and disciples may have been with Jesus.

Although it is impossible to know Jesus's thoughts at that time, considering what they may have been can help bring to life what transpired. As Jesus walked in the temple courts, He may have contemplated that the temple was His and His Father's house. He may have contemplated the reason for the festival: it was a celebration of the temple's rededication following its defilement by Antiochus IV Epiphanes. He may have thought about how the temple had been and continued to be polluted by the greedy money changers, corrupt priests, and other corrupt Jewish leaders. He may have contemplated the lighted menorah in the temple and in every home during this eight-day festival and may have then thought about His teaching that He was the Light of the World.

He may also have contemplated the events that would transpire in Jerusalem just a few months hence, including His atoning sacrifice amid the olive trees in Gethsemane. He may have pondered His coming Crucifixion and His glorious Resurrection. He may also have gazed at the Mount of Olives, from where He would ascend to His Father after teaching His disciples for forty days following His death.[8] Further, He may have contemplated the people of Jerusalem, feeling sadness because many had rejected Him. He knew He would be rejected again. Perhaps when John indicated that Jesus

---

7. See *HarperCollins Bible Dictionary*, s.v. "Solomon's Portico." According to Josephus, Solomon's Court "was a portion of Solomon's Temple, which had been left standing by Nebuchadnezzar"; however, many modern scholars question Josephus's claim (see Dummelow, *Bible Commentary*, p. 792).

8. See Acts 1:9, 12.

was in Solomon's Porch in the winter, John was referring not only to the temperature but also to the cold hearts of many of the Jews.

While Jesus was in Solomon's Porch, He was confronted by certain Jews, presumably leaders and perhaps even members of the Sanhedrin. They claimed they were uncertain about who He really was, and they asked Him to tell them "plainly" whether He was the Christ. It is possible that some of these Jews were sincere in their request; however, given the events that followed, it is likely that many of them wanted Jesus to clearly declare that He was the Christ so that they could accuse Him of blasphemy and consequently seek to have Him killed. Of course, Satan was at the heart of this desire, and he wanted more than anything to thwart the Father's plan, including Christ's atoning sacrifice. The words these Jews used—"If thou be the Christ"—were similar to the words of temptation Satan used at the beginning of Christ's ministry more than two and a half years earlier.

Jesus responded to the Jews by stating that He had already declared (perhaps to these very Jews) who He was but that they had not believed. He then declared that the way He lived, what He taught, and the miracles He performed bore witness of Him but that these Jews had refused to believe. Rather than seeing God's hand in Christ's miracles, these Jews claimed the miracles were performed by the power of Beelzebub. These Jews had unbelieving hearts and impure motives.

Jesus then told these Jews that they did not believe Him because they were not His sheep. In contrast, Jesus's sheep heard His voice and followed Him. Jesus further told these questioning Jews that He would give eternal life to those who believe in Him and follow Him and that they would not perish, be taken from Him, or falter. Jesus likewise affirmed that no one could take the disciples from the Father, for the Father "is greater than all." As Dummelow pointed out, "No power of the world or of Satan can pluck believers out of Christ's hand; only their own unfaithfulness to grace received can do this. The Father is superior to all hostile powers, and therefore believers can never be lost through the power of the enemy."[9]

The truth of Jesus's statement is evident in the fact that following His death, neither the Jews nor the Romans could cause those who truly believed

---

9. Dummelow, *Bible Commentary*, p. 792.

in Christ to abandon Him, even when they faced martyrdom. Likewise, neither humans nor the power of Satan could stop Christ from atoning for the world, and because of the Atonement, those who believe in Christ, follow Him, and endure to the end will receive eternal life.

Jesus then declared, "I and my Father are one." In some other versions of the Bible, this verse is stated as "the Father and I are one,"[10] placing the Father before the Son. The *NIV Study Bible* gives the following explanation regarding the use of the word *one* in this verse: "The Greek is neuter—'one thing,' not 'one person.' The two are one in essence or nature, but they are not identical persons. This great truth is what warrants Jesus' 'I am' declarations (see [John] 8:24, 28, 58 and note on [John] 6:35; see also [John] 17:21–22)."[11] Regarding Jesus's declaration, Edersheim stated: "Rightly understood, it is not only the last and highest announcement, but it contains and implies everything else. If the Work of Christ is really that of the Father, and His Working also that of the Father, then it follows that He 'and the Father are One' ('one' is in the neuter). This identity of work (and purpose) implies the identity of Nature (Essence); that of working, the identity of power."[12] In addition, Talmage wrote: "The reference to what had been before told was a reminder of His teachings on the occasion of an earlier sojourn among them, when He had proclaimed Himself as the I AM, who was older and greater than Abraham, and of His other proclamation of Himself as the Good Shepherd."[13] Of course, Christ and His Father are one in purpose, not one physically.[14]

Jesus was the divine Son of God, born of Mary in Bethlehem. Jesus was conceived by the "power of God"[15] and was of the Father. In addition, Jesus was subject to His Father,[16] and Jesus's will was "swallowed up in the will of the Father."[17] Under the direction of the Father, Jesus created this earth, and He subjected Himself to becoming mortal, in part that He might better

---

10. See, for example, the New Jerusalem Bible and the New Revised Standard Bible.
11. *NIV Study Bible*, p. 1614.
12. Edersheim, *Life and Teachings of Jesus the Messiah*, p. 634.
13. Talmage, *Jesus the Christ*, p. 456.
14. See John 17:20–23.
15. Mosiah 15:3.
16. See Mosiah 15:5.
17. Mosiah 15:7.

understand how to succor all. According to the Father's plan, Jesus atoned for the sins of all and brought about the resurrection of all humankind. Throughout His mortal ministry, He was taught and directed by the Father. Jesus and the Father are indeed one in nature and purpose.

Christ's declaration of being one with the Father is worth reflecting on over and over again. It points to the Father's plan of salvation for each of His children and to Christ's Atonement as part of that plan. Christ supported this plan in the premortal world. His declaration is the central message of Jesus's encounter with the Jews in Solomon's Porch and can give all people hope.

The Jews at least partially understood what Christ meant when He declared that "I and my Father are one," for they took up stones with the intention of killing Him. Jesus then asked them to identify which of His good works was the reason they desired to stone Him. Though Jesus's miracles testified of the Father and of Jesus as the Son of God, these Jews had chosen not to believe. They responded that the reason they intended to stone Him was not that He had performed miracles but "that thou, being a man, makest thyself God." Jesus stood before them as a man. It was winter, and He was likely cold, as they likely were, and He walked and talked as they did. They were ignorant of His birth in Bethlehem of Judea, the location where the Messiah was prophesied to be born. He had not come with power to overthrow their oppressors, as they had assumed that the Messiah would. They thought He was simply a man. Their hearts were hardened, and they could not spiritually feel Christ's divine nature and authority, nor spiritually discern the many witnesses given. They were not His sheep.

Jesus responded with a scripture from Psalms: "I have said, Ye are gods."[18] This verse refers to ancient Israelite judges being God's representatives and holding His delegated authority.[19] If the Jews did not consider it blasphemy for Jehovah to refer to these judges as gods, how could these Jews accuse Jesus of blasphemy for claiming to be the Son of God? Their inconsistency was obvious; many of these Jews may also have been judges themselves.

The Greek word for *blasphemy* is *blasphēmia*, which means "injurious speaking,"[20] that is, to "injure the reputation of another." Particularly in

18. Psalm 82:6: "I have said, Ye are gods; and all of you are children of the most High."
19. See Edersheim, *Life and Times of Jesus the Messiah*, p. 634.
20. Young, *Analytical Concordance*, s.v. "blasphemy."

the Old Testament, the term *blasphemy* "means showing contempt or a lack of reverence for God."[21] The Lord told Moses, "And he that blasphemeth the name of the Lord, he shall surely be put to death."[22] According to the above definition, Christ's declaration that He was the Son of God and that He and the Father were one was not blasphemy because it did not show contempt or a lack of reverence for God. It was not until New Testament times that blasphemy was interpreted to include "claiming divine attributes for oneself,"[23] as Jesus was doing in stating that He was the Son of God.

How could the long-sought-for Messiah possibly be guilty of blasphemy? Under the rabbinical law, the claim that Jesus had blasphemed could only be sustained if Christ was not the Son of God. Although these Jews thought that Jesus was not the Son of God, notwithstanding His many miracles, they were prepared to stone Him without conducting any meaningful investigation, obtaining the required witnesses, holding the prescribed trial, or obtaining permission from Rome.

Jesus then referred again to His works being a witness of His divinity. In all cases, Jesus's miracles helped those in need and did not bring evil upon the recipients. As a result of Jesus's statement, the Jews needed to claim that Jesus's healing miracles were not good; such a claim was entirely untenable.

Perhaps this discussion of works as a witness of Christ's divinity was the precursor to Jesus raising Lazarus from the grave, which would be another great witness to the Jews that Christ was the Son of God.

Because Jesus had said that He was the Son of God and that the Father was in Him and He was in the Father, the Jews sought to take Him, presumably to bring Him before the Sanhedrin for trial and death, but He escaped by some means. It is possible that Roman representatives were watching the exchange and that the Jews present were frightened because Roman officials had not given approval to kill Him. Or perhaps there was divine intervention because Christ's mortal mission was not yet complete.

The Jews had the scriptures containing prophecies of the coming of Christ. The Jews had the witness of Christ's many miracles, which the Jews could not duplicate. They had the witness of the Spirit of Christ as He stood

---

21. *HarperCollins Bible Dictionary*, s.v. "blasphemy."
22. Lev. 24:16.
23. *HarperCollins Bible Dictionary*, s.v. "blasphemy."

before them and spoke with them, but they could not discern who He was or His divinity. These Jews failed to believe and even sought the life of the Son of God, who came to earth to redeem them and all others. Although the mortal Christ is not on the earth today, people can receive the witness of the Holy Spirit, whose mission is to witness of the Father and the Son[24] and who whispers to the soul. These whispers are often more enduring than a single open vision. Just as the Jews of Jesus's day had agency to choose whether to believe, so do people today.

The Apostle John concluded his account of this event by testifying that everything John the Baptist said of Jesus Christ was true. In testifying of John the Baptist's words, the Apostle John was likewise testifying that Jesus was the Son of God.

Jesus Again in Perea (John 10:40–42)

After the Festival of Dedication, Jesus left Jerusalem and went to the place where John the Baptist first baptized people. The Gospel of John's record is as follows:

> **John 10:40–42.** And [Jesus] went away again beyond Jordan into the place where John at first baptized; and there he abode. And many resorted unto him, and said, John did no miracle: but all things that John spake of this man were true. And many believed on him there.

The Gospels do not record what occurred during the brief time between when Jesus left Jerusalem and arrived where John the Baptist had first baptized.[25] The location was likely in the area of Bethabara in Perea, on the east side of the Jordan River, and was possibly Bethany,[26] which was about two miles from Jerusalem. If Jesus was in Bethany, He may have stayed at the home of His friends Mary, Martha, and Lazarus. The location where John the Baptist first baptized was presumably where or near where Christ began His public ministry by being baptized,[27] demonstrating His commitment to being obedient to His Father's commands and completing His mission

---

24. See D&C 20:27; 2 Ne. 31:18; 3 Ne. 11:32; 1 Cor. 12:3.
25. See Matt. 3:6; Mark 1:5.
26. See Dummelow, *Bible Commentary*, p. 792.
27. See Matt. 3:13; Mark 1:9; John 1:28; see also 1 Ne. 10:9.

on earth.[28] This location was also where John the Baptist had preached to prepare the people to hear Jesus's words.[29] Many who heard John preach were touched by his message of repentance and his witness of the Lamb of God.[30] John's impassioned testimony would perhaps always burn in their hearts. John had sealed his testimony of Christ with his own blood,[31] and Christ likely thought of John as He arrived at this area.

After Jesus arrived, many people came to Him. They remembered John's preaching and believed that his testimony of Jesus was true. The record indicates that many people who came to Jesus at this time "believed on him," which suggests that they had not only heard John the Baptist preach but had also heard Jesus teach. He likely also healed those with afflictions. Jesus's time with these believing individuals was likely tender and a stark contrast with His exchange with the critical, unbelieving Jews in Solomon's Porch.

While in this area, Jesus may have also felt peace because He was away from those in Jerusalem who sought His life. Additionally, He may have reflected on His impending Atonement and death, which would occur approximately three months later.

Parable of Laborers in the Vineyard (Matt. 20:1–16)

At some point in Jesus's ministry, He gave the parable of the laborers in the vineyard.[32] Matthew's Gospel places the parable after Peter asked Jesus, "Behold, we have forsaken all, and followed thee; what shall we have therefore?"[33] Jesus's response is recorded in the final three verses of chapter 19, and then chapter 20 begins with this parable. The parable is directed to the Apostles and all others who are called to sacrifice for Christ's sake.[34] The parable adds dimension to Jesus's response in the final verses of chapter 19. Rather than quoting the entire parable at the

---

28. See 2 Ne. 31:7.
29. See Matt. 3:1–12; Mark 1:2–8; Luke 3:2–18.
30. See Matt. 3:5–6; Mark 1:5; Luke 3:21.
31. See Matt. 14:10–11; Mark 6:27–28.
32. In Matthew's account, this parable follows immediately after and appears to be an outgrowth of Peter's question and Jesus's response in Matthew 19:27–30. However, Matthew's account is not always chronological.
33. Matt. 19:27.
34. See Matt. 19:27–29; Mark 10:29–30; Luke 18:29–30.

beginning of this section, the parable is divided into parts, with each part immediately followed by commentary:

> **Matthew 20:1.** For the kingdom of heaven is like unto a man that is an householder, which went out early in the morning to hire labourers into his vineyard.

As with some of the other parables Christ gave, this parable begins with a glimpse into the kingdom of heaven. Presumably, Jesus was attempting to foster in the Apostles development of the character needed to inherit the kingdom of heaven.

The Apostles knew that it was common for a householder who had fields to go into the marketplace to hire laborers to assist with the required work. In this parable, the householder represents God, the vineyard is His kingdom, and the laborers are His servants. The householder sought laborers early in the morning, presumably at sunrise, which occurred at around six o'clock and was when the workday typically began. Hiring laborers at an early hour implies there was much work to do. The laborers were not the householder's regular employees, nor did they aspire to be. Upon hearing this parable, the Apostles may have remembered Christ's words when He called and ordained them as Apostles: "Ye have not chosen me, but I have chosen you, and ordained you, that ye should go and bring forth fruit, and that your fruit should remain."[35] In the parable, the laborers were presumably ready to work.[36]

> **Matthew 20:2.** And when he had agreed with the labourers for a penny a day, he sent them into his vineyard.

The householder did not force the laborers to work for him. Rather, he offered a wage in return for the work, and the laborers had agency regarding whether to accept the offer. The work would last throughout the day, and since the laborers would be working in a vineyard, the work was presumably

---

35. John 15:16.
36. The Apostles were the first "hired" or called in Jesus's time but were not the first on earth "hired," for there were many laborers from Adam's day to Christ's day.

arduous or tedious. The laborers would earn a penny, or a denarius, which was the common wage for a day's labor.[37]

Matthew 20:3–4. And he went out about the third hour, and saw others standing idle in the marketplace, and said unto them; Go ye also into the vineyard, and whatsoever is right I will give you. And they went their way.

There was more work to be done in the vineyard than those originally hired could complete, so the householder went again to the marketplace, this time at around nine o'clock. He saw individuals who were willing to work but had not yet received employment for the day. He hired them and said he would pay them an appropriate amount at the end of the day, but he did not specify what the amount would be. The laborers had to trust that the householder would pay them fairly. They probably did not expect to earn as much as would the laborers the householder initially hired.

Matthew 20:5–7. Again he went out about the sixth and ninth hour, and did likewise. And about the eleventh hour he went out, and found others standing idle, and saith unto them, Why stand ye here all the day idle? They say unto him, Because no man hath hired us. He saith unto them, Go ye also into the vineyard; and whatsoever is right, that shall ye receive.

Those who stood in the marketplace during the sixth, ninth, and eleventh hours were willing to work, and they accepted the opportunity when the householder presented it to them. As with those hired during the third hour, the householder promised these later groups of laborers that he would pay what he determined was right. Their agreement to labor in the vineyard required faith that the householder would be fair in his payment. It is evident that there was considerable work to do in the vineyard and that all the laborers could contribute, no matter when they were hired.

The willingness of those hired to work in the eleventh hour has particular spiritual significance for people in the latter days. The Lord told Joseph Smith, "For behold, the field is white already to harvest; and it is the eleventh hour, and the last time that I shall call laborers into my vineyard."[38] The latter days are the eleventh hour referred to in the parable. People on the

---

37. Edersheim, *Life and Times of Jesus the Messiah*, p. 762.
38. D&C 33:3.

earth today are the last laborers in the Lord's vineyard and must work with haste to complete the work before the sun sets.

God has dominion over all the earth and all His children. He knows the work that needs to be done and the laborers who are needed to contribute to it at various times. God sends people to the earth at the time when the labor they can provide is most needed.

> **Matthew 20:8–9.** So when even was come, the lord of the vineyard saith unto his steward, Call the labourers, and give them their hire, beginning from the last unto the first. And when they came that were hired about the eleventh hour, they received every man a penny. But when the first came, they supposed that they should have received more; and they likewise received every man a penny. And when they had received it, they murmured against the goodman of the house, saying, These last have wrought but one hour, and thou hast made them equal unto us, which have borne the burden and heat of the day.

The householder directed his steward, who represents Christ, to pay the laborers, starting with the laborers hired in the eleventh hour and ending with the laborers hired in the first hour. Had the laborers hired in the first hour been paid first, an important lesson would have been missed because they would have gone their way without knowing what the others had been paid. After learning that all the laborers were paid the same amount, the first laborers murmured and perhaps felt some resentment and jealousy toward the other laborers. Even though all laborers received the same wages, the first laborers could not object that they were not paid enough, because they were paid what the householder had promised to pay them. They could only object that other laborers were paid too much. Those of the third, sixth, ninth, and eleventh hours did not murmur because they had not bargained for any specified amount. The parable does not indicate how the laborers hired in later hours felt about being paid the same wages as those hired the first hour.

> **Matthew 20:13–15.** But he answered one of them, and said, Friend, I do thee no wrong: didst not thou agree with me for a penny? Take that thine is, and go thy way: I will give unto this last, even as unto thee. Is it not lawful for me to do what I will with mine own? Is thine eye evil, because I am good?

Reward in the world to come is not dependent on when a person is called to serve. There will not be a greater reward for laborers who served with Christ than for those who served in the millennia before or after Christ's mortal ministry. In addition, it does not matter whether a person accepts the gospel while young or in later years. It does not matter if life is seemingly cut short by accident or illness. If people labor diligently and for the right reasons, they will not be disappointed in the heavenly reward they receive. A person's desire to build up the kingdom of God and serve others should be an outgrowth of who the person is. The goal should not be to receive a reward but to become perfect, as Christ directed.[39] When becoming perfected is the goal, the reward will follow.

The Jews believed that they would receive a position in the kingdom of heaven because of their works and obedience and that they did not need the grace of God. However, the cumulative number of good works is not what really matters. People cannot buy their way into heaven or put God in their debt. The things that matter are character, belief in Christ, and commitment to follow Him. People are refined and strengthened as they serve and as the Holy Spirit works in their lives. As the prophet Nephi said in the Book of Mormon, "For we know that it is by grace that we are saved, after all we can do."[40]

In the parable, the laborers presumably did not have equal talents and abilities to work. Some were likely younger and stronger and could work harder and faster. Some may have had infirmities limiting their ability to work. The laborers were likely assigned different tasks, based on their abilities. Whereas some may have been asked to prune, others may have been assigned to water or fertilize. Some may have been assigned to repair and mend the stakes that held the grapevines. Some would have been needed to harvest the grapes, whereas others would have been needed to carry the heavy loads of grapes to where they would be stored. Everyone was necessary, and all needed to work together in order for the vineyard to be healthy and produce a bountiful harvest.

Likewise, those who labor in the kingdom of God have different strengths, talents, weaknesses, capabilities, and opportunities and are asked

---

39. See Matt. 5:48.
40. 2 Ne. 25:23.

to serve in different capacities. The important thing is how a person serves and the Godlike character he or she develops. Each person's contribution is important in helping the Church fulfill its divine mission of bringing souls unto Christ. As the Apostle Paul said to the Corinthian Saints, "For the body is not one member, but many. If the foot shall say, Because I am not the hand, I am not of the body; is it therefore not of the body? And if the ear shall say, Because I am not the eye, I am not of the body; is it therefore not of the body? If the whole body were an eye, where were the hearing? If the whole were hearing, where were the smelling? But now hath God set the members every one of them in the body, as it hath pleased him."[41]

Moreover, people often view their existence as limited to mortality. It is not. No matter how long a person's mortal life lasts, in the postmortal life there will be enough time for all to serve that there will be no meaningful difference in the length of service. Moreover, the breadth of the Atonement can make up for any deficiencies in time, talents, and opportunities to serve in mortality.

In the parable, the laborers hired in the first hour murmured because they thought they deserved to earn more than the laborers who were hired later. They lacked a complete understanding of the purposes of the householder. Though the first laborers believed they should receive more, in heaven no one will think that they should receive a greater reward than they have been given, for God is "perfect and just." He is also merciful.[42] Farrar stated that one of the lessons in this parable is "the truth that, while none who serve God shall be defrauded of the just reward, there could be in heaven no murmuring, no envyings, no jealous comparison of respective merits, no base strugglings for precedency, no miserable disputings as to who had performed the maximum of service, or who had received the minimum of grace."[43]

Regarding mortal and heavenly equality, the Lord has said: "Be equal in the bonds of heavenly things, yea, and earthly things also, for the obtaining of heavenly things. For if ye are not equal in earthly things ye cannot be equal in obtaining heavenly things."[44]

---

41. 1 Cor. 12:14–18.
42. See Alma 42:15.
43. Farrar, *Life of Christ*, p. 453.
44. D&C 78:5–6.

In the parable, after the first laborers murmured, the householder asked a piercing question that applies to all: "Is thine eye evil because I am good?" Jealousy and pride, no matter how they arise, have no place in the kingdom of heaven. People are not diminished when someone else receives blessings from God, and all people should rejoice with the individual. Conversely, Satan's view is that people are diminished when someone else receives a heavenly reward. This perspective is one of the principal reasons he tempts humankind to falter and fail.

Matthew 20:16. So the last shall be first, and the first last: for many be called, but few chosen.

The first part of the householder's concluding statement is something the Lord had previously taught the Jews: "The last shall be first, and the first last." During Jesus's mortal ministry, He preached the gospel to the Jews. After His death, the Apostles and others took the gospel to the Gentiles. In the latter days, the gospel will first go to the Gentiles and then to the Jews. In giving the parable, the Lord presumably wanted to remind His disciples that the gospel is for all dispensations of humankind; He may also have wanted to provide a glimpse of what His disciples' future responsibilities would entail.

The final seven words of the parable—"for many be called, but few chosen"—were likewise a reminder to His disciples that to be among the chosen, their hearts must not be on the world or their wages or even their reward in heaven but on serving the Lord, learning from Him, and becoming like Him.

A final comment about this parable: This parable is not just about being employed in the Lord's service, being satisfied with the wages received, not murmuring, or becoming perfected; the parable is also about the holiness and mercy of God; His plan of happiness; and the Atonement of Christ, which can lift, sanctify, and help people become worthy servants. God knows each of His children, including their strengths and weaknesses. He is the one who can declare that His children's efforts have been sufficient.

Notes to Chapter 46

1. Antiochus IV Epiphanes. Josephus gave the following account of Antiochus IV Epiphanes taking possession of Jerusalem and looting and profaning the holy temple:

> Now it came to pass, after two years, in the hundred and forty-fifth year, on the twenty-fifth day of that month which is by us called Chasleu . . . that the king [Antiochus IV Epiphanes] came up to Jerusalem, and, pretending peace, he got possession of the city by treachery. . . . But, led by his covetous inclination (for he saw there was in it a great deal of gold, and many ornaments that had been dedicated to it of very great value,) and in order to plunder its wealth, he ventured to break the league he had made. So he left the temple bare, and took away the golden candlesticks, and the golden altar [of incense,] and table [of shew-bread,] and the altar, [of burnt-offering;] and did not abstain from even the veils, which were made of fine linen and scarlet. He also emptied it of its secret treasures, and left nothing at all remaining; and by this means cast the Jews into great lamentation, for he forbade them to offer those daily sacrifices which they used to offer to God, according to the law. . . . And when the king had built an idol altar upon God's altar, he slew swine upon it, and so offered a sacrifice neither according to the law, nor the Jewish religious worship in that country. He also compelled them to forsake the worship which they paid their own God, and to adore those whom he took to be gods; and made them build temples, and raise idol altars, in every city and village, and offer swine upon them every day.[45]

2. Judas Maccabeus. According to the *HarperCollins Bible Dictionary*, Judas Maccabeus was

> the third of the five sons of Mattathias. The nickname Maccabeus . . . probably derives from a word for "hammer." After Antiochus IV Epiphanes polluted the temple in 167 BCE, Mattathias moved with his family to Modein (1 Macc. 2:1–4). When officers of Antiochus sought to force Mattathias and his family to commit apostasy, Mattathias rose up in defense of the law

---

45. Josephus, *Antiquities*, 12.5.4.

and the covenant, killed an officer, and led his sons into the wilderness in revolt (2:15–48). Upon the death of his father, Judas successfully led Israel in numerous battles against the Syrians. . . . Judas continued to lead Israel in battle with great success, liberating Jews from surrounding territories and even making a treaty with Rome.[46]

3. Judas Maccabeus's defeat of Antiochus IV Epiphanes and restoration of the temple. Josephus gave the following account of the restoration of the holy temple at Jerusalem:

> When, therefore, the generals of Antiochus's armies had been beaten so often, Judas assembled the people together, and told them, that after these many victories which God had given them, they ought to go up to Jerusalem and purify the temple, and offer the appointed sacrifices. But as soon as he, with the whole multitude, was come to Jerusalem, and found the temple deserted, and its gates burnt down, and plants growing in the temple of their own accord . . . he and those that were with him began to lament. . . . When therefore he had carefully purged it, and had brought in new vessels, the candlestick, the table [of shew-bread,] and the altar [of incense,] which were made of gold, he hung up the veils at the gates, and added doors to them. He also took down the altar [of burnt offering,] and built a new one of stones that he gathered together, and not of such as were hewn with iron tools. So on the five and twentieth day of the month Casleu . . . they lighted the lamps that were on the candlestick, and offered incense upon the altar [of incense]. . . . Now it so fell out, that these things were done on the very same day on which their divine worship had fallen off, and was reduced to a profane and common use, after three years' time . . . but it was dedicated anew, on the same day.[47]

4. Festival of Dedication. The *HarperCollins Bible Dictionary* states that the Festival of Dedication is

> also known as Hanukkah (hahn'uh-kuh) . . . On the twenty-fifth of Chislev, 164 BCE, three years to the day after the pollution of the altar, the new altar was dedicated with sacrifices, song, music and joyous worship for eight days. Judas and the people determined that those eight days of dedication

---

46. *HarperCollins Bible Dictionary*, s.v. "Judas."
47. Josephus, *Antiquities*, 12.5.6.

should be celebrated annually. It was apparently the relighting of the temple candelabras that led to the festival also being called the "Festival of Lights." That name is further associated with a postbiblical story about a small cruse of holy oil discovered at the cleansing of the temple that was miraculously able to light the temple lamp for eight days.[48]

---

48. *HarperCollins Bible Dictionary*, s.v., "dedication, festival of."

Chapter 47

JESUS RESTORES LAZARUS TO LIFE AND IS CONDEMNED TO DEATH

After Jesus left the Festival of Dedication in Jerusalem, where the Jews had illegally sought to stone Him, He and His disciples went east to Perea, "again beyond Jordan into the place where John at first baptized; and there he abode."[1] While in Perea, Jesus received word that His beloved friend Lazarus was gravely ill in Bethany. By the time Jesus arrived in Bethany, Lazarus had died. After meeting with Lazarus's sisters and then going to the place where Lazarus was buried, Jesus restored Lazarus to life. This miracle and the events surrounding it evidence Jesus's divinity and His deep love, empathy, and compassion.

This miracle was a powerful witness to the Jews that Jesus was indeed the promised Messiah and the Son of God and that He had power over death. Many Jews witnessed the miracle and thereafter believed in Him. Ironically, this miracle, which could not be logically disputed or explained away, was also the final motivation for the chief priests and Pharisees to formally resolve to put Jesus to death.

Jesus had previously restored life to Jairus's daughter in Capernaum[2] and to the widow's son in Nain.[3] However, the circumstances of these earlier

---

1. John 10:41. John the Baptist baptized in "Bethabara beyond Jordan" (see John 1:28; 3:26). Bethabara is also referred to as Bethany (see *HarperCollins Bible Dictionary*, s.v. "Bethabara"). This Perean Bethany should not be confused with the Judean Bethany, near Jerusalem (see *HarperCollins Bible Dictionary*, s.v. "Bethany"; see also Farrar, *Life of Christ*, p. 453).

2. See Matt. 9:23–25.

3. See Luke 7:11–17.

miracles differed in some respects from the miracle of restoring life to
Lazarus. When Jesus restored Lazarus's life, many Jews were present, some
of whom believed and some of whom were Jesus's enemies and sought His
life. In addition, this miracle occurred in Bethany, which was located on the
southeastern slope of the Mount of Olives and only about two miles from
Jerusalem,[4] which was the ecclesiastical center of Judaism and where the
Sanhedrin met.[5]

John, the only Gospel writer to record this event, devoted a significant
portion of his record to events involved in this miracle, indicating the
importance of this occurrence to John.

Lazarus Is Restored to Life (John 11:1–46)

John's account of Jesus restoring life to Lazarus begins with a report of
Lazarus's illness and a description of his family:

> **John 11:1–4.** Now a certain man was sick, named Lazarus, of Bethany, the
> town of Mary and her sister Martha. (It was that Mary which anointed
> the Lord with ointment, and wiped his feet with her hair, whose brother
> Lazarus was sick.) Therefore his sisters sent unto him, saying, Lord, behold,
> he whom thou lovest is sick. When Jesus heard that, he said, This sickness
> is not unto death, but for the glory of God, that the Son of God might be
> glorified thereby.

Martha, her sister Mary, and their brother Lazarus6 lived in Bethany,
which may have been twenty miles or more from where Jesus was in Perea.
Lazarus lived with his sisters, and there is no mention that he had a wife
or children. Presumably, his sisters and others believed that his life was cut
short. That tragedy would likely have added to Mary and Martha's grief
and sorrow. Jesus was close to them and loved them, and they loved Him.
Martha and Mary sent urgent word to Jesus that Lazarus was very sick, with
the implication that He should come to them quickly. They may have hoped
that Jesus would heal Lazarus. In response to this message, Jesus told the

4. See *HarperCollins Bible Dictionary*, s.v. "Bethany."
5. See Smith, *Bible Dictionary*, s.v. "Sanhedrin."
6. See Edersheim, *Life and Times of Jesus the Messiah*, p. 691; see also *HarperCollins Bible Dictionary*, s.v. "Martha," "Mary," and "Lazarus."

messenger to report back that "this sickness is not unto death, but for the glory of God, that the Son of God might be glorified thereby." Presumably, the messenger was to relay Jesus's response to Mary and Martha and did so with haste.

John 11:5–6. Now Jesus loved Martha, and her sister, and Lazarus. When he had heard therefore that he was sick, he abode two days still in the same place where he was.

Notwithstanding Jesus's love for Mary, Martha, and Lazarus, He remained where He was for two days after learning about Lazarus's illness. Jesus did so because He knew that waiting would lead to a public opportunity to glorify God and further demonstrate His divine Sonship. Jesus had likewise been patient on previous occasions, using the resulting opportunities to teach lessons. For example, He had slept during the tumultuous storm on the Sea of Galilee and thereafter calmed the wind and waves.[7] Before traveling to Mary and Martha's home in Judea, Jesus likely continued to teach and to heal people in Perea.

One may wonder what the disciples said to Him or among themselves after hearing the report of Lazarus's serious illness and the plea for Jesus to come to Bethany. After continuing His ministry in Perea for two more days, Jesus knew it was now time to go to Bethany:

John 11:7–10. Then after that saith he to his disciples, Let us go into Judaea again. His disciples say unto him, Master, the Jews of late sought to stone thee; and goest thou thither again? Jesus answered, Are there not twelve hours in the day? If any man walk in the day, he stumbleth not, because he seeth the light of this world. But if a man walk in the night, he stumbleth, because there is no light in him.

When Jesus told His disciples that it was time to return to Judea, they reminded Him that only a short time prior, Jews had sought His life in the temple courts in Jerusalem, which was located in Judea. They may have also reminded Him that He was well-known to the Jews in Judea and that to return to that region would likely result in His death.

In response, Jesus told His disciples that the workday lasted twelve hours (presumably from 6:00 a.m. to 6:00 p.m.). Figuratively, He was indicating

---

7. See John 8:22–24.

that it was His day to work and that those who sought to take His life would not be able to do so until it was time for Him to voluntarily give it up. Further, Jesus was reminding His disciples that He was going to diligently continue His mortal ministry until the end of His life (figuratively, until the night came). His enemies could not cut short His time—or mission—on earth. He further told His disciples that those who believed in and followed Him would not stumble, because He was the Light of the World. Those who would not believe in and follow Him would spiritually stumble in darkness because they did not recognize Him as the true Light. The disciples needed to increase their faith in Him as the Son of God with divine power to prevent individuals from killing Him if it was not His will.

Jesus then reminded the disciples why He would return to Judea:

John 11:11–15. These things said he: and after that he saith unto them, Our friend Lazarus sleepeth; but I go, that I may awake him out of sleep. Then said his disciples, Lord, if he sleep, he shall do well. Howbeit Jesus spake of his death: but they thought that he had spoken of taking of rest in sleep. Then said Jesus unto them plainly, Lazarus is dead. And I am glad for your sakes that I was not there, to the intent ye may believe; nevertheless let us go unto him.

Jesus explained that He would return to Judea so that He could awaken Lazarus from his "sleep." Upon hearing Jesus's words, the disciples mistakenly thought that Lazarus had fallen asleep from his serious illness. In response, Jesus plainly told them that Lazarus was dead. Jesus then hinted at why He had delayed going to visit Lazarus: by waiting until Lazarus had died, what He would do afterward would be another witness of His divinity to Mary, Martha, and Lazarus; to His other disciples present; and to other Jews who witnessed the miracle. The great miracle that was to come would buttress the faith of many who were present. Witnessing this miracle would strengthen His disciples in preparation for challenges in the future. Further, because the miracle of restoring Lazarus to life was witnessed by many of the Jews and occurred so near Jerusalem, the chief priests quickly learned of this marvelous witness of Jesus's divinity. Nevertheless, they formally determined to take His life and the life of Lazarus,[8] and the chief priests

---

8. See John 12:9–11.

would therefore be left without excuse when they ultimately stood before God to be judged.

The Gospel of John next describes the valiant commitment of the Apostle Thomas to Jesus's decision to travel to Judea, where He would be in harm's way.

John 11:16. Then said Thomas, which is called Didymus, unto his fellow disciples, Let us also go, that we may die with him.

Thomas indicated that he was willing to endure persecution and possibly even death in order to follow and support Jesus.[9] The other disciples' response to Thomas is not recorded, but presumably they also accepted the serious risk involved in traveling to Bethany with Jesus. John's record continues:

John 11:17–19. Then when Jesus came, he found that he [Lazarus] had lain in the grave four days already.[10] Now Bethany was nigh unto Jerusalem, about fifteen furlongs off: And many of the Jews came to Martha and Mary, to comfort them concerning their brother.

The Jewish custom was to bury a deceased person on the day of the death.[11] Jesus and His disciples likely left Perea on the morning of the second day after Jesus received the report of Lazarus's illness, and they may have completed the approximately twenty miles to Bethany by that evening. The group may have lodged outside of Bethany that night, for John later

---

9. Sometimes, Thomas is criticized for his later skepticism that other disciples had seen the risen Lord. At that time, Thomas stated: "Except I shall see in his hands the print of the nails, and put my finger into the print of the nails, and thrust my hand into his side, I will not believe" (John 20:25). Thomas's courageous statement in John 11:16 indicates that he was not of little faith.

10. It likely took at least a day for the messenger to travel to Bethany in Perea, locate Jesus, and deliver the message of Lazarus's illness. If Jesus stayed in Perea for two days, it took a day for Jesus and His disciples to travel to near Bethany in Judea, and Lazarus had lain in the tomb for four days when Jesus arrived, then presumably Lazarus died the same day the messengers left. Of course, it is unknown how long it took the messenger to find Jesus and how long it took Jesus to travel to near Bethany in Judea.

11. See Edersheim, *Life and Times of Jesus the Messiah*, p. 692.

recorded that "Jesus was not yet come into the town."[12] He went to the tomb the next day, perhaps in the morning or early afternoon.[13]

Many Jews came to comfort Martha and Mary, some of these Jews were likely prominent and from Jerusalem. Even though Lazarus and his sisters were close friends of Jesus, they were apparently not considered apostates of the local synagogue and were not ostracized by Jews in Jerusalem.

John next recorded Martha's reaction when she heard that Jesus was coming:

John 11:20–30. Then Martha, as soon as she heard that Jesus was coming, went and met him: but Mary sat still in the house. Then said Martha unto Jesus, Lord, if thou hadst been here, my brother had not died. But I know, that even now, whatsoever thou wilt ask of God, God will give it thee. Jesus saith unto her, Thy brother shall rise again. Martha saith unto him, I know that he shall rise again in the resurrection at the last day. Jesus said unto her, I am the resurrection, and the life: he that believeth in me, though he were dead, yet shall he live: and whosoever liveth and believeth in me shall never die. Believest thou this? She saith unto him, Yea, Lord: I believe that thou art the Christ, the Son of God, which should come into the world. And when she had so said, she went her way, and called Mary her sister secretly, saying, The Master is come, and calleth for thee. As soon as she heard that, she arose quickly, and came unto him. Now Jesus was not yet come into the town, but was in that place where Martha met him.

After Martha received word that Jesus was near Bethany, she went to meet him. Mary, who had not heard of Jesus's arrival, remained at home. One can only imagine Martha's thoughts and feelings upon seeing Jesus and knowing that He had responded to her request to come help her brother. Upon reaching Jesus, Martha told Him, likely with great emotion, love, and faith: "Lord, if thou hadst been here, my brother had not died. But I know, that even now, whatsoever thou wilt ask of God, God will give it thee." There was no criticism in her words. Even though Jesus had not immediately hastened to Bethany and had sent word that Lazarus would not die from his sickness, Martha still believed that Jesus was the Son of God. Even though

---

12.   John 11:30; see also v. 20; Farrar, *Life of Christ*, p. 454.

13.   This assumption is based on the fact that many people were with Mary and Martha when Jesus arrived. Many Jews were present and had come from Jerusalem to comfort the two sisters, a fact that further suggests it was late morning or early afternoon.

Lazarus had lain in the tomb for four days, Martha's words expressed a glimmer of hope that Jesus could even now ask God to restore life to her brother. Perhaps there was also a spirit of prophecy in Martha.

Jesus then told Martha that Lazarus would rise again. Martha understood Jesus's words to mean that Lazarus would eventually be resurrected, as would all people. Jesus then declared, "I am the resurrection, and the life: he that believeth in me, though he were dead, yet shall he live: and whosoever liveth and believeth in me shall never die." Christ was explaining that He had been given the power of resurrection by the Father and was implying that those who believe in Him would have eternal life in the kingdom of heaven.

And then, Jesus asked Martha: "Believest thou this?" Presumably, Jesus was asking Martha to look deep within herself and consider the circumstances surrounding her brother's death and ensure that she could say both to Jesus and to herself that she believed. In responding, she confirmed her belief with a profound declaration: "Yea, Lord: I believe that thou art the Christ, the Son of God, which should come into the world." Her response was deep and unequivocal despite the emotionally painful circumstances she was in. Unlike Martha, many people who lose a loved one decide to curse God because they lack understanding of why the loved one was not spared. Martha's declaration, born of faith gained before and confirmed in the midst of deep sorrow, can provide inspiration for people today who mourn the loss of others.

Martha then went back to Bethany to find Mary. After arriving, Martha secretly told Mary that Jesus had arrived and had asked to see Mary. Upon hearing this news, Mary quickly went to where Martha had spoken with Jesus.

John continued his account as follows:

John 11:31–32. The Jews then which were with her in the house, and comforted her, when they saw Mary, that she rose up hastily and went out, followed her, saying, She goeth unto the grave to weep there. Then when Mary was come where Jesus was, and saw him, she fell down at his feet, saying unto him, Lord, if thou hadst been here, my brother had not died.

When Mary left her home, the Jews who had been comforting her followed her, assuming that she was going to Lazarus's tomb to mourn. Instead, Mary went to Jesus, and when she reached Him, she fell down at

His feet and wept. She, as with Martha, was filled with deep emotion. Even though Jesus had not cured Lazarus's illness, she loved Him, believed in Him, and worshipped Him.[14] With language identical to that of her sister, Mary said: "If thou hadst been here, my brother had not died." She did not express doubt; rather, she expressed sorrow because of her brother's death, and she also declared her unshaken faith in Christ.

John's record continues with the following:

> **John 11:33–37.** When Jesus therefore saw her weeping, and the Jews also weeping which came with her, he groaned in the spirit, and was troubled, and said, Where have ye laid him? They said unto him, Lord, come and see. Jesus wept. Then said the Jews, Behold how he loved him! And some of them said, Could not this man, which opened the eyes of the blind, have caused that even this man should not have died?

When Jesus saw Mary and others crying, He sorrowed and was deeply moved. Jesus was also troubled because He knew that some present did not believe in Him and were aligned with the Sanhedrin, whose members would later cause His death.[15] Nevertheless, Jesus loved all people with a love beyond mortal understanding.

Jesus then asked where Lazarus had been laid to rest. Although Jesus knew the answer, He wanted those with Him to take Him to the tomb so they would be present when He performed the miracle. Then, as the Gospel of John indicates, "Jesus wept." These two simple words convey a multitude of feelings that poured from the Master's soul as tears streamed down His face. He likely wept because He felt the love that Mary, Martha, and others present had for Lazarus. Jesus likely wept because of the abiding faith of these two sisters, who had lost their younger brother. Jesus likely wept because He loved this faithful friend, who had died. Jesus likely also wept because He knew that His prayers to the Father would be heard and that Lazarus would soon be miraculously brought back to life.

Some of the Jews present asked whether Jesus could have prevented Lazarus's death, given that Jesus had previously given sight to the blind.

---

14. She later anointed the Lord with ointment and wiped His feet with her hair (see John 11:2; 12:3).

15. Compare with 3 Ne. 17:14, which states, "Jesus groaned within himself, and said: Father, I am troubled because of the wickedness of the people of the house of Israel."

Perhaps they thought that He could have even healed Lazarus from a distance, just as He had done when healing the Centurion's servant from palsy in Capernaum.[16] They did not know that an even greater miracle was yet to come.

John's record continues as follows:

John 11:38–40. Jesus therefore again groaning in himself cometh to the grave. It was a cave, and a stone lay upon it. Jesus said, Take ye away the stone. Martha, the sister of him that was dead, saith unto him, Lord, by this time he stinketh: for he hath been dead four days.[17] Jesus saith unto her, Said I not unto thee, that, if thou wouldest believe, thou shouldest see the glory of God?

Upon arriving at the cave that Lazarus had been laid in, Jesus groaned again, perhaps because some with little faith concluded that Jesus's authority was limited. According to Talmage, "This manifestation of malignant unbelief caused Jesus again to groan with sorrow if not indignation."[18]

Jesus then asked that the stone in front of the cave's entrance be taken away.[19] Martha responded that because her brother had been dead for four days, he would stink.[20] She may have also thought that opening the tomb would desecrate it, just as people today would likely think that a grave would be desecrated if someone asked that the dirt be removed, that the casket be raised, and that it be opened. Though Jesus likely understood her concern, He reminded her that if she believed, she would see the glory of God. Jesus presumably wanted to make her faith even stronger than it was. Because of

---

16. See Matt. 8:5–13.

17. Edersheim wrote, "It was the common Jewish idea that corruption commenced on the fourth day, that the drop of gall, which had fallen from the sword of the Angel and caused death, was then working its effect, and that, as the face changed, the soul took its final leave from the resting place of the body" (see Edersheim, *Life and Times of Jesus the Messiah*, p. 699).

18. Talmage, *Jesus the Christ*, p. 461.

19. Martha, Mary, and Lazarus were presumably a family of prominence and means, as suggested by the fact that many Jews came to give comfort and to mourn and the fact that Lazarus was laid to rest in a private tomb instead of in the cemetery where common people were buried.

20. "It was the common Jewish idea that corruption commenced on the fourth day, that the drop of gall, which had fallen from the sword of the Angel and caused death, was then working its effect, and that, as the face changed, the soul took its final leave from the resting-place of the body" (Edersheim, *Life and Times of Jesus the Messiah*, p. 699).

Jesus's statement, Martha presumably dared not disbelieve, but she may have also wondered how Jesus's promise would be fulfilled.

John's account next states the following:

> **John 11:41–44.** Then they took away the stone from the place where the dead was laid. And Jesus lifted up his eyes, and said, Father, I thank thee that thou hast heard me. And I knew that thou hearest me always: but because of the people which stand by I said it, that they may believe that thou hast sent me. And when he thus had spoken, he cried with a loud voice, Lazarus, come forth. And he that was dead came forth, bound hand and foot with graveclothes: and his face was bound about with a napkin. Jesus saith unto them, Loose him, and let him go.

Imagine the thoughts of those who rolled away the heavy stone and the thoughts of those who witnessed. Those who moved the stone must have had faith that Jesus had directed them to do so for a wise purpose. Almost all present would have wondered what Jesus's purpose was. Did He want to go into the tomb? If so, for what reason? Some may have wondered whether opening the tomb would desecrate the grave. Some may have wondered about Lazarus's condition after four days in the tomb. Some may have wondered, like Martha, about whether a foul odor would come from the tomb. Most would not have expected the marvelous miracle that would shortly follow.

With the stone rolled away, Jesus expressed gratitude to His Father for hearing and answering Jesus's prayers. To all who heard, this expression was a witness of the Father, of Jesus doing the will of the Father, and of God always hearing Jesus's prayers. This expression was also a witness that prayers are answered and that Christ and the Father are separate and distinct beings. Jesus then said in His prayer that He recognized that the miracle would occur so that those who were present would hear His words and that thereby some would believe that He was indeed sent by the Father. Further, by calling upon His Father, Jesus confirmed to those present the declaration He had made to the Jews who were at Solomon's Porch a few weeks before that "the works that I do in my Father's name, they bear witness of me."[21] Moreover, His prayer to the Father implicitly confirmed His miracles were of God, not of Beelzebub, as the leaders of the Jews had falsely claimed.

---

21. John 10:25.

After Jesus concluded His communion with His Father, Jesus "cried with a loud voice, Lazarus, come forth." Obedient to the voice of the Master, Lazarus came forth! He was wrapped in burial clothes, with a cloth covering his face. Jesus directed that someone, presumably Mary or Martha, remove the burial napkin and loose the burial clothes that bound Lazarus. His coming forth provided an undeniable witness of the power of Jesus Christ, the Son of God.

What Lazarus first said or later reported of his experience is unknown. Likewise, it is unknown what his sisters may have said to him or to Jesus. It is certain, however, that Lazarus thereafter testified of his restoration to life. And many believed.

In none of Jesus's actions was there unnecessary display or aggrandizement. Further, He involved others in the miracle, and their help required effort. For example, He could have easily found the grave Himself, but He inquired. He could have caused the stone to be rolled away, just as He had stilled the wind and waves on the sea. He could have caused the burial clothes to be removed, but He invited others to complete this task. Involving those present may have enabled the import of the miracle to more deeply penetrate their souls.

The scriptural record is silent as to what happened afterward. There is no mention of how Lazarus was loosed or what praise and worship he and others offered. Including this information might have detracted from the miracle.

It is evident that Martha and Mary's faith amid sorrow was honored in that Jesus restored life to their brother. The fact that Lazarus honored Christ's call to "come forth" and thus leave the spirit world is a testament of Lazarus's abiding faith, obedience, and willingness to submit to the will of God and Christ "for the glory of God, that the Son of God might be glorified thereby."[22]

John's record then describes the responses of those who witnessed the miracle:

John 11:45–46. Then many of the Jews which came to Mary, and had seen the things which Jesus did, believed on him. But some of them went their ways to the Pharisees, and told them what things Jesus had done.

---

22. John 11:4.

Many of the Jews who witnessed the miracle chose to believe, whereas others chose not to. The same happens today. Some see miracles for what they are, whereas others see only science or eventually forget the miraculous nature of events. Some recognize spiritual impressions as coming from the Holy Ghost, whereas others seek to attribute impressions to the imaginations and power of the mind.

Faithful Lazarus's illness and then death raise the question of why some who are good experience great challenges. To aid in understanding, often one needs to see beyond the present and sometimes even beyond mortality. Mortals' limited vision of the eternities, both before and after this life, can obscure the lessons Heavenly Father knows that all people need to learn from the challenges and trials of mortality. As explained in Isaiah 55:8–9, "For my thoughts are not your thoughts, neither are your ways my ways, saith the Lord. For as the heavens are higher than the earth, so are my ways higher than your ways, and my thoughts than your thoughts."[23]

One of the fundamental purposes of mortality is for people to learn, grow, and be refined through their experiences. As recorded in Isaiah 48:10, the Lord said: "Behold, I have refined you, but not as silver; I have tried you in the furnace of affliction."[24] This principle applies to all people, no matter how righteous they are. Moreover, God does not measure people against each other but against themselves, given their unique challenges, trials, and potential.[25]

Other scriptures provide further insight. Lehi in the Book of Mormon taught, "It must needs be, that there is an opposition in all things. If not so . . . righteousness could not be brought to pass, neither wickedness, neither holiness nor misery, neither good nor bad."[26] As the Lord told Adam, people must "taste the bitter, that they may know to prize the good."[27] Further, the Lord revealed to Joseph Smith, "And it must needs be that the devil should tempt the children of men, or they could not be agents unto themselves; for if they never should have bitter they could not know the sweet."[28] Further,

---

23. Isa. 55:8–9.
24. See also Zech. 13:9; 1 Pet. 1:7.
25. See Matt. 5:45.
26. 2 Ne. 2:11.
27. Moses 6:55
28. D&C 29:39.

Jacob in the Book of Mormon taught: "But, behold, the righteous, the saints of the Holy One of Israel, they who have believed in the Holy One of Israel, they who have endured the crosses of the world, and despised the shame of it, they shall inherit the kingdom of God, which was prepared for them from the foundation of the world, and their joy shall be full forever."[29]

No matter a person's circumstances, to progress it is essential to have faith, as did Mary, Martha, and Lazarus. As the Prophet Ether said in the Book of Mormon, "Wherefore, whoso believeth in God might with surety hope for a better world, yea, even a place at the right hand of God, which hope cometh of faith, maketh an anchor to the souls of men, which would make them sure and steadfast, always abounding in good works, being led to glorify God."[30]

Heavenly Father wants all His children to progress as far as they can. Ultimately, those who are good and bear their crosses with faith, doing all they can with what they are given, will receive exaltation. Those who lose faith when adversity arises will receive a lesser reward or will merit punishment. God knows each person's heart and the depth of his or her challenges, and He is both just and merciful.

Restoring Lazarus to life was and is a marvelous witness of the divinity of Jesus Christ and of His power and glory. Likewise, this miracle was also a witness of the Father and of His love and concern for His children.

The account's record of the faith of Martha and Mary stands among the greatest in all of scripture. These two sisters must have experienced a tremendous and almost overwhelming challenge to their faith when Lazarus died even though Jesus had told the messenger that "this sickness is not unto death." The depth of this trial of their faith cannot be overstated. Lazarus too retained his faith through serious illness. He and his sisters each needed to look deep into their hearts to determine whether they still believed. After their trial of faith, the miracle came.[31] Their faith can inspire people today who face doubts, do not understand certain Church doctrines or events, or see a seeming conflict between science and religion. Restoring life to Lazarus is a message of hope!

---

29. 2 Ne. 9:18.
30. Ether 12:4.
31. See Ether 12:6.

The words of the hymn "Be Still, My Soul" can give comfort when people experience tragedy or questions, lack understanding, and need peace:

> Be still, my soul: The Lord is on thy side;
> With patience bear thy cross of grief or pain.
> Leave to thy God to order and provide;
> In ev'ry change he faithful will remain.
> Be still, my soul: Thy best, thy heav'nly Friend
> Thru thorny ways leads to a joyful end.
> Be still, my soul: Thy God doth undertake
> To guide the future as he has the past.
> Thy hope, thy confidence let nothing shake;
> All now mysterious shall be bright at last.
> Be still, my soul: The waves and winds still know
> His voice who ruled them while he dwelt below.
> Be still, my soul: The hour is hast'ning on
> When we shall be forever with the Lord,
> When disappointment, grief, and fear are gone,
> Sorrow forgot, love's purest joys restored.
> Be still, my soul: When change and tears are past,
> All safe and blessed we shall meet at last.[32]

Chief Priests and Pharisees Conspire to Put Jesus to Death (John 11:47–53)

After certain of the nonbelievers told the Pharisees about the miracle Jesus performed, the Pharisees and chief priests met to discuss what they should do regarding Jesus and His many miracles. The following is John's account:

John 11:47–53. Then gathered the chief priests and the Pharisees a council, and said, What do we? for this man doeth many miracles. If we let him thus alone, all men will believe on him: and the Romans shall come and take away both our place and nation. And one of them, named Caiaphas, being the high priest that same year, said unto them, Ye know nothing at all, nor consider that it is expedient for us, that one man should die for the people, and that the whole nation perish not. And this spake he not of himself: but being high priest that year, he prophesied that Jesus should die for that

---

32. *Hymns*, no. 124, lyrics by Katharina von Schlegel, trans. by Jane Borthwick.

nation; and not for that nation only, but that also he should gather together in one the children of God that were scattered abroad. Then from that day forth they took counsel together for to put him to death.

The group's major concern was not whether Jesus's miracles actually occurred or whether Jesus was guilty of a crime worthy of death but was whether the Roman government would strip them of their "place"—that is, their power, positions, and prestige among the people and the resulting wealth.

Caiaphas reminded the other chief priests that "it is expedient for us, that one man should die for the people, and that the whole nation perish not." The Jewish leaders also expressed concern that a split in the religious beliefs of the Jews would lead the Roman government to "take away our . . . nation" (meaning that Judaism would not be permitted to operate as a religion) and that, consequently, their nation would suffer further.[33] In addition, the Jewish leaders feared that the people would make Christ a king and thus threaten Israel's existence as a nation,[34] for the Roman government would not tolerate Israel having a king who might rival the Roman emperor.

The majority of the chief priests and Pharisees allowed Satan to plant murder in their hearts, just as Cain had allowed Satan to do.[35] Those at the meeting did not talk of whether Christ's miracles resulted in good or whether Christ was good and of God. These leaders did not investigate whether Lazarus's life truly had been restored. They were spiritually dead. Moreover, they did not discuss whether Christ had committed a sin worthy of death. The chief priests and Pharisees were the overseers of the law,[36] yet they ignored Jehovah's command to Moses on Sinai: "Thou shalt not kill."[37] Their hearts were hard, their eyes could not see, and their ears could not hear.

After some discussion, Caiaphas told the others: "Ye know nothing at all."[38] He was totally devoid of moral principle and acted without regard to guilt or compliance with Jewish law regarding trials; rather, he cared only

---

33. See Talmage, *Jesus the Christ*, p. 464.

34. See Farrar, *Life of Christ*, p. 459.

35. See Moses 5:29–33.

36. See *HarperCollins Bible Dictionary*, s.v. "council, the."

37. Ex. 20:13.

38. Caiaphas was appointed as high priest in AD 18 by the Roman governor Valerious Gratus and remained in that position until AD 36–37, when Vitellius, Pontius Pilate's successor, deposed Caiaphas (see *HarperCollins Bible Dictionary*, s.v. "Caiaphas").

about preserving his own station. He stood before the group as judge and jury to convict Jesus and sentence Him to death without so much as the trial or witnesses that Jewish law required.

Caiaphas made no claim of receiving divine instruction or even inspiration. Rather, Caiaphas used Rome as a weak excuse. However, neither Caesar nor the Roman governor Pontius Pilate had given warning regarding Christ or His followers. The Roman government ruled many nations, including Israel, during the time of Christ. The people in these nations worshipped various gods, and the Roman government tolerated this worship. The objective was to maintain relative peace within and collect taxes from all of Rome's jurisdictions.[39] Fear of Roman retribution was likely not the real reason for Caiaphas's statement or the decision of those at the meeting but was merely a pretext for the real motive of preserving their authority and wealth.

Of Caiaphas's declaration, John wrote: "And this spake he not of himself: but being high priest that year, he prophesied that Jesus should die for that nation; and not for that nation only, but that also he should gather together in one the children of God that were scattered abroad." Caiaphas was unaware of the import of his words—namely, that Jesus would die not only for the Jews but for all of the children of God. The events of the meeting must have been reported to John or someone close to him by one or more of those present at this meeting, perhaps Nicodemus[40] or Joseph of Arimathea.

Things were now put into motion to take Jesus's life. Those at the meeting did not realize that Jesus's death was part of the divine plan of God and that Christ agreed to this part in the premortal world. Further, the judgment of the chief priests and Pharisees against Jesus would ultimately become a judgment against the Jewish nation for its unbelief in Jesus and growing wickedness. As Jesus had said in the Sermon on the Mount: "For with what judgment ye judge, ye shall be judged: and with what measure ye mete, it shall be measured to you again."[41] And so the Jewish nation was judged and consequently destroyed by the Roman Empire.

---

39. See Lyon, *Apostasy to Restoration*, p. 21.
40. See Edersheim, *Life and Times of Jesus the Messiah*, p. 700.
41. Matt. 7:2.

Jesus Goes to Ephraim (John 11:54)

Jesus likely heard about the meeting shortly afterward, for He no longer walked openly among the Jews. The Pharisees and the chief priests had directed that anyone who knew where Jesus was should report the information so that He could be taken.[42] Those who did know Jesus's whereabouts remained silent. Jesus and some of His disciples departed from Bethany and traveled to Ephraim, which was about twenty miles north of Jerusalem. All that is known of Jesus's time in Ephraim is provided in a single verse:

> **John 11:54.** Jesus therefore walked no more openly among the Jews; but went thence unto a country near to the wilderness, into a city called Ephraim, and there continued with his disciples.

Jesus presumably spent close to three months in Ephraim.[43] Ephraim was sufficiently far away from Jerusalem for Jesus to avoid detection by the Pharisees and chief priests and to likely experience relative calm, free from persecution and the threat of death. While in Ephraim, Jesus likely prepared His disciples for what was to come and for their responsibilities following His death. After His sojourn in Ephraim concluded, Jesus walked toward Jerusalem a final time with His Apostles.

Notes to Chapter 47

1. **Lazarus's funeral.** Those who attended the funeral likely included friends from Bethany and surrounding areas, as well as hired mourners. The funeral would have included an oration, and each friend would have parted from Lazarus by saying, "Depart in peace."[44] As the funeral procession moved to the tomb, the men presumably would have been on one side, with the women on the other.[45] A large stone would have been placed in front of the entrance to the

---

42. See John 11:57.
43. This estimate is based on the fact that Jesus raised Lazarus from the dead during the last winter of His life and that He returned to Jerusalem in the spring for the Passover.
44. See Edersheim, *Life and Times of Jesus the Messiah*, pp. 694, 696.
45. See Edersheim, *Life and Times of Jesus the Messiah*, p. 696.

tomb, and the stone would have been whitened, as was the custom.[46] Given the time of year, the temperature was cold.

2.   **Lazarus after being restored to life.** Six days before the final Passover before Jesus's death, He traveled to Bethany on His way to Jerusalem. While in Bethany, He ate with Mary, Martha, and Lazarus. It was at this time that Mary anointed Jesus's feet with costly spikenard and wiped His feet with her hair.[47] Many Jews came to the home of Mary, Martha, and Lazarus, in part to see Jesus and in part to see Lazarus because of the miracle he had received. The chief priests conspired to put Lazarus to death because many of those who saw Lazarus and heard his account of being restored to life believed in Jesus and deserted their Jewish faith.[48] Although the scriptural record is silent, it is presumed that the chief priests were not successful in taking Lazarus' life, for such would have somewhat frustrated Jesus's success in restoring Lazarus to life.

3.   **Caiaphas's position as "high priest that same year."** Farrar stated: "Some have seen an open irony in the expression of St. John (xi,49), that Caiaphas was High Priest 'that same year,' as though the Jews had got into this contemptuous way of speaking during the rapid succession of priests—mere phantoms set up and displaced by the Roman fiat—who had in recent years succeeded each other. There must have been at least five living High Priests, and ex-High Priests at this council—Annas, Ismael Ben Phabi, Eleazer Ben Hanan, Simon Ben Kamhith, and Caiaphas, who had gained his elevation by bribery."[49]

4.   **Rome and religion.** During Christ's public ministry, the Roman government did not recognize His gospel as a religion separate from Judaism. Some thought Christianity was an offshoot of Judaism and could potentially lead to discord among the Jews, something the Roman government did not view favorably. In addition, the government's attitude was that if a religion had not been accepted as one of the state-recognized religions, it had no right to exist, have property, construct buildings, or hold public or private worship services.[50]

---

46. See Edersheim, *Life and Times of Jesus the Messiah*, p. 696.
47. See John 12:1–8.
48. See John 12:9–11.
49. Farrar, *Life of Christ*, p. 460n1.
50. See Lyon, *Apostasy to Restoration*, pp. 21–22.

Chapter 48

THE FINAL JOURNEY TOWARD JERUSALEM

After departing Bethany, Jesus "walked no more openly among the Jews."[1] The chief priests had formally conspired to take His life and had declared that anyone who knew of His whereabouts must report the information so that the Jewish leaders "might take him."[2] Presumably, Jesus and His disciples spent the rest of the winter and the early spring somewhat secluded in Ephraim,[3] which was in the mountains about twenty miles to the north of Jerusalem. Ephraim overlooked the roads that Jews generally took when traveling from Galilee to Jerusalem along the Jordan Valley. From the mountains in or near Ephraim, Jesus may have seen caravans of people as they began to make their way to Jerusalem to purify themselves before the commencement of the Feast of the Passover.[4]

The time had now come for Jesus and those who were with Him to leave the peace and relative security of Ephraim and to travel to Jerusalem so they could attend the last Passover to occur before Jesus was crucified. As the group traveled, Jesus taught of His death and Resurrection, restored sight to Bartimaeus, dined with Zacchaeus, and gave the parable of the ten pounds. Before arriving in Jerusalem, Jesus also stopped in Bethany, where Mary anointed Jesus's head and feet prior to His great and final sacrifice.[5]

---

1. John 11:54.
2. John 11:57.
3. Ephraim may be the place referred to as Ephrain in 2 Chronicles 13:19 or Ophrah in 1 Samuel 13:17 (see Dummelow, *Bible Commentary*, p. 795).
4. See Farrar, *Life of Christ*, p. 462.
5. The trip from Ephraim to Bethany and then to Jerusalem would have totaled a little over thirteen miles, with approximately thirty-three hundred feet in elevation gain.

Jesus Foretells His Death and Resurrection (Matt. 20:17–19; Mark 10:32–34; Luke 18:31–34)

One can only imagine Jesus's thoughts as He descended the hills and traveled toward the Jordan Valley. He knew that His destination was Jerusalem, where He would give His final witness. He may have looked back on the last three years of His life and pondered the time He had spent teaching His disciples, performing miracles, and touching peoples' lives in other ways. He may have contemplated Gethsemane, where He would suffer for the sins of all humankind. He knew that He would thereafter endure the insult of illegal arrest and unjust condemnation to death. He may have contemplated the cruelty of the scourging and the agony of being crucified—experiences that would demonstrate to all of humankind that He had overcome the world and all that Satan could devise. He may also have contemplated that His Resurrection would serve as the pinnacle of His witness to the world that He was the Son of God and that He had completed what He had promised to do.

All three synoptic Gospels indicate that on the way to Jerusalem, Jesus taught His disciples about His death and Resurrection. He may have done so with great emotion, and His words likely caused great solemnity among Jesus's disciples as they traveled. The following is Mark's account:

> **Mark 10:32–34.** And they were in the way going up to Jerusalem; and Jesus went before them: and they were amazed; and as they followed, they were afraid. And he took again the twelve, and began to tell them what things should happen unto him, saying, Behold, we go up to Jerusalem; and the Son of man shall be delivered unto the chief priests, and unto the scribes; and they shall condemn him to death, and shall deliver him to the Gentiles: and they shall mock him, and shall scourge him, and shall spit upon him, and shall kill him: and the third day he shall rise again.

The disciples' amazement may have resulted from the fact that Jesus was returning to Jerusalem even though people there sought His life and He had taught His disciples of His coming death. The gravity of returning to Jerusalem likely rested deeply on each of them.

Wanting to teach and forewarn His disciples about what was to occur in Jerusalem, Jesus explained that He would be delivered into the hands of

Jewish leaders and then to Gentiles, who would mock, scourge, and spit on Him and kill Him. Then, on the third day He would be resurrected. The disciples, however, "understood none of these things: and this saying was hid from them, neither knew they the things which were spoken."[6] The inability to understand may have resulted from the hope that Jesus, as the promised Messiah, would come to Jerusalem in glory and also from the fear that something terrible would occur. Further, they had no frame of reference to understand Jesus's Resurrection since no one had previously been resurrected.

Just as Jesus instructed His disciples of His coming death and subsequent Resurrection, people today have been instructed by Him through His prophets that He will return to the earth in His glorious Second Coming. The scriptures are replete with prophecies of this great and dreadful day of the Lord. Further, just as Jesus's disciples during His mortal ministry did not understand His prophecy of His Resurrection, many people today fail to understand or center their thoughts on the signs of His Second Coming. Some focus on things of a more immediate nature, whereas others simply do not understand or believe. What Christ taught His disciples on the road to Jerusalem is a warning to all people that they should always remember and be prepared both physically and spiritually for what is to come. If they are prepared and believe in Christ, they will look forward to His Second Coming.

The Mother of James and John Desires That Her Sons Sit on Jesus's Right and Left Hands (Matt. 20:20–28; Mark 10:35–45)

The group who traveled with Jesus included Salome, who was the wife of Zebedee and the mother of Apostles James and John.[7] It is unknown whether Salome was with Jesus and the others in Ephraim or whether she joined them as they traveled to Jerusalem for the Feast of the Passover. The following is

---

6. Luke 18:34.

7. Salome and other women provided for Jesus and some of His other disciples in Galilee. Presumably, these women devoutly believed in Jesus and cooked, mended clothes, and completed other tasks for Jesus and the others. She and her husband may have contributed funds to Jesus's ministry, using money from the family fishing business. The business presumably did well financially, as indicated by the fact that the business included a boat and employees. (See *HarperCollins Bible Dictionary*, s.v. "Salome"; Mark 1:20.)

Matthew's account of Salome[8] worshipping Jesus and then expressing her desire that her sons sit on Jesus's right hand and left hand in heaven:

Matthew 20:20–28. Then came to him the mother of Zebedee's children with her sons, worshipping him, and desiring a certain thing of him. And he said unto her, What wilt thou? She saith unto him, Grant that these my two sons may sit, the one on thy right hand, and the other on the left, in thy kingdom. But Jesus answered and said, Ye know not what ye ask. Are ye able to drink of the cup that I shall drink of, and to be baptized with the baptism that I am baptized with? They say unto him, We are able. And he saith unto them, Ye shall drink indeed of my cup, and be baptized with the baptism that I am baptized with: but to sit on my right hand, and on my left, is not mine to give, but it shall be given to them for whom it is prepared of my Father. And when the ten heard it, they were moved with indignation against the two brethren. But Jesus called them unto him, and said, Ye know that the princes of the Gentiles exercise dominion over them, and they that are great exercise authority upon them. But it shall not be so among you: but whosoever will be great among you, let him be your minister; and whosoever will be chief among you, let him be your servant: even as the Son of man came not to be ministered unto, but to minister, and to give his life a ransom for many.

Jesus surely knew and loved Salome for the sacrifices she made in supporting Him and those who followed Him. Jesus knew that Salome had a deep belief in Him and would even be with Him as He hung on the cross.[9] Nevertheless, she may not have completely recognized that many great prophets had served the Lord before her sons were called as Apostles. In light of her sons' valiant service and deep belief, it may be somewhat understandable that Salome had the courage to ask that James and John be able to sit next to Jesus after He ascended to heaven.

In response, Jesus said that Salome did not understand the import of what she had asked. Jesus then asked James and John whether they were able to "drink of the cup that I shall drink of, and to be baptized with the baptism that I am baptized with." His words were not a reproach but

---

8. Mark's account does not mention Salome; in his account, the two sons make the request themselves. If Salome made the request, James and John may have acquiesced, which may be the reason Mark did not mention Salome.

9. See Matt. 27:55–56; Mark 16:1.

an inquiry encouraging them to look deep within themselves. They each responded that they were able to endure what Jesus would soon endure. However, even though Jesus had recently explained what was to happen to Him, they did not fully understand and they certainly could not undertake what Jesus would soon undertake.

Jesus then stated that they would suffer persecution for His name's sake but that Heavenly Father, not Jesus, would be the one to decide who would sit on His right and left hand. Apparently, Salome and these two Apostles had failed to consider the work and sacrifice of the great prophets who had come before, such as Adam, Enoch, Noah, Moses, and Abraham, and had not thought of the mighty prophets who would come after. Salome and her sons had also apparently failed to completely understand all the implications of Peter's question and Jesus's response of "what shall we have therefore"[10] after teaching the rich young ruler. Further, the mother and sons had failed to understand all the implications of the parable of the laborers in the vineyard.

Matthew recorded that upon hearing the request regarding James and John, the other ten Apostles "were moved with indignation." Similarly, Mark recorded that the other Apostles were "much displeased."[11] Jesus did not share these feelings but, rather, took this opportunity to teach. He called the Apostles together, presumably as a loving father and mother would call together their contentious children in order to teach, correct, and admonish. He began by telling the Apostles that political rulers exercised authority over those in their realms, a fact that the Apostles were familiar with. Jesus then told them that His disciples should never seek to exercise authority over others. Instead, they were to minister and serve others. Instead of seeking honor and position in heaven, His disciples were to focus on being humble and serving others while in mortality.

Jesus next reminded His disciples that even He, the Son of God, came to the earth to minister, not to be ministered to, and ultimately to sacrifice His life. Jesus was the greatest of all, but His entire life was one of absolute humility. He was the example the Apostles should follow. As they heard Jesus's words, they must have thought about all the times they had witnessed

---

10. Matt. 19:27.
11. Mark 10:41.

Jesus's profound humility, love, compassion, and mercy for all humankind. His focus was always on others, especially individuals in need. Now, His focus centered on the events that would demonstrate His love even more deeply: His atoning sacrifice, Crucifixion, and Resurrection.

In moments of reflection, some may ask themselves or plead with their Heavenly Father to help them understand what they need to do in order to become more like Christ. Doing so is, of course, good and proper. One way to become more Christlike is to ensure that they are focusing on ministering to others, whether formally or informally, rather than on obtaining accolades, high positions, wealth, or possessions. Even in times of distress or challenge, people should be less concerned about their needs than about the needs of others. Christ set the example and taught this vital lesson to Salome, His Apostles, and presumably other disciples while traveling to Jerusalem.

Jesus Restores Bartimaeus's Sight (Matt. 20:29–34; Mark 10:46–52; Luke 18:35–43)

Jesus and the rest of the group then continued their journey toward Jerusalem. As they traveled on a road in the Jordan Valley, they reached the city of Jericho, which is about twenty miles east of Jerusalem and about six miles from the northern tip of the Dead Sea.[12] The tropical climate, abundance of water from flowing springs, and vegetation earned Jericho the description of "city of palm trees" in the Old Testament.[13] Joshua's Israelite army conquered the city when its outer walls collapsed by the power of God.[14] Herod the Great built a winter palace in or near Jericho.[15] Additionally, many scholars believe Jericho was designated as a residence for thousands of priests and Levites who performed temple duties in Jerusalem. In Jesus's day,

---

12. The Dead Sea is approximately 1,294 feet below sea level (see *HarperCollins Bible Dictionary*, s.v. "Dead Sea").

13. Deut. 34:3; Judg. 3:13.

14. See Josh. 6.

15. See *HarperCollins Bible Dictionary*, s.v. "Jericho."

many people stopped in Jericho when traveling to Jerusalem for festivals such as the Passover.[16] Mark's account of Jesus coming to Jericho is as follows:

Mark 10:46–52. And they came to Jericho: and as he went out of Jericho with his disciples and a great number of people, blind Bartimaeus, the son of Timaeus, sat by the highway side begging. And when he heard that it was Jesus of Nazareth, he began to cry out, and say, Jesus, thou Son of David, have mercy on me. And many charged him that he should hold his peace: but he cried the more a great deal, Thou Son of David, have mercy on me. And Jesus stood still, and commanded him to be called. And they call the blind man, saying unto him, Be of good comfort, rise; he calleth thee. And he, casting away his garment, rose, and came to Jesus. And Jesus answered and said unto him, What wilt thou that I should do unto thee? The blind man said unto him, Lord, that I might receive my sight. And Jesus said unto him, Go thy way; thy faith hath made thee whole. And immediately he received his sight, and followed Jesus in the way.

Jesus arrived in Jericho about a week before His final Passover. Farrar posited that Jesus arrived on a Thursday, with the Passover occurring the following Thursday.[17] Jesus was now accompanied by a multitude of people, perhaps in part because word had spread that Jesus had restored Lazarus to life. Those in Jericho who believed surely would have welcomed Jesus to the city as the long-sought-for Messiah and may have waved palm leaves as He entered.

As Jesus walked in the city, Bartimaeus, who was blind, begged by the side of the road.[18] How he had gotten to the road is unknown, though it is likely that family members or friends helped him. Additionally, how long he had been blind is unknown. Certainly, he had little hope for any future beyond begging for money to purchase sustenance. Thus he spent the day

16. Smith, *Bible Dictionary*, s.v. "Jericho."

17. See Farrar, *Life of Christ*, pp. 464–465. Some scholars have asserted that Jesus arrived in Jericho on a different day. There are slight differences in the synoptic Gospels concerning the timing of what took place in Jericho. Matthew and Mark indicated that Jesus met Bartimaeus as He departed Jericho, whereas Luke stated that this meeting occurred when Jesus came near Jerusalem. Given that Jesus subsequently ate in Zacchaeus's house in Jericho, it seems reasonable to conclude that Jesus healed the blind man either at the time He entered Jericho or while He was still in it.

18. Both Mark's and Luke's accounts reference one blind man (see Mark 10:46–52; Luke 18:35–43), whereas Matthew's account references two blind men (see Matt. 20:30–34).

begging by the side of the highway, where he might receive a small amount to sustain himself.

Bartimaeus presumably would have heard any praise and adoration coming from the crowd and must have heard from the multitude that Jesus was among the group. As Jesus approached, Bartimaeus cried out: "Jesus, thou Son of David, have mercy on me." Bartimaeus's use of the appellation "Son of David" indicates that he recognized Jesus as the Messiah. Even though many tried to quiet him and told him to not disturb the Master, he cried out even more. One can almost hear the desperation and hope in his voice as he petitioned for Jesus's help.

Amid the presumed noise of the multitude, Jesus heard Bartimaeus, just as He hears all who call to His for help. Jesus stopped and asked that Bartimaeus come to Him. Individuals relayed the message to Bartimaeus and told him to "be of good comfort." These words likely brought much-sought-for hope. Bartimaeus then removed "his garment," which may have been dirty from the dust and dirt of the road; he likely wanted to be a little cleaner before going to Jesus. Bartimaeus may have approached Jesus with someone's help, enabling one or more people to be of service in the miracle that was to come. It is also possible that Bartimaeus was able to approach Jesus on his own because he heard the Savior's voice or the voice of others who spoke for Him. As with Bartimaeus, all can hear and approach Jesus if they truly desire to.

Jesus then asked what Bartimaeus would like Him to do. Jesus may have wanted the man to look deep within himself and test his faith, for Jesus certainly knew what Bartimaeus desired: the miracle of sight.

Mark and Luke recorded that the miracle occurred with Jesus only speaking a few words. According to Mark, Jesus said: "Go thy way; thy faith hath made thee whole." According to Luke, Jesus said: "Receive thy sight: thy faith hath saved thee."[19] Matthew alone recorded that Jesus touched Bartimaeus's eyes.[20] Whatever the case, the miracle came because of Bartimaeus's faith. How he gained the faith to receive his sight is unknown. He must have been taught about Jesus by someone who believed.

---

19. Luke 18:42.
20. See Matt. 20:34.

Imagine Bartimaeus's joy as he looked at Jesus, the multitude, and the world around him. Not only did he see physically but he also saw spiritually, for he thereafter followed Jesus. Luke's account notes that Bartimaeus and all who witnessed the miracle praised God.[21] And presumably the faith of those present increased even more.

Even though Jesus must have been filled with deep anxiety about what awaited Him in Jerusalem, He ministered to the one. His boundless mercy and compassion never diminished, no matter the circumstances, and He always made time to help those in need. As Jesus had said to His disciples as He left Ephraim, He came to minister to others, not to be ministered to.

Jesus Declares That Salvation Has Comes to Zacchaeus (Luke 19:1–10)

While in Jericho, there was more for the Master to do. Luke recorded the following:

Luke 19:1–10. And Jesus entered and passed through Jericho. And, behold, there was a man named Zacchaeus, which was the chief among the publicans, and he was rich. And he sought to see Jesus who he was; and could not for the press, because he was little of stature. And he ran before, and climbed up into a sycomore tree to see him: for he was to pass that way. And when Jesus came to the place, he looked up, and saw him, and said unto him, Zacchaeus, make haste, and come down; for to day I must abide at thy house. And he made haste, and came down, and received him joyfully. And when they saw it, they all murmured, saying, That he was gone to be guest with a man that is a sinner. And Zacchaeus stood, and said unto the Lord; Behold, Lord, the half of my goods I give to the poor; and if I have taken any thing from any man by false accusation, I restore him fourfold. And Jesus said unto him, This day is salvation come to this house, forsomuch as he also is a son of Abraham. For the Son of man is come to seek and to save that which was lost.

---

21. Luke 18:43.

Zacchaeus was called a sinner by the Jews likely because he was appointed by the Roman government to be the chief publican[22] in the city and because he presumably gained his wealth from taxing the people.[23] He had a deep desire to see Jesus, presumably because he had heard of Him and also perhaps because he had received inspiration to see Jesus. However, Zacchaeus's short stature prevented him from catching a glimpse of Jesus. Instead of simply waiting in the crowd, with the hope of seeing Jesus, Zacchaeus acted in the best way he could: he climbed a "sycomore tree"[24] in order to see Jesus from above. Likewise, some people today cannot see Christ because of the press and noise of the crowd.

As Jesus was passing by, He looked at the tree and saw Zacchaeus. Jesus called him by name and then said, "Make haste, and come down; for to day I must abide at thy house." One can only imagine what Zacchaeus thought in response. He may have wondered, "I am typically despised by the Jews, yet Jesus—a Jew—recognized me, knew my name, and spoke to me. Am I worthy to have the Messiah eat in my home? What will I feed Him and His Apostles? How do I show proper honor and respect? Will I be able to talk with Matthew, who was once a publican?" People today might likewise wonder what they would think if they found out that Jesus and His Apostles would be visiting for dinner. Just as Jesus knew Zacchaeus's name, Jesus knows all other people's names[25] and is willing to figuratively come to them regardless of whether they are despised by others.[26]

Zacchaeus climbed down from the tree and responded to Jesus's words with great joy. The multitude murmured because Jesus and His companions

---

22. Jericho was the home of a number of publicans, who secured revenue for the Roman government in order to purchase a type of balsam that grew in the area and to regulate exports and imports between Judea and Perea. Since Jericho was in the province of Judea, Zacchaeus was presumably under Pontius Pilate's direction. (See Farrar, *Life of Christ*, pp. 456, 465.)

23. Somewhat ironically, the name Zacchaeus is a Greek derivation of the Hebrew word that means "pure" (see *HarperCollins Bible Dictionary*, s.v. "Zacchaeus"; Young, *Analytical Concordance*, s.v. "Zacchaeus").

24. This tree may not have been what today is commonly called a sycamore tree; rather, the tree was likely an Egyptian fig tree (see Farrar, *Life of Christ*, p. 466n4).

25. See Isa. 40:26.

26. See Isa. 40:26.

were going to eat with a publican, whom most Jews classed as a sinner.[27] Zacchaeus may not have cared that the multitude murmured, for Jesus had shown him respect. And because Jesus respected Zacchaeus, he would respect himself. It is reasonable to assume that Jesus's tenderness and awareness of Zacchaeus lifted him to a higher spiritual plane. It is also reasonable to assume that what was base in him was driven away and that what was noble came forth.

Zacchaeus then declared to Jesus, presumably in the hearing of the multitude, "Behold, Lord, the half of my goods I give to the poor; and if I have taken any thing from any man by false accusation, I restore him fourfold." Zacchaeus was not only generously giving to the poor but was also willing to pay twice the amount the law required as restitution if he had erred.[28] Zacchaeus' goodness was acknowledged by Christ, who said: "This day is salvation come to this house." Jesus never discriminates against those who others claim to be sinners. His love, compassion, mercy, and gospel are for all.

Jesus also declared that Zacchaeus was of the lineage of Abraham. Jesus was presumably referring to Zacchaeus being a literal descendent since he was likely a Jew. Jesus may also have been indicating that Zacchaeus was now a spiritual descendent of Abraham, entitling Zacchaeus to all the blessings promised to Abraham's posterity.[29]

The very reason that Christ came into the world was to save those who are lost. His ultimate method of doing so would involve suffering in Gethsemane and dying on the cross. Perhaps Jesus's triumphal entry in Jerusalem was not nearly so sweet as was hearing Zacchaeus declare his belief in Jesus and his sincere expression of repentance. That which was lost had been found, and the multitude had been richly taught.

Luke's record does not describe the subsequent meal at Zacchaeus's home. It is assumed, however, that God's hand was over all that occurred and that Zacchaeus and his family, if he had one, were blessed beyond measure.

---

27. Though Jews typically considered publicans to be sinners, Jesus had found among the publicans some of His most eager listeners and had even selected one of them, Matthew, to be an Apostle.

28. See Ex. 22:7.

29. See Abr. 1:18–19; 2:8–11.

Jesus Gives the Parable of the Ten Pounds (Luke 19:11–27)

Likely as Christ and His disciples were heading toward Bethany before reaching Jerusalem, He gave the parable of the ten pounds.[30] In giving the parable, He may have drawn on fairly recent Jewish political events in Judea. As a brief summary of the pertinent history, after Herod's death, his son Archelaus traveled to Rome to claim the throne but was opposed by his brothers and a delegation of fifty Jews. As a result, Archelaus was away from Jerusalem for a time and his younger brothers were in charge. Eventually, Caesar decided that none of the brothers would be king but, rather, that the land would be divided into territories, with each brother governing over a separate area.[31] Many of those who heard the parable presumably knew of these events.

Luke alone recorded this parable:

Luke 19:11–27. And as they heard these things, he added and spake a parable, because he was nigh to Jerusalem, and because they thought that the kingdom of God should immediately appear. He said therefore, A certain nobleman went into a far country to receive for himself a kingdom, and to return. And he called his ten servants, and delivered them ten pounds, and said unto them, Occupy till I come. But his citizens hated him, and sent a message after him, saying, We will not have this man to reign over us. And it came to pass, that when he was returned, having received the kingdom, then he commanded these servants to be called unto him, to whom he had given the money, that he might know how much every man had gained by trading. Then came the first, saying, Lord, thy pound hath gained ten pounds. And he said unto him, Well, thou good servant: because thou hast been faithful in a very little, have thou authority over ten cities. And the second came, saying, Lord, thy pound hath gained five pounds. And he said likewise to him, Be thou also over five cities. And another came, saying, Lord, behold, here is thy pound, which I have kept laid up in a napkin: for I feared thee, because thou art an austere man: thou takest up that thou layedst not down, and reapest that thou didst not sow. And he saith unto him, Out of thine own mouth will

---

30. This parable has strong parallels to the parable of the talents, which will be discussed in volume 4, chapter 58, of this series.

31. For more information regarding the political background, see note 1 at the end of this chapter.

I judge thee, thou wicked servant. Thou knewest that I was an austere man, taking up that I laid not down, and reaping that I did not sow: wherefore then gavest not thou my money into the bank, that at my coming I might have required mine own with usury? And he said unto them that stood by, Take from him the pound, and give it to him that hath ten pounds. (And they said unto him, Lord, he hath ten pounds.) For I say unto you, That unto every one which hath shall be given; and from him that hath not, even that he hath shall be taken away from him. But those mine enemies, which would not that I should reign over them, bring hither, and slay them before me.

Luke's record states that Jesus gave this parable because He was close to Jerusalem and because "they"—either the Jews with Him at Jericho or His disciples more generally—"thought that the kingdom of God should immediately appear." That is, they thought that the Messiah would come with power. Those who believed Jesus to be the Messiah hoped He would free them from Roman bondage and thereby bring about the kingdom of God. They needed to learn that Christ's political kingdom was not going to come immediately and that Israel would not be freed from Roman rule when Jesus entered Jerusalem.

In the parable, the nobleman symbolizes Jesus, the Only Begotten Son of God. The nobleman gave each of his ten servants, who symbolize Jesus's disciples,[32] one pound—a substantial amount of money. [33] Likewise, the Apostles and the Seventy had each been individually called[34] and ordained; each had been given priesthood authority, which was of substantial spiritual

---

32. The number ten may be symbolic of disciples; for example, ten lepers were healed by Jesus (see Luke 17:12–19) and ten virgins waited for the bridegroom (see Matt. 25:1–13). The servants may also symbolize the Apostles. It is interesting that the parable of the ten pounds describes ten servants, whereas Christ had twelve Apostles. However, one of the Apostles was Judas, who betrayed Christ and would no longer serve, and another of the Apostles, John, was given a very different mission from the other Apostles: to remain on the earth and help build up the kingdom of God until the Savior's return.

33. *Pound* is "the term used by the NRSV [New Revised Standard Version of the Bible] for *mina* in a parable of Jesus related in Luke 19:13–26. A mina was equal to 100 denarii, making it equivalent to about a hundred times a typical days' wage" (*HarperCollins Bible Dictionary*, s.v. "pound").

34. As Jesus explained to the Apostles, "Ye have not chosen me, but I have chosen you, and ordained you, that ye should go and bring forth fruit, and that your fruit should remain" (John 15:16). After Jesus called the Seventy, He "sent them two and two before his face into every city and place, whiter he himself would come" (Luke 10:1).

value; and each had a mission to bring souls unto Christ. In the parable, the servants were to put the money to use so that the nobleman would have an increase when he returned. Similarly, the disciples needed to put their talents and individual callings to good use in building up the kingdom of God, particularly following Jesus's death and Resurrection.

In the parable, the nobleman went into a far country to receive His kingdom. Similarly, following Jesus's Crucifixion, He left mortality and ultimately ascended to His Father and there received His kingdom and glory.[35] Like the nobleman in the parable, Jesus will return again to the earth to rule and reign forever.[36]

When the nobleman returned, he asked each servant to explain what he had done with the pound he had received. One servant had gained an additional ten pounds, and another servant had gained an additional five pounds. Consequently, the nobleman gave these servants authority over ten cities and five cities, respectively. Their rewards were far greater than the additional pounds they had earned for the nobleman. Because they had proven responsible over a few things, they became rulers over many things.[37] Likewise, all people who diligently serve Jesus will receive rewards far greater than they expect.

One servant did nothing with his pound but place it in a napkin because he feared the nobleman. In addition, the servant implicitly criticized the nobleman for gaining a reward earned for him by others.[38] Also implied in the parable is that this servant lacked humility and gratitude for the opportunity he had been given to serve the nobleman. And because of fear of the nobleman, the servant had failed to act and magnify what he had been entrusted with. In response, the nobleman condemned the servant as wicked, took the pound from him, and gave it to the servant who had increased his pound to ten.

---

35. See John 20:17; Luke 24:50–51; Acts 1:9–11.

36. See D&C 76:110, 119.

37. See Matt. 25:21; Luke 12:44.

38. The conduct of the third servant is somewhat similar to that of Satan when he rebelled in the premortal world (see Moses 4:3). Presumably, Satan's followers in the premortal realm also thought and acted similar to this third servant.

Just as an accounting was required of the servants in the parable, there will be an accounting of every person's life at the day of judgment. Each person will receive the reward he or she merits. Similar to the first two servants in the parable, the righteous will receive the reward of becoming kings and queens over various dominions.

At the end of the parable, the nobleman directed that those who opposed his reign should be slain. Similarly, many Jews rejected Jesus as their heavenly king. In fact, a few days after Jesus gave this parable, many Jews told Pilate: "Away with [Jesus], away with him, crucify him." Pilate responded, "Shall I crucify your King?" In answer, the chief priests said, "We have no king but Caesar." Later, Pilate directed that a sign stating "Jesus of Nazareth the King of the Jews" be placed on the cross, and the chief priests said to Pilate: "Write not, The King of the Jews; but that he said, I am King of the Jews." Pilate responded, "What I have written I have written."[39] When Christ returns to the earth, the wicked will be destroyed. As Nephi prophesied in the Book of Mormon: "For the time speedily cometh that the Lord God shall cause a great division among the people, and the wicked will he destroy; and he will spare his people, yea, even if it so be that he must destroy the wicked by fire."[40]

This parable was not only for Jesus's disciples but for all who would serve in the generations thereafter, because those who serve should do so diligently and according to their talents, strengths, circumstances, and opportunities.

Jesus Travels to Jerusalem (Luke 19:28)

After Jesus gave the parable of the ten pounds, He made His final assent to Jerusalem.

Luke's account simply states the following:

Luke 19:28. And when he had thus spoken, he went before, ascending up to Jerusalem.

Many people were likely traveling the same road as Jesus was, headed to Jerusalem for the Passover. The road from Jericho to Jerusalem was rocky

---

39. John 19:15, 19, 21–22.
40. 2 Ne. 30:10.

and dangerous and involved ascending more than thirty-three hundred feet. The trek was not like Jesus's prior travels along the beautiful shores in Galilee. The trek was also dangerous, with robbers often lying in wait for the opportunity steal from travelers who were unwary or weak. The journey was likely even more difficult for Jesus because He knew what lay ahead for Him in Jerusalem. Jesus was the only mortal who could endure atoning for all people, being rejected and betrayed, being subjected to an illegal and hypocritical trial, and being scourged and crucified. Each difficult step along the road to Jerusalem may have reminded Him of the challenges He would soon face.

Many Look for Jesus during the Passover (John 11:55–57)

As previously noted, many Jews traveled to Jerusalem to purify themselves at the temple in preparation for the Passover, particularly because men were not permitted to eat the Passover meal while ceremonially unclean.[41] The Jews did not realize that these steps were symbolic of Jesus's Atonement, death, and Resurrection. Upon arriving in Jerusalem, many of these individuals looked for Jesus. The following is John's record:

> **John 11:55–57.** And the Jews' passover was nigh at hand: and many went out of the country up to Jerusalem before the passover, to purify themselves. Then sought they for Jesus, and spake among themselves, as they stood in the temple, What think ye, that he will not come to the feast? Now both the chief priests and the Pharisees had given a commandment, that, if any man knew where he were, he should shew it, that they might take him.

As individuals stood in the temple, they speculated about whether Jesus would attend the Passover. Presumably, they were aware that the chief priests and the Pharisees had ordered that anyone who knew where Jesus was must report this information so that the Jewish leaders could take Him.

John may have recorded this information simply to explain the events taking place in Jerusalem at the time. However, John may have also wanted

---

41. See Dummelow, *Bible Commentary*, p. 795; see also Num. 9:10. The purification process included ritual washing, either by immersing the entire body or by washing the hands with a cup of pure water; shaving the head; and offering a prescribed sacrifice (see Dummelow, *Bible Commentary*, p. 795; see also *HarperCollins Bible Dictionary*, s.v. "purity").

to teach later generations a lesson. Just as the Jews wondered whether Jesus would attend the Passover, many people today speculate about Jesus and His Second Coming. Some may wonder whether Jesus ever existed and, if so, who He was. Some may wonder whether Jesus is the Son of God and whether He will return to the earth, as prophesied. Those who believe the prophecies may wonder when, where, and how He will come; whether the signs of His coming have begun; and what catastrophic events will yet precede His return. Others may wonder why He did not come in the year 2000. Christ has plainly said that He will "come in a day when he looketh not for him, and in an hour that he is not aware of,"[42] and only the Father knows when the Second Coming will occur.[43]

Mary Anoints Jesus (Matt. 26:6–13; Mark 14:3–9; John 12:1–8)

Jesus likely arrived in Bethany on Friday before nightfall, when the Jewish Sabbath began.[44] Nothing is said in the scriptural record regarding what transpired or where Jesus stayed when He arrived. On Saturday, He may have contemplated the fact that this Sabbath was the last one He would have in mortality. He may have also contemplated many of the previous Sabbath days, including those on which He taught in the synagogues and healed people through His touch or His words. He may also have pondered about His commitment to atone for all humankind, as He had promised to do in the premortal world. The following is John's record:

> **John 12:1–8.** Then Jesus six days before the passover[45] came to Bethany, where Lazarus was which had been dead, whom he raised from the dead. There they made him a supper; and Martha served: but Lazarus was one of them that sat at the table with him. Then took Mary a pound of ointment of spikenard, very costly, and anointed the feet of Jesus, and wiped his feet with her hair: and the house was filled with the odour of the ointment. Then

---

42. Matt. 24:50.

43. See Matt. 24:36.

44. Many scholars believe that in that year, the seven-day Passover began on Thursday, which was the fourteenth day of Nisan (see Talmage, *Jesus the Christ*, p. 476; Edersheim, *Life and Times of Jesus the Messiah*, p. 720).

45. Matt. 26:1–13 and Mark 14:1–9 indicate that Mary anointed Jesus on Tuesday or Wednesday of the week of Christ's death, but John's chronology is more likely correct.

saith one of his disciples, Judas Iscariot, Simon's son, which should betray him, Why was not this ointment sold for three hundred pence,[46] and given to the poor? This he said, not that he cared for the poor; but because he was a thief, and had the bag, and bare what was put therein. Then said Jesus, Let her alone: against the day of my burying hath she kept this. For the poor always ye have with you; but me ye have not always.

The meal that John's account refers to probably occurred on Saturday evening, after the Sabbath had ended. Matthew's and Mark's accounts indicate that the meal was held in the house of Simon the leper. He must have already been healed of his leprosy; otherwise, he would have been considered unclean and would not have been allowed to be around those who were considered clean. Jesus may have healed Simon of this loathsome disease on some previous occasion. Many have speculated that Simon was related to Martha, Mary, and Lazarus—perhaps even their father—since they were at the meal and Mary served it. Alternatively, Lazarus may have simply lived near the siblings and had a home large enough to accommodate a rather large gathering, including the siblings, Jesus, and at least some of His Apostles.

When a large group gathered at a home for supper, it was not unusual for a number of others to observe from outside. It is not a surprise, therefore, that many observers were present at this supper, perhaps in a porch area; they had come to see both Jesus and Lazarus, whom Jesus had restored to life.[47]

What happened next would be known by people in all generations to come. Mary took an alabaster flask[48] containing spikenard, which was a very costly ointment, and then poured it on Jesus's head, according to Matthew and Mark,[49] and His feet, according to John. She then lovingly wiped his feet with her hair. To anoint a guest's head with ordinary oil was a sign of honor, and to anoint both head and feet indicated special honor. To anoint a guest's head and feet with costly spikenard was an act of reverence and homage rarely rendered even to kings.[50] Mary's worshipful love of Jesus was likely

46. A laborer typically earned the equivalent of one pence per day of work (see Edersheim, *Life and Times of Jesus the Messiah*, p. 721).

47. See John 12:9–11.

48. Matthew 26:7 and Mark 14:3 call the container a box; John's description is more accurate.

49. See Matt. 26:7; Mark 14:3.

50. See Talmage, *Jesus the Christ*, pp. 478, 487n7.

overflowing as she performed this great service for Him. She undoubtedly remembered Jesus mercifully restoring life to her brother approximately three months earlier, and that thought would have added to her reverence of Christ.

It is unknown when, where, or how Mary acquired the spikenard. She may not have known when she purchased the spikenard how she would use it, but she may have acquired it because of inspiration from the Holy Ghost, given Jesus's subsequent statement about the spikenard's purpose and the fact that three of the Gospel writers recorded this event.

When Mary anointed Jesus's head and feet with the spikenard, Judas Iscariot asked why this valuable oil had not been sold so that the resulting money could be given to the poor. John's account indicates that Judas did not ask because he cared for the poor but because he was in charge of the bag containing money for Jesus and the Apostles and he stole from the bag.

Likely with deep emotion, Jesus responded: "Let her alone: against the day of my burying hath she kept this. For the poor always ye have with you; but me ye have not always." Both Matthew and Mark added that Jesus said Mary had "wrought a good work on me."[51] She may not have used all the oil in anointing Jesus at that time; she may have been inspired to keep some so that she could anoint Jesus's body following His death.[52]

Mary's faith, love, and worshipful spirit sharply contrasted with Judas's evil heart. As one of Jesus's Apostles, Judas outwardly appeared to be good. However, good is never evil, and evil is never good; in the end, good will triumph over evil, just as Christ would soon triumph over sin and death and just as Judas would soon take his own life.

Christ then prophesied, "Verily I say unto you, Wheresoever this gospel shall be preached throughout the whole world, this also that she hath done shall be spoken of for a memorial of her."[53]

---

51. Mark 14:6; see also Matt. 26:10.
52. See Dummelow, *Life of Christ*, p. 795.
53. Mark 14:9; see also Matt. 26:13.

The Chief Priests Conspire to Put Lazarus to Death (John 12:9–11)

As previously indicated, many people knew that Jesus was at Simon's house in Bethany. They came to see Jesus and also to see Lazarus since he had recently been raised from the dead. John's record continues as follows:

> **John 12:9–11.** Much people of the Jews therefore knew that he [Jesus] was there: and they came not for Jesus' sake only, but that they might see Lazarus also, whom he had raised from the dead. But the chief priests consulted that they might put Lazarus also to death; because that by reason of him many of the Jews went away, and believed on Jesus.

The faith of those who saw Jesus and Lazarus would soon be tested in that the one who had restored Lazarus to life would shortly be put to death Himself. At that time, some who disbelieved in Christ or whose faith was shallow asked why, if He were indeed the Son of God, He did not miraculously come down from the cross.[54] Others asked why He could save others but not Himself.[55] Still others said that since He trusted God, let God save Him.[56]

Knowing that Lazarus was a remarkable witness of Jesus's power to raise the dead, the chief priests conspired to kill Lazarus.[57] Those who were supposed to be the keepers of the law now once again stood in defiance of the sixth commandment: "Thou shalt not kill."[58] These chief priests disregarded the same commandment in seeking Jesus's death. Soon, Christ would triumphantly enter Jerusalem and would permit the Jewish leaders to carry out their wicked resolution to put Him to death. By suffering in Gethsemane and allowing Himself to be killed, He would bring about the resurrection of all humankind and thus fulfill His mission in mortality.

---

54. See Matt. 27:39–40; Mark 15:30.

55. See Matt. 27:42; Mark 15:31.

56. See Matt. 27:43; Mark 15:32.

57. The chief priests may have been conspiring to put Lazarus to death since almost immediately after Jesus restored Lazarus to life.

58. Ex. 20:13. The scriptures are silent regarding whether Lazarus was indeed killed.

Note to Chapter 48

1. **Political background of Judea in relation to the parable of the ten pounds; Pilate's position at the time of Christ's death.** Shortly after Christ was born, Herod died and a dispute arose between his three surviving sons as to who should take Herod's place as king. Archelaus, who was the eldest surviving son, assumed he would become king, as directed in his father's last will. Archelaus's brother Antipas, whom Herod's previous will indicated would become king, challenged Archelaus's appointment.

Before Caesar had confirmed Archelaus's appointment as king, Archelaus put down a claimed insurrection by having his army mercilessly slay three thousand men while they attended the Feast of the Passover.[59] Archelaus left for Rome to obtain Caesar's decree confirming Archelaus's right to the throne as the eldest son. While he was in Rome, his younger brothers, Antipas and Philip, were in charge in Judea. The Jews sent fifty ambassadors to Rome to oppose Archelaus's confirmation as king.[60] These fifty joined many other Jews who were in Rome to ask Caesar that the throne be withheld from Archelaus because he was ruthless and the Jews would not support him. This request was a fairly daring move. Because of this request and other disruptions in Judea, Caesar withheld the title of king from all three brothers. Instead, he gave Archelaus the title of ethnarch and half of the territory, including Judea, Idumea, and Samaria. Caesar split the other half between the two younger brothers, whom Caesar gave the title of tetrarch. Antipas received Galilee and Perea, and Philip received Batanea, Trachonities, and Auranitis.[61]

Archelaus was ruling in Judea when Joseph, Mary, and the young Jesus were in Egypt or on their return to Israel. Rather than be in Archelaus's jurisdiction and risk Jesus's life, the family returned to Nazareth, which was in Herod Antipas's jurisdiction.[62] While Archelaus was ethnarch, he rebuilt

---

59. See Josephus, *Antiquities*, 17.9.3.
60. See Josephus, *Antiquities*, 17.9.1.
61. See Josephus, *Antiquities*, 17.11.4.
62. See Matt. 2:22.

the royal palace in Jericho and stayed there in the winter.[63] The palace was still in use when Jesus traveled through Jericho on His way to Jerusalem.

Archelaus's reign was relatively disastrous and lasted only approximately ten years—both Jews and Samaritans petitioned that he be removed because of his brutality.[64] His territory then became a Roman province under a prefect named Coponius. Later, Pontius Pilate became the fifth governor of the territory, and he ruled during Jesus's public ministry and for several years after Jesus's death.[65]

---

63. Archelaus also diverted half of the water that the city of Neara used so that the palm trees he had ordered to be planted could be watered (see Josephus, *Antiquities*, 17.13.1).

64. See Josephus, *Antiquities*, 17.8.2.

65. See *HarperCollins Bible Dictionary*, s.v. "Herod, 2 Herod Archelaus"; s.v. "Pilate, Pontius."

Bibliography

Books of the Maccabees (King James Bible and Douay Rheims versions). Enhanced Ebooks, 2014.

Callister, Tad R. *The Infinite Atonement*. Salt Lake City, UT: Deseret Book, 2000.

Chandler, Walter M. *The Trial of Jesus from a Lawyer's Standpoint*. 2 vols. 1908. Reprint, Leopold Classic Library, 2015.

Clarke, Adam. *Clarke's Commentary*. Vols. 1 & 3: Matthew–Revelation. Nashville, TN: Abingdon, 1810, 1824.

Cornwall, J. Spencer. *Stories of our Mormon Hymns*. Salt Lake City, UT: Deseret Book, 1975.

Dummelow, John R. *The One Volume Bible Commentary*. New York: MacMillan, 1975.

Edersheim, Alfred. *The Life and Times of Jesus the Messiah*. Peabody, MA: Hendrickson, 1997.

Farrar, Dean. *The Life of Christ*. Quiver ed. London: Cassell and Company, 1896.

Geikie, Cunningham. *The Life and Words of Christ*. 2 vols. New York: Appleton, 1883.

HarperCollins Bible Dictionary. Edited by Mark Allan Powell. New York: HarperCollins, 1989.

Holzapfel, Richard Neitzel, and Thomas A. Wayment, eds. *The Life and Teachings of Jesus Christ*. 3 vols. Salt Lake City, UT: Deseret Book, 2006.

Huntsman, Eric D. *The Miracles of Jesus*. Salt Lake City, UT: Deseret Book, 2014.

Hymns of The Church of Jesus Christ of Latter-day Saints. Salt Lake City, UT: The Church of Jesus Christ of Latter-day Saints, 1985.

Jewish Encyclopedia. 1901–1906. http://www.jewishencyclopedia.com.

Keil, Carl F., and Friedrich Delitzsch. *Commentary on the Old Testament.* 10 vols. 1996. Edinburgh: Clark, 1866. Reprint, Peabody, MA: Hendrickson, 1996.

Josephus. *The Works of Flavius Josephus.* Translated by William Whiston. Grand Rapids, MI: Kregel, 1971.

LDS Bible Dictionary. In the Holy Bible. Salt Lake City, UT: The Church of Jesus Christ of Latter-day Saints, 1979.

Lundwall, N. B., comp. *Lectures on Faith.* Salt Lake City, UT: Bookcraft, 1999.

Lyon, T. Edgar. *Apostasy to Restoration.* Salt Lake City, UT: Deseret Book, 1960.

McConkie, Bruce R. *Mormon Doctrine.* 2nd ed. Salt Lake City, UT: Bookcraft, 1966.

McConkie, Bruce R. *The Mortal Messiah.* 6 vols. Salt Lake City, UT: Deseret Book, 1980.

Merriam-Webster. http://merriam-webster.com.

NIV Study Bible. Grand Rapids, MI: Zondervan, 1995.

Sachar, Abram Leon. *A History of the Jews.* 5th ed. New York: McGraw-Hill, 1975.

Smith, Joseph Jr. *History of the Church.* 7 vols. 1839–1856. Reprinted Salt Lake City, UT: Deseret Book, 1976.

Smith, Joseph Fielding. *Answers to Gospel Questions.* 5 vols. Salt Lake City, UT: Desert Book, 1979.

Smith, Joseph Fielding, comp. *Teachings of the Prophet Joseph Smith.* Salt Lake City, UT: Deseret Book, 1964.

Smith, William. *The New Smith's Bible Dictionary.* Edited by Reuel G. Lemmons. Garden City, NY: Doubleday, 1966.

Talmage, James E. *Jesus the Christ.* Salt Lake City, UT: Deseret Book, 1915. Reprinted, Covenant Communications, 2006.

The Church of Jesus Christ of Latter-day Saints. *Preach My Gospel.* Salt Lake City, UT: The Church of Jesus Christ of Latter-day Saints, 2004.

The First Presidency and the Quorum of the Twelve Apostles. "The Family: A Proclamation to the World." Salt Lake City, UT: The Church of Jesus Christ of Latter-day Saints, 1995.

Trench, Richard C. *Notes on the Miracles of Our Lord.* New York: Appleton, 1853.

Young, Robert. *Young's Analytical Concordance to the Bible.* 22nd ed. Edited by William B. Stevenson. New York: Funk and Wagnalls, 1970.

Wikipedia. http://www.wikipedia.org.

Index

About the Author

Steven R. McMurray grew up in Salt Lake City, Utah. He graduated from the University of Utah with a juris doctor degree in 1971 and has practiced law in Salt Lake City ever since. He has a Martindale-Hubble rating of AV (the highest possible) and is listed in Best Lawyers of America.

From 1964 to 1966, Steve served as a full-time missionary for The Church of Jesus Christ of Latter-day Saints in the Scottish Mission. Afterward, he taught early morning seminary for four years. In 1971 (before MTCs were established), he developed a missionary preparation class and then taught it for five years. For this class, he developed extensive outlines of gospel topics, particularly oriented toward teaching those interested in learning about the Church. Upon request, he provided copies of his outlines to the Church. He also taught at an institute for four years and was a host on Temple Square in Salt Lake City for nine years.

He has served as a counselor in a stake presidency, a member of a high council, a bishop, a branch president, a counselor in a bishopric, an elders quorum president, a counselor in a stake mission presidency, and a stake missionary. He has also taught Gospel Doctrine several times and has served as a priesthood quorum instructor and a young men's advisor. Steve and his wife, Lorna, who are the parents of nine children, served in the Australia Melbourne Mission. Upon returning from Australia, Steve began writing this book, which has taken over six years and has been one of the spiritual highlights of his life.

9 781949 974072